LIVING ON THE VOLCANO

Michael Calvin is one of the UK's most accomplished sports writers. He has worked in more than eighty countries, covering every major sporting event, including seven summer Olympic Games and six World Cup finals. He was named Sports Writer of the Year for his despatches as a crew member in a round-the-world yacht race and has twice been named Sports Reporter of the Year. He was the *Independent on Sunday*'s chief sports writer when it closed in March 2016. He has held similar positions with the *Daily Telegraph*, *The Times* and *Mail on Sunday*.

His book, *The Nowhere Men*, won the Times Sports Book of the Year prize in 2014. He became the first author to receive the award in successive years, when *Proud*, his collaboration with former Wales and British Lions rugby captain Gareth Thomas, was named Sports Book of the Year in 2015.

LIVING ON THE VOLCANO

MICHAEL CALVIN

arrow books

1 3 5 7 9 10 8 6 4 2

Arrow Books
20 Vauxhall Bridge Road
London SW1V 2SA

Arrow Books is part of the Penguin Random House group of companies
whose addresses can be found at global.penguinrandomhouse.com.

Penguin
Random House
UK

First published by Century in 2015
First published in paperback by Arrow Books in 2016

www.penguin.co.uk

A CIP catalogue record for this book is available from the British Library

ISBN 9780099598657

Typeset in Minion by Palimpsest Book Production Ltd, Falkirk, Stirlingshire

Printed and bound in Great Britain by Clays Ltd, St Ives plc

Penguin Random House is committed to a sustainable future
for our business, our readers and our planet. This book
is made from Forest Stewardship Council® certified paper.

For Mum and Marielli. Golden links in the chain.

Contents

Acknowledgements

Gareth Ainsworth was the last to leave the training ground, as usual. It had been a sunny day, and he walked me through the ground-floor gymnasium to a fire exit which led to the car park. There, in the far corner, was a vintage Ford Mustang, a vivid orange fashion statement from the sixties. It gleamed defiantly, and took me back to my childhood, when my friend Tony Wilson's father, John, had a similar model, dark blue. Its lines were sleek and its noise was seductive. We used to cram into the back seat and travel to the Northamptonshire village of Brafield to watch stock car racing.

Ainsworth shared my reverie. 'That car is my pride and joy,' he confessed. 'I saw the sun this morning and had to get it out of the garage. That's the rock 'n' roll in me I guess. I've still got a bit of the wild thing left in me . . .'

Such an apparently inconsequential exchange captured the mood of many of the conversations I had during the research for this book. Football managers are categorised by the profundity of their pronouncements. They endure character assassination, casual dismissal and crass judgements.

They are rarely allowed to be themselves. I thank every manager featured in these pages for the privilege of their candour and the authenticity of their responses. Since they inhabit a small, overheated world, news of what I was up to spread. Each was interested in my perception of their peers; curiosity merged with rivalry.

They were amazingly generous with their most precious luxury, their time. A phrase from the ancient Chinese poet and philosopher Lao Tzu – 'Leadership is the ability to hide your panic from others' – often filtered through my brain. The pressure under which they work was tangible and, at times, terrifying.

I am hugely flattered and eternally grateful that Arsène Wenger should contribute a foreword to this book. He is the last of his type, a dynastic manager whose belief in winning being a consequence of excellence, rather than its solitary justification, is wonderfully counter-intuitive in an age in which idealists are no longer accepted at face value.

He has his moments, when he is consumed by the strength of his feelings, but I have come to regard him as football's equivalent of a favourite teacher, who moulds lives and shapes personalities by his passion for his subject, the breadth of his knowledge, and the subtlety of his communication skills. Is it really so wrong to promote, pursue and protect a principle? I think not.

My thanks must go, first and foremost, to Dan Tolhurst, Arsenal's Head of Football Media Operations. Dan has been at the club almost as long as Arsène, and his reputation for proactivity is rightly renowned. I've been fortunate to work with some of the best club media staff in the business.

Special thanks, in strictly alphabetical order, to Ben Campbell (MK Dons), Richard Dorman (Exeter City), Max Fitzgerald (Bournemouth), Colin Gibson (Derby County), Jim Lucas (Southampton), Matt McCann (Liverpool), Fraser Nicholson (Stoke City), Mark Rowan (Everton), Ralph Shepherd (Notts County), John Simpson (WBA), Deano Standing (Millwall) and Jonathan Wilsher (Swansea City).

I've been struck, during the process of writing the book, by the breadth and sensitivity of the support system operated by the League Managers Association in what is such a splintered, insecure profession. Thanks, especially, to Richard Bevan, Sarah Collins, Alison Betson and Dr Sue Bridgewater for giving context to my research.

You would not be reading this without the faith and professionalism of Ben Dunn and his team at Century, which includes Ajda Vucicevic, Natalie Higgins and

Philippa Cotton. I thank them for their encouragement and support. The working relationship we established on my previous book, *The Nowhere Men*, has incalculable value. Thanks, also, to my literary agent, Paul Moreton, for his guidance.

There really should be an additional name on the front cover. Caroline Flatley is, spiritually at least, my co-author. Her transcription of the endless hours of interviews was a miracle of patience and precision; all told they totalled nearly 350,000 words. She is an acute judge of character, despite the aberration of putting up with me, and her observations on individual managers helped focus my thoughts.

Life at home, with an expanding family that includes Marielli, my first grandchild, is unremittingly hectic. Consequently, I made a pragmatic retreat to the village of Hartington, in the Derbyshire Peak District, to write. Thanks very much to Kate and Rob Tenty for the use of their cottage, and their directions to the local pub, the Devonshire Arms.

As usual I must offer thanks and apologies, in equal measure, to my wife, Lynn, my children, Nicholas, Aaron, William and Lydia, and their partners, Vicky, Jo and Brad. They've tolerated my tantrums and shared my obsession. Writing books is an exquisite addiction, and I must confess I am hooked.

Michael Calvin, May 2015

Foreword by Arsène Wenger

Managing a football team has changed dramatically over the 30 years or so since I first took charge of a first team, in France with Nancy.

The challenges for a 'modern day' manager are consistently evolving. Football is ever-increasingly popular, worldwide. It is watched by millions and involves heavy investment by broadcasters and commercial organisations alike.

However, the fundamentals of a successful football manager remain the same. There are many factors in measuring that success, but the key ingredients will always be the passion an individual has for the sport; man management; the ability to evolve and adapt; and, of course, an eye for talent.

I have respect for every single manager in football, throughout all levels, as we all suffer. We are all striving for the perfect performance and the perfect season, and we all feel the intense pain after every defeat. That is why it is so important to try to enjoy those short post-match victorious moments as much as we can, before our minds move to the next match.

There is a growing trend within the game for clubs to change managers more frequently, as there is so much pressure for short-term results. I am always sad when a manager loses their job. Clubs need stability, and having been at Arsenal for almost 19 years now, I have been given the time to create a culture at the club, which is so important.

Although it is often challenging, I have enjoyed every minute of being a manager of a football club. I grew up in a football environment, as my parents ran a restaurant bar in Alsace, in France, where all the local football teams would congregate before and after matches. I grew up around football people. I enjoyed listening and learning from them and this gave me my passion for the game.

I'm really looking forward to reading this book, a study of a completely unique way of living – being a football manager.

Best wishes,

Arsène Wenger

1

Intolerance of Uncertainty

A padded electrode was placed on either side of Martin Ling's head. He was emotionally exhausted, still and submissive. His world was dark, denuded of basic human comfort. His final sentient thought, as he lost consciousness following an anaesthetising injection in his right wrist, was: I hope this works.

Electroconvulsive therapy, or shock treatment to use the term which has enduring echoes of the asylum, involves triggering an epileptic fit by passing an electric current through the brain. The aim is to combat severe depression, but the procedure is increasingly unfashionable, since it is ineffective in around half of patients and relapses are common.

Once Ling was unconscious, another injection, containing a muscle relaxant, was administered. A mouth guard was inserted, to prevent him biting his tongue. A series of high-voltage surges, up to 70 pulses

1

a second for between three and five seconds, caused his body to stiffen. Each seizure lasted between 20 and 50 seconds.

He went through the process five times, at the Priory Hospital in Roehampton in early 2013, after enduring a series of acute panic attacks, during which he was convinced he had a brain tumour and was suffering a cardiac arrest. He had fleeting thoughts of suicide, of running into traffic on the northbound carriageway of the M5 in Somerset, or steering his car into the path of an oncoming lorry on the A10 near his home in Hertfordshire.

'ECT is barbaric, but only people who have been that low will understand you will try anything in that situation,' he says, in a muted monotone which testifies to the latent power of reminiscence. 'You go into a black hole. It feels like you are living in a fog. You can see nothing. It is so black, totally black. It is as if the world is going to end.'

Ling is an unobtrusive figure as he sits, drinking a tall, slender cup of latte, in the bar area of the suburban hotel in which he used to conduct individual interviews with prospective players for the three clubs he managed over the course of a decade, Leyton Orient, Cambridge United and Torquay United. Football is his life force, his workplace.

He prides himself on the accuracy of his untutored insight into the human condition, his instinct for weakness and the effectiveness of his compassionate approach to the insecurities of the lower-division footballer. He looks younger than his 48 years, despite the grey hair which frames a boyish face, reddened by the exertions of an afternoon's coaching on a clear, cold February day in 2015.

'My man management is the best part of my management. It is the most important part of the job, because at the clubs I've worked we've had to take some wrong 'uns that others wouldn't touch. I know I can find someone's on–off switch. In the lower leagues you have to be absolutely everything to all men. I have always believed in honesty, in creating the right atmosphere.'

He understands the complexities of candour, the stigma his story represents in a profession underpinned by desperate ambition, absurd pretension and ritual sacrifice. Admissions of a history of mental health issues are, he admits, 'a coffee stain' on a strong CV. They deter potential employers, who have bought into the mythology of modern football management.

Men like Ling are expected to be a cross between a sage and a stand-up comedian, a patriarch and a pithead rabble-rouser. They are prisoners of perversity, expected to dispense summary justice despite being utterly disposable. Their names and faces are overfamiliar, due to the tyranny of a ceaseless news cycle, yet they remain resistant to anything other than superficial scrutiny.

They have the trappings of cartoon kings, with courtiers who dance attendance, oblivious to the irrelevance of their self-importance. They are accustomed to addressing the public on their own terms, and tend to shy away from substantive analysis of their personal and professional priorities.

Who are they? Why do they submit themselves to illogical, often malevolent judgement? What coping strategies do they utilise? Where, and from whom, do they derive their greatest inspiration? Which philosophies are the most effective? How do they salve their consciences, when it proves impossible to reconcile career and family? Will they change, as the world changes around them?

Arsène Wenger likens the job to 'living on a volcano: any day may be your last'. He speaks with the authority of being the longest-serving manager in the English game, having been at Arsenal for nearly 19 years. The average lifespan of a Football League manager is 17 months, a sentence reduced to eight months in the charnel house of the Championship.

My aim is to look beyond the brand names, to scratch the sheen and reveal the realities of the role. The tabloid foot soldier who breathlessly informed Ling that his east London birthplace had inspired a pre-written headline for his life story – 'From Custom House to the Madhouse' – was an unwitting accomplice, since he hardened Ling's determination to make full disclosure, whatever the consequences. He is an archetypal survivor.

His inner strength has been taken for granted since his playing career began at Exeter City as 'a little, mouthy cockney' aged 16. The only apprentice of his intake to be offered a professional contract, he was scoured by the bitter tears of five friends who were rejected. They asked his advice and shared their fears without shame. He was an alpha male, even in adolescence.

'I was the starlet in the group, I suppose. I knew enough then to know if you tell someone at that level they are not going to be a footballer, they probably will not become one. If you are let go by Arsenal, Man United or Chelsea, you can filter down. If you get released by Exeter, it is much more difficult. The percentages are against you. You're not going to make it.'

Ling had a good career as a creative midfield player, featuring in more than 600 matches across all four divisions, including a showreel season in the Premier League at Swindon Town. He had a quick wit, which could be cruel or self-deprecating given the circumstances, and was at ease in the testosterone frenzy of the dressing room.

'Part of your survival mechanism in football is humour. I was always social secretary. I was the centre of every joke. I used to win the yellow jersey for worst trainer on Fridays at training. Why did I become a manager? Very good question. If someone said to me at twenty-nine I'd become one I'd have laughed in their face.

'But at thirty I thought: what am I going to do at thirty-five? I wasn't really a student of the game. I was an off-the-cuff type of player who used to listen to the coach but not too intently, because I played a free role. A few of the lads went on a C licence course at Southend, so I decided to give it a go. It suited my aptitude for getting men to do what I wanted them to do.

'I've never been enthralled by coaching dynamics, doing special Monday sessions to titillate the group. I'm more about character, charisma, how you bubble people up. Give me any group of players and I can make them feel better about themselves. I can't break down why, because just as I went past people on instinct as a player, I manage by instinct and empathy.

'I can smell a dressing room. I know the bad eggs. I know the people I can make better. I know the people who are beyond help, but I will always look for the good in them first. If the bad bits stay unchanged I will get rid of them. An awful lot of coaches fall into the trap of seeing more faults in a player the longer they have them. Just tell me what the fuck he can do, rather than what he can't do.'

Ling's rite of passage came at the age of 34, as a youth coach at Orient. He was summoned to a meeting to decide the future of a borderline prospect, striker Jabo

Ibehre. The scene summarised the hierarchical nature of any football club: manager Tommy Taylor dominated the room from a leather reclining chair situated behind his desk.

Ling sat in a reverential semicircle with the senior coaches, Paul Brush and Paul Clark, and Taylor's most trusted scout, Len Cheesewright, who sensed the discomfort of the younger man. He spoke with the authority of someone who had discovered Laurie Cunningham and Glenn Roeder for Orient, and Sol Campbell for Tottenham: 'Let the kid speak first.'

The memory stimulates a smile: 'Jabo was sixteen. I advised them to move him into the first team group. I said: "If I'm making this decision I'd give him a two-year contract. I'll tell you for why. Every club we play on a Saturday would take him." I could hear everyone take a deep breath. Clarkie said: "Not for me. He doesn't listen and he doesn't learn. I'd give him three months, max." Paul Brush gave him six.

'My back is up. I am fighting my corner. I say, "He is a quiet boy. He will struggle. He will find it a bit intimidating, but he will have a career." Tommy turned to me and said: "You may sit in this chair one day. Would you be making the same decision?" "Yes, I would." And I did sit in that same chair. It was a lovely black leather one. We had it ten years.

'I will always admire Len, God rest his soul. He went: "He works with him every day. Listen to what the young lad is telling you." I was wet behind the ears. Jabo was six foot two but he couldn't head the ball. He didn't get a lot of goals, but he was powerful, strong, and held it up well. He was timid but that changed, over time.

'Could he control it? Did he know what he was doing with it? No. But did the other team? No. His biggest strength is that he is uncoachable. Let him do what he's gonna do. He was in the first team in the play-off final at the Millennium Stadium as a seventeen-year-old. He's thirty-two now. He was never going to make the top leagues, but he's still played around four hundred and fifty games.

'I learned a big lesson that day. Never chuck the runt of the litter out. I was eight stone wet through when I went to Exeter. Nicky Shorey was our ninth-rated scholar, the last one we took in his year, and he ended up playing for England. You never know what might happen when you try to get people thinking better about themselves.'

Chances, when presented, must be seized. Ling owes his managerial career to Barry Hearn, who had found both Taylor and Brush wanting, and was receiving insufficient value from his annual £500,000 indulgence in a lower-league club of limited means. Their initial telephone exchange can be found in no HR manual, or any formal employment strategy, but it summarises how things work in football.

'Lingy. I want you to take the job but I don't want you to be our manager.'

'That's lovely, Bal. Thanks.'

'You've got the job on a twenty-four-hour caretaker basis.'

'OK. How about if I change your mind?'

'I like that answer, son.'

Ling is smiling, once again, at the memory: 'He moved me to a week, then a month. Then at Christmas, after doing the job since September, he gave me an eighteen-month contract. I was thirty-six. Was I ready? No. Did I learn on my feet? Yes. That was my strength. I make decisions quickly.'

He became accustomed to authority, comfortable with the power he wielded. He was treated deferentially, even by his family. When his father was rushed back into hospital following what appeared to be a routine operation, he was met in the waiting room by his mother, brother and sister. They craved his guidance, relied on his strength.

'They'd been there a while. Mum just said: "The consultant wants to see you. You make the decision for the family." Dad's bowel had been cut and he was fighting for his life. The doctors were telling me things, giving me eventualities I felt I couldn't share. Mum just said: "You will deal with it. It will be all right."'

You will cope. You're my man. The roll call of responsibility. Disturbed sleep. Tightness across the chest and shoulders. Irritability. The silent signs. One in five people suffers stress on a daily basis. It is annually responsible for the loss of 13 million working days, at a cost of £15 billion to the UK economy. One in four people will experience some kind of mental health issue over the course of a year. No football manager is an island.

Hearn trusted his manager; they shared a daily telephone call, usually at 10 p.m., when he was starting to monitor his American business activities. Ling gambolled on the pitch at Brisbane Road with his two children when Orient were promoted from League Two on the last day of his second full season in charge.

It ended in tears, of course. It invariably does so. They were shed by Hearn when he turned up, unannounced, at a post-match warm-down session one Sunday morning in January 2009. Ling saw the owner approaching, and murmured to Dean Smith, his assistant, 'Deano, we're gone.' His principal concern was for his son Sam, who was playing for Orient's Under 13s at the training ground.

'I know the news is going to go round like wildfire. Someone has to break it to him before he hears everyone talking about his dad. They were playing roll-on, roll-off subs, so no one gave it a thought when he came off and the coaches pulled him to one side. Orient was all my kids knew. They'd gone in the away end with my wife when we were on the road. Sam was constantly around the club with me. Honestly, do you know what he said when they told him? "Can I go back on and play . . ."

A peal of laughter dies quickly, forcefully, like a rogue wave hitting the shoreline: 'The time was right. Barry said it was the hardest decision he had ever taken, but I needed the change. I had thirteen solid years of Barry, five as his manager. If he liked you, he loved you. If he hated you, he really hated you. I count myself as one of his pals. We still play cricket and golf together. He was the best, because you knew where you stood. A problem never evolved because we talked every day. I just didn't realise I was going into a shithole club with a terrible chairman.'

He resigned after eight days at Cambridge United, citing 'irreconcilable differences' with chairman George Rolls, whose opaque operating practices aroused immediate suspicion. Rolls resigned within 24 hours, following an internal investigation into a disputed £10,000 facility fee for a pre-season friendly against West Ham. He was subsequently banned for five years by the FA, and fined £10,000 for no fewer than 3,076 breaches of FA betting regulations.

Ling was reinstated with the thanks of the club's board for his 'honesty, integrity and strength of character', yet the subliminal damage had been done. A world which would eventually turn black 'became grey'. His senses were dulled and his behaviour became illogical. The tipping point was mundane – a glance in the mirror confirmed he had forgotten to gel his hair – but it was enough for him to sweat profusely. He reported sick, without telling the club he was crying uncontrollably.

'I couldn't cope with leaving people out of the team. I knew I was upsetting them, spoiling their lives. I have done it throughout my career, and suddenly an everyday decision puts my life on the line. A problem the size of a pea becomes a volcano, through fear and anxiety. I tried a couple of glasses of wine to get to sleep, which was a recipe for disaster because alcohol feeds depression.

'I couldn't sleep but I stayed in bed. I wanted to hide away from the world, but I was scared of being in my own company. If my wife needed to go shopping, I'd beg her not to leave. I didn't really know what I was scared of, but I had an awful feeling of being alone. Managers are expected to be manly. They are expected to cope. But I'd lost Deano as my number two. We were really close mates.'

Smith, alerted by Caroline, Ling's wife, contacted Graham Mackrell and Richard Bevan at the League Managers Association. They arranged a consultation with leading psychotherapist Peter Kolb, who quickly detected the spiritual significance of Ling's sacking by Orient, and the associated trauma of his father's ill-health.

Ling returned to work after ten days, explaining he

had been laid low by a 'virus'. He was prescribed anti-depressants and underwent a course of cognitive behavioural therapy. Despite a panic attack on a train, after the specialist maintained his treatment was progressing well, his world gradually 'turned blue again'.

'My home life was sound, a lifesaver, but at work I had swapped security for volatility. For the next six months my old masseur Sandy Risley propped me up. He took me into work, talked me through things. I didn't feel right for a couple of months but my mood seemed to lift. I just thought it had gone away. I didn't know depression as I know it now. I thought I'd had a life experience, a little explosion.'

He left Cambridge in February 2011, a month after Smith had been appointed Walsall manager, and joined Torquay in June. He overachieved initially, reaching the League Two play-offs despite being given the strategic remit to avoid relegation. Obliged to raise £650,000 the following summer by selling the core of his team, his second season started poorly, and internal issues began to resurface.

'I was living with my brother-in-law, and couldn't get home to London during the week. I'd lost my driving licence for six months, for accumulating speeding points, so I had to use the train. I'd get back late on Saturday nights after matches, spend a lot of Sunday on the phone, and be on the five a.m. train back to Devon on Monday.

'I had my first dark moment in the October of 2012. It was a gut feeling that something wasn't right. When the fear moved from my gut to my heart and my head, I spoke to Graham at the LMA. He got me to a regional specialist, someone in Ashburton. It felt weird, speaking to him in his living room for an hour, completely unlike my previous experience of therapy.

'When we'd finished he said: "I think you've got IOU."

'"What's that?" I asked.

'"Intolerance of uncertainty."

'"Well," I told him, "I'm in a great job for that, ain't I?"'

Ling's laughter is a little bitter, less convincing this time, because 'things quickly snowballed out of control'.

Smith took advantage of a free Saturday with Walsall to watch Torquay lose 2–1 at Burton, but his eyes rarely strayed from the visiting team's technical area. 'I could tell Martin was not right again. He's normally loud and animated, but he was so subdued.' Smith called on the way home. 'Are you OK?' he asked. 'Not really,' Ling replied. 'I'm having those dark moments again.'

Fifteen days later, on Sunday, January 27, 2013, after completing preparations for the following day's West Country derby against Exeter City, Ling insisted on being taken to the Royal Devon and Exeter Hospital, to receive treatment for an imaginary brain tumour.

'I complained of pain in my head. I could sense my mother-in-law wanted to tell them "he's had depression", but she said nothing. They kept me in overnight, gave me a lumbar puncture. I knew there was nothing physically wrong with me but I wanted something to be wrong. I didn't want it to be depression again. Does that make sense? The doctors convinced me everything was clear, but I had to phone in ill to the club because people had seen me.

'Shaun [Taylor, his assistant] took the game, which we won one–nil. We gave the players Tuesday and Wednesday off, and I was OK until I decided to try to shoot back to London. I had another panic attack as soon as I got on the M5 at Exeter. My chest was heaving, and I was hanging on to the wheel for dear life, trying to get to Taunton services.'

Once there, he accosted an unsuspecting staff member and announced: 'I am having a heart attack. Please, please get me an ambulance.' He telephoned his wife, who tried to calm him down. 'I am dying. I am dying,' he shouted. 'Get someone to me now.' She called Shaun Taylor at his home in Exmouth, and told him her husband had a history of such episodes.

When Taylor arrived at the service station, Ling was in an ambulance, in meltdown, screaming: 'If I die, what is your name?' at the paramedic who was insisting there was nothing physically wrong with him. For a moment suicide seemed an attractive option. 'I had a fleeting thought: it is easier to run out of this service station, on to the M5 and bang, someone in an oncoming car will take me out. I knew deep down it was the depression coming back. Shaun scooped me up, and drove me to London while I spilled out my life story. I tried to tell him I would be back at work in ten days, but once I got home I was ordered to go to Harley Street.'

The tried and tested rescue chain, featuring his wife, Smith and the LMA hierarchy, secured an immediate appointment with Philip Hopley, brother of former England rugby international Damian, who founded and runs the RPA, the game's players' union. A specialist in forensic psychology who operates as the Priory's deputy medical director, Philip suspected Ling was in the midst of a mental breakdown, but allowed him a night's grace to see his children before he checked into the Roehampton hospital.

Ling has no coherent memory of his first three weeks there, though he has pieced together fragments of his experience, the subtle signs of being on suicide watch. His mobile phone charger was taken from him on admission. He was vaguely aware of the door of his private room clicking gently every half an hour, as nurses entered, to check on him without touching him.

Some senses were stimulated, since he can recollect the sound of footsteps along the corridor and the muffled buzz of patients queuing outside the medical room next door, at 7 a.m. for their medication. He attended art therapy sessions, in which six inmates were encouraged to express their deepest feelings through painting or drawing.

'When you draw, all the fear comes tumbling out. You make this picture, and you think: where the fuck did that come from? Those of us who were in a better place had nice bright pictures, in bold colours. Mine had slashes of black, black, black. I was in a dark, dark place.'

Football's life cycle continued, oblivious to his torment. Smith was pulling into the Priory car park to visit Ling when he heard on the radio that Paul Dickov had resigned as Oldham manager. He had urged him not to do so the previous day, when his Walsall side had won 3–1 at Boundary Park. His personal mantra – 'family, friends, perspective' – had rarely seemed more relevant.

He was unprepared for what he was about to witness. Smith failed to recognise his friend as he walked past him in a refreshment area. Ling's face was pinched, aged. His body was hunched, desiccated. After they met and returned to Ling's room, Smith instinctively drew back the curtains. Ling recoiled from the light. Their splintered, hesitant conversation, refracted through the fog of confusion, is reminiscent of a parent cajoling a reluctant child.

'Let's go for a walk.'

'I can't.'

'Who says you can't?'

'Just can't.'

'Have you ever asked anyone?'

'Well, no.'

'I am going to see someone.'

Smith received permission from the nursing staff, and took him outside the grounds, into the surrounding streets. He took the precaution of stationing Robert Jacobs, a mutual friend, outside by the kerb, 'just in case'. Ling remembers it as 'the most physically painful walk of my life'. Smith is consumed by an image of 'a ninety-year-old man, shuffling along'.

The regime at the Priory is designed to stimulate. Patients undergo other therapies, including music and yoga. Groups of twelve discuss their strategies for coping in times of stress. Some confessed to a reliance on cocaine, others on sex. Ling realised for the first time that his default position, when he felt despondent or vulnerable, involved alcohol. He was not a problem drinker, but his drinking represented an avoidable problem. He gave up, on the spot.

ECT became a viable option almost by chance. He met an outpatient, 'a blonde-haired girl from Brentwood called Kate. I noticed her because she had a cockney accent like me. I asked why she came and went, three times a week, and she spoke of the treatment as an old-fashioned remedy. She believed it would work.

'I knew I was not getting any better. Philip was telling

me my mood was not where it should be. It was all a little *One Flew Over the Cuckoo's Nest*, but he asked me to go away and read the leaflets about ECT. They didn't scare me. At that stage if you'd said to me: "Put your head in that fire for half an hour and you will feel a bit lighter," I would have done so.

'After the fourth session, something amazing happened. Oh my God! I just felt a light had come from somewhere. Brightness had come into my life. I know it doesn't work on everyone, but I swear that was a massive part of my recovery. It was as if they had jump-started my brain. Ever since that day, I've felt well.

'I began to get phone calls, from Sir Alex Ferguson, Sam Allardyce, Chris Hughton. I sensed that was the LMA putting out the message: "One of our members is in trouble. We need some help here." It was the start of the realisation that my peers do care for me.

'I began to wonder if others had gone through the same thing. Philip told me: "You are not the biggest and best to sit in that chair." He might have been trying to normalise it, but there is no doubt the LMA have a very quick way to get to the right people.

'The last few days in the Priory were quite funny, to be honest. I went back to the coping strategy group and announced: "Here we are. Two sex addicts, a couple of druggies and a bunch of drinkers. We should have a great party tonight." My sense of humour was coming back. That was the first sign I was getting better. I could laugh again.'

Reality was rather more sombre. Internet message boards, the bane of any football manager's life, were ablaze with conjecture that Ling was suffering from either cancer or alcoholism. The Torquay board knew the stress-related nature of the manager's problem, which was kept in house, but they appeared reluctant to acquiesce when he asked to resume his role.

'I was supposed to go back when I declared I was well. I felt great and ready to go. By then, Shaun had taken six games, and they deemed him not strong enough to be a manager. He had won the first match, but lost the next five. We had started to drift, and the bottom two were starting to creep up. They told me they felt they needed to fetch someone in to look after my position when I was not there.'

On February 20 Alan Knill, the former Rotherham, Bury and Scunthorpe manager, was appointed interim manager until the end of the season. When Ling protested, he was assured in writing he would resume his duties on April 28, the day after Torquay's final fixture at home to Bristol Rovers. It failed to ease his reservations.

'I was getting phone calls. Alan had brought Chris Brass in as his assistant. Shaun was reduced to bibs, balls and cones. Damien Davey, my physio, called, saying "Mart, this doesn't sit right with me."' I told him I'd been categorically told the job was mine, and that we would go again the following season.'

Torquay duly survived, finishing 19th in League Two, two points ahead of relegated Barnet, after accumulating seven points in their last three games. Ling's career prospects were crystallised the following day by two contrasting telephone calls. First, there was a message on his answerphone left by Davey at 2 a.m., containing the warning: 'I've been told not to stay in your camp, because Alan is going to be the manager.'

The second call was from Thea Bristow, widow of Paul, a fan who invested in the club when the couple had won £15 million on the National Lottery. Ling understood her loyalty in attempting to maintain her husband's legacy by acting as chair of the club, but felt she was naive as to football's manipulative ways.

Such sympathy lasted only as long as it took her to awkwardly read a pre-prepared statement that his services were no longer required due to 'footballing reasons'. He shot back, 'What other reasons are there?', without receiving an adequate answer. The LMA secured payment for the remainder of Ling's contract, but the wider world regarded him as just another casualty. His was the fifty-fifth of 63 managerial changes in the four divisions that season.

Knill subsequently met Ling at an LMA dinner, when he insisted he would not have taken the job had he had any indication Ling was so ill. He was sacked by

Torquay in the aftermath of defeat by Plymouth on New Year's Day 2014. He would be out of work for only 25 days, when he would benefit from a more celebrated manager's misfortune.

2

From King to Clown

Aidy Boothroyd entered his ground-floor office, a dead man walking. His tie hung limply and loosely, revealing the top three buttons of his white shirt undone. His black suit trousers, soaked by incessant rain, clung to his calves. He had just been sacked by Northampton Town, the bottom club in the Football League.

The blinds were drawn. He ignored a plastic tray of savoury snacks, samosas, spring rolls and battered prawns, and leaned down to pull a beer from a small, cheap refrigerator. The silence from his six senior staff, who stood self-consciously or sat inelegantly on a black leather sofa, was respectful but oppressive.

No one knew the precise details, the tearful *coup de grâce* applied by a director acting on the orders of owner David Cardoza, who had monitored the 4–1 home defeat by Wycombe Wanderers on his mobile telephone from a sunlounger in Dubai, but everyone knew the outcome.

An inquest was an unnecessary embarrassment. When Gareth Ainsworth, the Wycombe manager, completed his media duties and headed for the office for the conventional post-match drink with his opposite number, he was warned off by a firm but friendly steward. 'Not now,' he was told.

A Premier League manager at 35, Boothroyd was touted as the next big thing, an innovative coach and dynamic, challenging personality. He was spoken of as a mini-Mourinho, a future England manager. On this dank, dismal evening, six weeks from his 43rd birthday, he was being blithely dismissed by strangers as a has-been.

'Well, this is awkward,' he said, as he took a long, deep swig from the bottle. His contemplation of fate was interrupted by the arrival of his wife, Emma. 'Come on, Adrian,' she said, using the full version of the Christian name she favours. 'We're going.' He shook hands solemnly, in a mine of mutual commiseration, and headed out, past the ticket office and up the stairs towards the car park on a plateau overlooking Sixfields stadium.

Nathan, his 14-year-old son, was waiting in the family Audi estate car. Like many boys, he harbours dreams of becoming a professional footballer. Small in stature but smart and engaging like his father, he had acted as my tour guide when I first visited Northampton, nine months earlier. He sat in on our interviews and had an endearingly proprietorial air. Now, though, he acted his age. When his dad asked, 'Are you all right?' he burst into tears.

Boothroyd radiated paternal concern and spoke with affecting tenderness: 'Listen, mate, watching what happens to your dad is a lesson in life for you, because you've always got to remain true to who you are and what you do. Always understand that people are going to put you on a pedestal if you do that, and they're going to knock you off it when you're down, particularly in this job. Don't be upset about it. Treat it as just another chapter.'

The short speech stayed with him. 'Nathan has sat on an open top bus, watching twenty-five thousand people come out on to the streets of Watford to greet us when we beat Leeds to reach the Premier League. He's sat in the dressing room as a young kid, listening to me talking about how we're going to deal with Drogba, Rooney, Fabregas. What an education he's had.

'Now he's seen his dad get the sack at Northampton Town, a League Two club. After being a king, he's a clown. That's what I tried to tell him in the car: he has seen the highs and lows. I think – well, I hope – that it's going to make him a more rounded person. It is interesting that when I look at his life, it condenses my career as a coach.

'The contrasts are huge, from can do no wrong, to this. He still loves being around football, but he killed me the other day. He's come in the front room. There's me and Emma sat there, and he's gone "Dad, my knee's bollocksed." She's gone straight for me. "That's because he goes to work with you! Private school education and he comes out with that!"'

As soon as Boothroyd departed from his old office, Andy King, his erstwhile assistant, perched on the edge of the manager's desk. 'Right, what are we doing on Monday?' he asked, monitoring injuries, training plans and the availability of match analysis.

Personal loyalty was no longer an issue, since he was expected to fend for himself. Installed as caretaker manager, his first team talk involved a revealing imprecation: 'Win this, or I'll be painting and decorating next week.' He failed to win any of his five matches in charge, but didn't require a refresher course in the spreading rate of white emulsion; he moved on quickly, to become Karl Robinson's chief scout at MK Dons.

Chris Wilder, a dour, distant man with a reputation for producing functional football teams, joined Northampton from Oxford United. His first act was to install Alan Knill, Martin Ling's nemesis, as his assistant. In other professions, the role reversal – Wilder had been Knill's number two at Bury – might have triggered tension and invited discord.

However, football management is a network of

enduring allegiances and frigid marriages of mutual convenience. The pair had known each other for 20 years, since playing together at Southampton. They shared a car, commuting from their Yorkshire homes, and stayed two nights a week in the Holiday Inn Express at junction 15 on the M1.

The modern mania for treating the Gaffer as Godhead ignores the mundane nature of the trade. Boothroyd, typically, began coaching unpaid at Mansfield's Centre of Excellence. He needed to be similarly resourceful at Peterborough, where his diligence and intelligence impressed Kit Carson, a quietly revered figure in youth football.

As Under 19 coach, he 'became a marketing guy for a bit', persuading a local garage to donate a car, raffled, so he could employ a sports scientist. He was already distancing himself from the journeyman defender whose playing career ended at the age of 26, when he broke his leg badly in suitably unpretentious surroundings and faintly farcical circumstances.

'It was in 1996, at Meadow Lane. I'm playing right back for Peterborough. We were in a relegation fight at the time with Notts County. I've gone to clear a ball with my left foot. My leg's straight and Shaun Derry's come in to block the ball. He's gone high, caught the shin. I span round, landed on the floor. My left leg just felt very numb. I went to get back up, but the feeling in it still hadn't come back. Then I thought, right, OK.

'I saw the physio running on. He said: "That's it, mate, you're done." I was stretchered off, and placed in the tunnel because the ambulance wasn't there. I'm lying on the floor for five, ten minutes. People are just walking past, doing their job. It was like a *Carry On* film. Eventually, they took me to the Queen's Medical Centre in Nottingham.

'It was a strange feeling. I'd never had a serious injury, and it's almost a novelty at first. You get a bit of attention, but within a few days you're thinking, God, how long's this going to be? How long am I going to take to come back? But it's probably the best thing that ever happened to me, because it made me think about what I was going to do. Through a strange quirk of fate Shaun Derry got my coaching career going.

'It's funny how things go around in this game. Years later I was first-team coach at Leeds, under Kevin Blackwell and Sam Ellis. It was a time of transition, with a lot of players coming through, and about three-quarters of the way through the season Shaun joined us on loan from Sheffield United. One of the first things I did was to get all the players together and make sure he was fined for ending the career of one of the brightest stars in English football. He got fined a tenner. So that's the sum of my football career, ten pounds.'

Swings swung and roundabouts continued on their circular journey to nowhere. While Derry was starting his first managerial job at his old club, Notts County,

Boothroyd, like many unemployed managers, was reassembling the jigsaw of his career in order to find shape and structure. He relished the chance to recalibrate, but also missed the job like a lost limb.

He developed the habit of going for a long run, or submitting himself to a punishing gym circuit, at 3 p.m. on Saturdays; he needed the physical release because 'my body clock tells me it is game time'. He rationalised the chemical imbalance simply, admitting: 'Before a game your senses go mad. After a game, I'm not listening.

'It got to a stage where my missus stopped organising nights out on Saturday. One day we were all set to go out with Geoff Thomas and his wife, another couple, and a guy called Charlie Craddock, the leukaemia specialist who saved Geoff's life. On my way home from the game I called Emma and said I couldn't be arsed. She made me phone Geoff to explain. I said, "Listen, mate, we got beat." He was fine about it, but said, "Don't let football spoil your life."

'I put the phone down and thought, what the fuck are you doing? Here's a guy who has cheated death twice. That's what life is all about, not getting fucking beat last minute by whoever. We went out and had a great time, but the reason I tell that story is twofold. Football does take you out of reality. But the other side of it is when you're at the end of the season, and you've got that trophy above your head, there is nothing like it. It is incredible. Anyone who has ever won anything will chase it and chase it and chase it.'

Seen through the prism of inactivity, even the bad times are good. Boothroyd's formative years as a coach were spent developing and delivering a technical plan at Norwich City and West Bromwich Albion. He embraced the star system at Watford, where he morphed into the character he mocks as 'Mr Big Wig', but had more humble obligations when he defied advice and attempted to address Northampton's customary under-achievement.

'They call it time in the trenches, don't they? One day I'm under the stand fixing a flood. Mr Big Wig is fixing a fucking flood, looking for the stopcock so he can switch it off. Now, my wife will tell you if anything goes wrong in the house I'm straight on the phone to someone. I haven't got a clue about DIY or things like that, but needs must.

'The next thing, I'm being reminded I've got a meeting with a guy at Northampton University because I'm trying to get a training ground. Then I go to the Saints at Franklin's Gardens to meet the rugby groundsman who's going to do the work on the training ground. Suddenly, it is five o'clock and I haven't even started football stuff yet.

'A break gives you the time to come out of the hamster's wheel. It's a great period for growth, for thinking and reflecting. We don't get enough of that, because managing is relentless, absolutely relentless. You're not going to get any better unless you reflect on what you've done. I love reading, because books are built to last. I write a lot of things down, to aid my understanding.

'I went to see Ivan Lendl at a coaching masterclass. He talked about himself as a player. The biggest thing which came across was how absolutely driven he was. He told a story about preparing for the US Open: he employed a guy who had just finished laying the centre court at Flushing Meadow to come and lay the same court in his garden, so that he could practise in an identical environment.

'Everybody laughed at him but he said, "To me, it's obvious." He had a restless, inquisitive mind. He jumped from one thing to another, from the benefits of cardiovascular work on Venice beach to developing endurance by being on his bike around LA. Then he got on to the power outputs of Eastern European speed skaters . . .'

Like Brendan Rodgers, who succeeded him as Watford manager, Boothroyd is a disciple of neuro-linguistic programming. Adept at reading the subtle signals of body language, he consciously regulates the pitch and tenor of his voice. Listening to him articulate his longing for self-improvement, I couldn't help but recall the private theatre of a League Cup tie at Sixfields, against MK Dons.

I watched the first half from the Northampton substitutes' bench, where one did not need to see Boothroyd's face to appreciate the dangers of his disapproval. His shoulders and back became visibly tense and hunched; his hands aimed tomahawk chops at an unseen foe, and he delivered a series of acidic asides. But was his evident anger a prop? Did its visibility have an ulterior motive? The half-time interval, when Northampton trailed 1–0 but should have been four goals adrift, delivered the answer.

He waited until his team had settled in the narrow rectangular dressing room before he lunged suddenly and punched the wall. 'Let's be fucking crystal clear,' he said, in a low, threatening voice, as his players tried desperately to retain eye contact, rather than follow the red and blue counters sent flying across the floor from a tactics board. 'You cannot kid me on.'

He dropped to his haunches in front of JJ Hooper, a young striker signed on a free transfer from Newcastle United. Their faces were no more than three inches apart.

'Who is the best striker Newcastle have ever had?'

'Erm, Alan Shearer, boss.'

'Why?'

'Power. Goals. Work rate, boss.'

'Exactly. The day it's not working is the day you work even harder. You work, and I will carry you home. You don't, and I'm driving you down to your mates in London. You can be a non-league player. Want that?'

Boothroyd did not wait for the impertinence of an answer. He turned on his heels, advancing four paces to confront Kevin Amankwaah, an experienced defender signed after a successful trial. He had the thousand-yard stare of an old pro who knew what was coming; he was braced for a barbed monologue.

'So, Mr Thirty-one-year-old, pleased with yourself now you've got your contract? The kid has done ten times more than you. You've not won a tackle, or a one v one. You've lost your headers, allowed that bunch of spineless cunts to ponce their way around you. You can put it in, or you can fuck off.'

After a more measured tactical analysis, completed by the challenge that 'this could be a turning point in your season', Boothroyd signalled to his physio to start tending the walking wounded. The silence was funereal. He moved into an alcove in which King and Tim Flowers, the goalkeeping coach, waited.

'Sorry, chaps, not a lot more to say,' he whispered, wringing his right hand. 'I think I've broken my finger.' We grabbed polystyrene cups of tea, poured from an ancient kettle, and headed down the tunnel. 'I do that a couple of times a year,' he confirmed, with an eerie sense of calmness. 'Sets the tone.'

A more nuanced explanation followed: 'I'd like to think I never did anything in an environment like that to make me feel better. I don't do that. Without getting all philosophical on you, it is good to get angry with the right person at the right time, with the right intensity in the right environment. It's important that you show your teeth sometimes, but there must be degrees of behaviour.

'I think a lot about the language I use, about the tonality I use when I'm addressing people. It's very rare that I'm going to raise my voice and point fingers, but it does need to be done. I felt in that instance I had a great opportunity to really mark down what is acceptable in this group and what isn't. That's why I went for the youngest player and one of the oldest players.

'It's important that you don't protect the babies, but you've also got to go after the A-type gorillas in your group. I've been in dressing rooms as a player when managers rant and rave and I think there does come a time when it goes over your head, so you've only got two goes at it a year. Did I get a reaction from the group? Well, I felt we did better in the second half, though we lost.

'Did I get a reaction from the kid? Well, as I understand it, without sounding like an egg, there are four levels of learning. Unconscious incompetence, conscious incompetence, conscious competence and unconscious competence. At that first level, if you don't know that you don't know, someone's got to fucking tell you. Once they know, and they are aware of it, you've got the chance to work with them.

'That was what the Alan Shearer stuff was all about. It told me he knows that it's about working hard, but he actually doesn't know what hard work is. You get that a lot with kids who come into professional football, from under twenty-one leagues especially. He's a typical kid in many ways. Very, very talented. Plays against the Newcastle youth team, gets picked up, gets a contract. He's in the Range Rover living the life, the wrong life.

'I got his mum and dad in, thanked them for coming, and told them I wanted to know about their son. So Mr Hooper says, "I think he's got in with the wrong crowd and I think someone like you will be good for him." So then his mum wades in. "He just needs a good mentor, he's a good boy deep down . . ."

'I shook their hands, and got him in. I said, "Right, let's be straight now. I think you're a lazy bastard, a big-time Charlie. I think you think you're better than you are, but you've got some talent and I want to help you to help yourself. This is what your dad thinks. This is what your mum thinks. I'm going to push you. I'm going to get on you."

'What's the first thing he does when I let him go? He walks into the physio room and wants a massage. It's not like, "Keep your head down, JJ, just get on with it." He's Premier League. He wants a massage. I get wind of it, because I want my staff to tell me everything. I don't want to have to deal with everything, but I like them to tell me how they would deal with it.

'I asked them what they thought of him. No real surprises: "He's fucking having himself . . . we need to be on him every day." I decided we hadn't got the time to do that.' Hooper never played for him again, but responded to Boothroyd's tough love by regenerating his career with Havant & Waterlooville. Amankwaah's contract was cancelled, and he joined Salisbury City before they were expelled from the Conference for failing to pay their debts.

It begs the question: did Boothroyd fail in his duty of care, or did they lack the maturity or moral courage to make the most of the opportunity he provided? On the balance of available evidence it is the latter, but the manager pays heavily for poor recruitment, and must listen to the quiet voice of his conscience.

'It's a human need to want to get better at something. Whilst we're fire-fighting, trying to get results, I think it's important every player thinks he's being looked after, thinks that he's valued. Now some people, depending on age and attitude, might say, "I'm not going to do that" or "You ain't going to make me better". They rarely say that, but you do get the odd one.

'Arsène Wenger once told me: "You can't possibly get round to every one of your players after a game and ask how they think they did, so players have to be good coaches." I knew what he meant. They have to have an understanding of your coaching philosophy, be on the same page as you.'

We are all products of our experience. Boothroyd continues to be defined professionally by the three and a half years he spent in charge of Watford. The public image, embroidered by new age principles and bold, self-aware statements of intent, disguised the insecurities of his relative inexperience at the time.

'I was frightened going in there. I wanted it, I was desperate for it, I knew I could do it, but I'd been knocked back by a few clubs. I had to do my team talk in front of people like Sean Dyche, a better player than I ever was, and Alec Chamberlain, who is older than me and has done more in the game. I had to convince others, who were good players but past their sell-by date. To go into that dressing room took a lot of bravado.

'Over time I did get complacent. I have always expected a lot of other people, because I push myself harder than anyone, but by the time I came out of there I was worn down, ready for a rest. I was emotionally done. I took criticism personally, whereas at the start I didn't even read it. My mum would phone and tell me I was in the paper and I'd not be bothered, and I'm like that again now.

'I know there is a stereotypical view of me. It's all about perception. My teams are tattooed with the long ball. I guess as you get a bit older, you learn to roll with it a bit more. But, at the same time, I'd be lying if I said that it didn't worry me, because actually, winning football matches is not as important as how you play the game.

'I don't regret any of the jobs I've done. I needed to work through all the nonsense at Watford, where they lauded me for doing a brilliant job, but didn't wait long to have a dig. When I left I thought I had a chance of perhaps getting a bigger team in the Championship. I thought, yeah, I'll hang on for it and was out for nearly ten months.

'I went for a couple of interviews, at Reading, Swansea and West Brom, but then I became quite cynical about the whole process. You go there to say hello, shake hands, but they've already decided who they want, or are very close to deciding who they want. It's usually up to that candidate to mess it up.

'I just look and think, well, what's your strategy, what's your structure, where do you want to be, what are you trying to do, what are you prepared to accept, what are you not prepared to accept? Those things are never written in stone, they're always fluid, so you never know where you are. You're on shifting sands all the time.

'Colchester was great, with a blinding chairman who couldn't do enough to help you. The old adage, don't pick the club, pick the chairman, has got to be right. But the way it's going there are going to be record numbers of us getting the sack every season. I can't see it changing until people start asking, "What exactly are we doing here?"

'There's no respect for the job, or the man in it. When you get owners telling the world what salary a manager is on, or making a play for the next guy, or the next guy after him, it totally undermines everything leadership and coaching are meant to represent. Everybody has an opinion, everybody thinks they can do it, and it isn't that easy, mate.

'You're managing people, managing expectations. When you think about it, football is about third or fourth down the list because you've got to survive first. Recruitment's got to be right, but before you recruit, you've got to get the money. In order to do that, you've got to be able to influence people. And you're trying to influence people who have little or no understanding of how it all works.

'They treat players and people like cattle, and they're not, they're human beings. If you want to get the best out of a human being you've got to find out what makes them tick. You've got to blend a team, find a formula you can work with. You've got to make mistakes together, grow together, and, at the end of it, you've got to win. You've got to win in a way that is acceptable to the public because they want to see their team play in a certain way and win in a certain way.

'It gets to the point sometimes where you think maybe I should go and do something different within football.

We go into it thinking we've got a chance to make a difference, but you reach the brink when the chairman gets emotional and you can't tell him to stick it. You've just got to take a deep breath and get on with it because you know that at some point the good times will come back. There's enough evidence out there to suggest if you keep going, something will come good.'

The subliminal nature of the message was so striking it was not entirely a surprise when, little more than two months after Boothroyd had condemned himself as a clown, he reinvented himself as a crown prince. His appointment as head coach to the England Under 20 team led to the recycling of 'Hoofroyd' insults and inaccurate sneering that he owed his elevation to having been best man at the wedding of Dan Ashworth, the FA's increasingly influential technical director.

'Did I know Dan Ashworth before I got this job? Course I did. We worked together at Peterborough, when I first broke my leg. His brother Paul, who incidentally was his best man, was the youth team coach and then became assistant manager of the first team, so of course paths cross. I went to Norwich and then, years later, I get to West Brom. I know I need someone who's going to be fantastic at organising. I'm the strategy guy and Dan's the structure guy.

'In he comes, but I leave him in the lurch, really, and go to Leeds. He turns Albion into this fantastic football club, with the help of lots of others, managers, coaches and chairmen, and then he joins the FA. This is where people miss the point. He's at the top of the chain and my job comes under Gareth Southgate.

'Dan comes in right at the end of my second interview, the last twenty minutes or so. If I'm not good enough for that job I'm not going to get it, whether I'm Dan's best mate, Trevor Brooking's best mate or Greg Dyke's best mate. The way I look at it is, I have a reputation in terms of building teams and developing young players.

'You're always going to get people having a pop. Everyone has an opinion, don't they? At the top a lot of it is bitterness and jealousy, but what do you do? Do you rise to it and have a row or do you say that's fine? Proof will be in the pudding. If I'm the wrong man, it'll come out in the end, won't it?'

The survivor has rediscovered scholastic intent. He is able to coach as a purist rather than manage as a pragmatist. His success will not be solely judged by results, but by the quality of the graduates from his squad and their longevity in international football.

'In terms of my career, I'm in an absolutely brilliant place, the best place. I could have fought it out and gone for a League One or League Two job. I might have got really lucky if I'd waited long enough and got a Championship job, because of my record at that level. I might have gone as somebody's number two, or become head of youth at a top club because of what I've done and the people I know.

'I'm working with better players now. That excites me, because I'm thinking more about the game, more about systems and playing against better, more strategic teams. I know how to win a game. I know how to spot and exploit a weakness. I can see where we've got a problem and I know how we can deal with it. I see that early because of the batterings I've had as a manager.

'Does it suit me? At this point in my life it's absolutely perfect. I can go to different games every week. I've got forty-odd days with my players. I can think about what I'm going to do with them. I'm contributing something towards a greater cause, if that doesn't sound too fluffy. We're going to be all right.'

That bleak day at Northampton seemed a lifetime ago. But for Ainsworth, whose team indirectly cost Boothroyd his job, the pressure was all too real. His career, and the future of the small club he had come to cherish, would be decided over the course of 90 memorably dramatic minutes.

3

Alive and Kicking

Two plastic buckets collected the slow, lazy leakage from an ancient air-conditioning unit on the wall behind Gareth Ainsworth's head. The red leatherette sofa wedged against the opposite wall, on which goalkeeping coach Barry Richardson had slept for six months, had understandably lost its showroom sheen.

'Want to see the reality of my life? Here you go,' Ainsworth said, proffering an invoice, made out to his home address, from the top of a fulsome in-tray. 'Items ordered,' it read. '24 × 8 ft full-sized football net. Heavy duty. Price (VAT excl.) £29.95. Immediate delivery.'

The Wycombe Wanderers manager had been shopping on eBay the previous evening. 'Had to be done. We needed a net for the training ground. I couldn't get one signed off so I paid for it. We've been trying to get the purchase order for the air conditioning signed off for three months. Now I need to find a ratchet set. Any ideas?'

He laughed softly. His office wasn't much, but it was home to a dream, an ideal. The training ground had an air of optimism, a sense of purpose. Players ate chilli and watched the Open Championship golf on a small television in an adjoining dining room, in which a poster proclaimed: 'A man has two names. One he is born with, and one he makes for himself.'

Ainsworth was making a name for himself as a quietly inspirational leader, a man of integrity, compassion and resilience. He dared to be different, acknowledging the importance of his Catholic faith, his passion for poetry and his love of the lost art of song writing. As lead singer of Road to Eden, the latest in a series of pub bands he fronted, he still harboured hopes of a secondary career as a rock god.

Languid, tousle-haired and earnest, he could have passed as a mid-life recruit to the seminary. He was 41, and retained his registration as a player, though he was in no hurry to spoil the statistical symmetry of having appeared in 600 games across all four divisions. To maintain fitness he braved the agricultural habits of Sunday League full backs, road-testing his reflexes on the wing for his village team. He could still hit a deceptively flighted cross which curled away from an overcommitted goalkeeper.

Together with assistant manager Richard Dobson, he

had spruced the place up over the summer. Whenever they had to do menial work, like carrying sprinklers, painting goalposts and attaching nets, they would indulge their imagination and lapse into a parallel universe, where armies of the night produce pristine pitches and six-course meals can be eaten off the dressing-room floor.

'Whenever we're doing something I'll put on an Arsène Wenger accent, and Dobbo will pretend he's Steve Bould. I'll say, "Come on, Bouldy, let's get these nets up," and he will nod, or say something daft. It's all to keep us going, because we know they wouldn't be doing that in a million years, but we have to here.

'I've still got cuts and scars on my hands where my fingers became trapped, and that's no joke. I'm not asking for a medal for that, because that's who I've always been. I'll always find a way to get something done. Now what I need to do is learn. I've got intuition, but I need this persona, this arrogance. I need to learn more technically, tactically.

'I have my ways of playing, and I would like to study the game more deeply, but this job consumes your life. It eats you up, it really does. You've got to have a really strong family to do it. Gary Waddock, whom I regard as my mentor, once said to me that it would be tough with three young kids, and he was right. I do make the effort to switch off when I can, but it isn't often.

'We got away to Lanzarote for ten days in the summer,

and the phone never stopped ringing. It was crazy, mayhem. My head's never on holiday. I'm always thinking about the team, thinking about selection. I'm on the sunbed with a book, writing down formations and squad numbers. The kids'll come up and ask me to go in the pool, so I play with them, but there are always calls, texts.

'My missus, Donna, is Venezuelan. She's so chilled, so laid-back. She says, "You've got to do it, and that's it." She trusts me, so that when I say I need to do something, I really need to do it. She understands and that's huge in football. Having a great family around you is vital, because so many have gone off the rails without that.'

He had clarity, certainty, despite the penury. It would have been so different had the events of May 3, 2014 not been so blissfully euphoric. I confess I travelled to Torquay, on a warm, redemptive day of blue skies and golden memories, in anticipation of history being made for all the wrong reasons. Had Wycombe lost they would have joined their hosts in a unique death roll, and left the Football League together. Ainsworth accepts that his managerial career would have been 'toast'. He cannot confirm conventional wisdom that Wycombe would have gone out of business, but he admits they were in 'big, very big money trouble'.

We don't deliver good news that often from the cheap seats in the press box, but the forest of raised thumbs at precisely 4.53 p.m., which signalled that Bristol Rovers had been beaten at home by Mansfield and Wycombe had avoided relegation by winning 3–0 at Plainmoor, triggered a wonderful form of madness.

Ainsworth swung from the crossbar. He flaunted a home-made banner which proclaimed 'Believe' and embraced players who were in danger of hyperventilation. The connoisseur of classic rock, hooked when his dad bought him a *Best of the Who* cassette for his 17th birthday, strutted his stuff as the public address system boomed out the Simple Minds anthem 'Alive & Kicking'.

By the time I reached Ainsworth, some 15 minutes after the formality of the final whistle, a seagull, one of hundreds scavenging on the post-match detritus of crisp packets, chip wrappers and burger cartons, had left a milky deposit on the shoulder of his shirt, which had already been impregnated by tepid water, energy drinks and cheap Prosecco.

They say it is a sign of good fortune, but he was too exultant to notice. 'Being a football manager does terrible things to your heart, but no one gets to feel how I feel right now,' he said, with a sense of wistfulness which bordered on spiritual fulfilment. 'I am going to stay as high as I can for as long as I can.'

He had been booed the previous Saturday, on a desultory lap of honour dictated by the traditions of the final home game of the season, but had subsequently been seized by an inexplicable serenity. He attended Mass, and was energised by the support of strangers. He made the fairy stories he read to his children the narrative of the build-up.

'I dug deep inside, because I thought, one chink of disbelief, one chink of doubt, and someone will see through you. I was given the best hotel room I had all year when we got to Torquay, and when I woke on the morning of the game I looked out over the Atlantic. It was just the most beautiful day. Everything's calm, and I just thought, we can do this.

'I'm getting a shiver down my spine now just talking about it. I rang Neal Ardley, who was a teammate of mine, and he was in exactly the same position managing AFC Wimbledon the previous year. He just said, "Don't let the emotion of the occasion take over." I'm a passionate guy, but I was really calm and methodical in the dressing room. Then, when I looked up and saw you guys in the press box with your thumbs up, I went crazy.'

I happened to follow the team bus out of the ground and along a narrow street of terraced housing. When it stopped at a traffic light, two fans, ecstatic stragglers, bowed low and offered to share their stash of supermarket lager. The driver's window opened, and a disembodied, tracksuited arm beckoned them over. The fans stood on tiptoe, attempted to embrace their unseen heroes, and settled for clasped handshakes.

It was the start of an unforgettable journey, the

reward for endless hours on the road at a club which paid a first-team player £100 a week, and consequently rationed overnight stays as though they had to be purchased in gold bullion. It was old school, beers with the boys instead of solitary confinement with Beats by Dre.

Ainsworth identified a local off-licence, 'but the boys had beaten me to it. By the time I got on the bus there were crates of this, bottles of that. I've looked after myself my whole career but I just thought, fair enough, get stuck in.'

The bus stopped again, in a lay-by two miles down the A38, to retrieve the team's boom box from the luggage compartment. Ainsworth had 180 messages when he turned his phone on, and its constant beeping throughout the first hour of the journey indicated that more members of the football community were iden-tifying with his achievement.

'I was responding to everyone who texted because they were people who really meant something to me. We all do the job because of days like that. I suppose you love recognition. I tried to tell people what a great day it had been, and it was probably a good thing it kept me so busy. Otherwise I wouldn't have been able to walk off the bus.

'We take the boom box everywhere we go, to blast the dressing room. That's probably from my Wimbledon days. The stereo wasn't loud enough on the bus, so we made sure we had a proper hi-fi. It was just awesome, people singing, the lads laughing. It had been nine months of hard graft, two months of real worry, and a few hours of just pure relief. The lads were crying at the end of the game, and some were still in tears.'

Once the hangovers cleared, there was a savage reckoning. Seven of the 18 players on the bus were released the following week. A total of 14 players left the club, and only five had guaranteed contracts for the following season. Thanks for saving us, lads. See you later.

'They scrapped for me and they gave it their all, but at the end of the day I look at the big picture. We finished ninetieth in the Football League. It was tough, after all that elation. Not a great time, all in all. It is cut-throat, but these are the decisions you have to make as a manager. You live and die by them.

'It took me a good few months to realise that as a manager I'm the most important person in my players' lives. Hard work got me through my career and I was lucky enough to get some decent moves. Now I can shape careers. That's a big responsibility to take on. Some of these guys have got no dads, no families and broken homes. They need this arm around them. You have to be a counsellor and a social worker as well as being a football manager.

'There's a young boy here who's lost people in his life close to him in the last couple of years. He's a top, top guy, but he just needs some love. He's a tough one on the outside, but I can see right through it. He just wants to do well and feel he can impress someone in his life. He wants to turn round and say, "See, I want you to be proud of me." That's hard to take sometimes.

'I've released pros, where they are trying to keep a straight face, but a tear runs down their cheek because they've blinked and they've welled up. They're not crying, and you want to say everything's going to be all right, but you can't. You can't lie to them, you have to be honest. You have to say, "Look, I don't think you've got what it takes. It's my opinion, but that's what counts at this club. Go and prove me wrong."'

He spoke from bitter experience, having been released from his boyhood club, Blackburn Rovers, on his 18th birthday – 'May 10, 1991, a day I will never forget' – by Don Mackay. He broke down in the manager's office, but had the inner steel and professional pride to wipe his eyes in the car park and go out to train as if nothing had happened.

He estimated that over 4,000 players were without a club in the summer of 2014, vastly more than the widely quoted figure of 600 or so whose profiles are registered on the PFA website. In a buyer's market, he had gone for quality rather than quantity, a blend of experience and unheralded youngsters suffocated by the pile 'em high principles of academies at bigger clubs.

'The amount of people in the game I have rung this summer, to check out a player's character, is phenomenal.

We'll see whether the research pays off, but I need good characters who can handle pressure, after last year. They've got to be able to take constructive criticism, specific instruction. They need to know what is going wrong, and how to put it right.'

He was imperceptibly maturing as a manager. He had taken the strategic decision to sacrifice a squad place, so that he could employ a sports scientist. Senior players were invited to the coaches' Monday morning debriefs. His working relationship with new chairman Andrew Howard, a self-confessed Leeds United fan whose financial acumen and entrepreneurial vision accelerated the development process, flourished.

'He's a good guy and I think he's a realist. He's spoken to me on trusting terms about what we want to achieve this season and how we can progress. There are plans being talked through for the years to come, and if I can be involved in them then that will be brilliant. It might be another Crewe Alexandra, where they let their managers stick around until they develop. I'm all for being part of that, but I'm sure any manager would say that, wouldn't they?'

He networked assiduously at the League Managers Association's traditional pre-season meeting, where he acquired knowledge almost by emotional osmosis. 'It was great. You've got the outspoken, opinionated ones, and the quiet ones who sit there and take it all in. You've got the deep thinkers, the believers in kinaesthetics, and the ones who are all energy and action. It's fascinating to see the characters mixing.

'People look out for their mates, don't they? Maybe it's the long hair, making me stand out, or maybe it's just having been in football for so long, but I've had a lot of managers come to me and ask if they can help in any way, and they truly mean it. A lot of them have been where I've been in League Two and realise how tough it can be.

'Steve Evans at Rotherham is not well known for helping a lot of people but he's always been brilliant with me. He loaned me a player last year when I was in dire straits. Mark Warburton is a fantastic guy, a really good down-to-earth bloke. Ian Holloway, my manager at QPR and Bristol Rovers, is a great example of someone you wanted to play for, not out of fear but because he was as open as could be.

'Towards the end he got shafted by the politics at Rangers. He feels everything so passionately that there's a real crossover between his life and football. He's a real leader of men. I'm not surprised he had the dignity to go at Palace. It takes a big man to say "let someone else have a go" and he's a big man.

'Roberto Martínez was my roommate at Walsall. He openly admits that he sometimes takes risks. I didn't take enough risks last season, which is strange, I suppose, as I'm seen as a rock'n'roll type of guy who will have a go. That could define the difference between success and failure. I never want to turn around and say I wish I'd taken that risk.

'John Still was at Lincoln as assistant when I was there with John Beck. My first game as Wycombe manager was against him, Dagenham and Redbridge away. We got beat three–nil. He took me to one side and said, "Winning and losing, please, don't let it affect you." There's real empathy between football managers. We all know the world we're in. Nobody ever wants to see someone get sacked.

'I have massive respect for John Beck. He'll always figure highly in my list of people to thank for my career. He taught me resilience, boldness, the power of doing something you think is right. It's not always going to come off first time but you keep at it, and avoid looking at failure as a bad thing. He was completely ahead of his time.

'Everyone looked at the long ball stuff and the cold showers in a negative way, but he introduced ice baths, which are routine now. John taught us about the importance of eating after training, hydrating. He would come in the day after a game and he, his assistant and the physio would massage us. These things just got overlooked.

'He works for the FA now, and even that got slated because of his style of football, but whatever the FA want to coach, John can get people to do it. He could get eleven people to run through a brick wall for him, with all their might. It's the same with Aidy Boothroyd. The way he gets a team to bond, the spirit he creates by doing something unorthodox, is fantastic.'

His days were full, 'but don't get the violins out'. He scouted three nights a week, routinely leaving home at 7 a.m. and returning at midnight. The range of his responsibilities was highlighted when he apologised for breaking off our conversation to go down to the ground, Adams Park, to broker a player's contractual compensation agreement.

Wycombe's problems, as a club run by a Supporters' Trust, were a consequence of the disconnection between a laudable principle and the daunting realities of life in the lower divisions. The chairman, an astute character who owned a local ice cream business and won titles as a sports car driver, gave Ainsworth a stability that had been lacking the previous season.

'It was a huge education, and probably too soon for me, if I'm honest. The Trust taking over the club sounds brilliant but that model, with a manager who only has a handful of games under his belt, doesn't really work at all. I sensed people were looking for experience, so the right decisions could be made, and nobody had it. I had a great staff and we decided to pull together, keep the footballing side tight, and let the other side of the club deal with itself. It wasn't a split, as such, but you've got to look after your men. I wasn't big enough to carry everything.

'The team and the results are what's important at any football club. Even at Manchester United, with their merchandising all across the world, the only thing that really matters is that result on a Saturday. We know we're the number one priority here, we know we're the public side of the club. Thank goodness the other side was looked after. It was close.

'I don't want to be a statistic, one of those guys who never get another job after their first go at it. I'm learning a helluva lot, some things quicker than others, and sometimes I'm learning the wrong things, rather than the right things. But it's coming together. We're getting there.

'I've never doubted myself, but I've always been the type of guy who wakes every morning and believes he can affect someone in a positive way. I've been through a lot in my life to realise that you have to get up and make the most out of every day. It is not so much doubt, but worry, in this job. You just worry. You worry about your team selection, your tactical approach. I worried about the opposition too much last year.

'When I was a player, and my manager did a big presentation on the opposition, I was the one thinking, surely it's what we do that matters. Being at the bottom of the league affects your mindset. I've got to be a lot tougher, and confident enough to step back and trust good people to do their jobs.'

Influences were starting to become tangible, instead

of theoretical. He would use the example of his father, who held down two jobs to feed the family, to reinforce his message that a robust work ethic was non-negotiable, and that playing professional football was a privilege. He would make a virtue of Wycombe's pitted pitch, ruined by rugby.

His Crazy Gang days would be significant, not for the anecdote every new recruit wanted to hear, about the infantile initiation ritual of having his shirt burned and his trousers cut up, but for the memories of his inner turmoil as he struggled to justify what was then an extravagant transfer fee of £2 million.

He would speak from experience in counselling an insecure player. He would recycle such war stories as the Wimbledon team storming Chelsea's dressing room, spoiling for a fight, to illustrate the need for collective commitment. He would attempt to recreate the cama-raderie of their Tuesday club, without risking the carnage of a drinking culture which can no longer be sustained.

His part in the 'complete farce' at QPR, where he was a serial caretaker manager, dealing with the wildly eccentric, wilfully ignorant Flavio Briatore, over-shadowed his quiet study of the science of physiotherapy when the madness was at its height. His players would be looked after, in body and soul. He had, after all, walked a mile in their boots.

He began to plan a series of so-called 'development

days' with his chairman, who shared his ambition to revive the club's youth programme, sacrificed out of financial expedience. The myth that footballers' viewing habits extend little further than MTV and *Match of the Day* would be challenged by a series of debates on social issues such as the radicalisation of youth.

Ainsworth's pet project was a trip to the battlefields of the Somme, where he sought to share the searing experience of helping to unveil the Footballers' Battalion Memorial at Longueval, the scene of primeval fighting in 1916.

He would not be one of those managers whose team talk at Accrington was stolen from Henry V's St Crispin's Day Speech at Agincourt. He lived with freeze-frame images of mass slaughter after visiting Caterpillar Valley Cemetery, where 3,795 of the 5,568 men buried or commemorated there are unidentified. It was impolite to ask, at such an early stage in his managerial career, but how would he like his professional epitaph to read?

'I'd like to be regarded as a good man manager who was honest and believed in what I did, right or wrong. I didn't give confusing messages or contradict myself. I wasn't a hypocrite. I believe in what I believe in. I do it my way and if that works, fantastic, and if it doesn't, that's life and you move on. I would like players to leave and say, "I enjoyed my time under Gareth, and he was honest. He was never a twat, he never lied to me."

'That's important, not just in club football but in life.

Those values are important to me as a person. I want to feel content inside. I want to bring the kids up right. Hopefully the players will see this and go, "Yeah, I'll play for Gareth because he believes in us so much." I don't think anyone would like to be known as a horrible person, but some are . . .'

He paused for several seconds, shelved private thoughts, and started to rummage around his desk. The season was upon him, and he needed to remind himself of the tyranny of the fixture list. He pushed it towards me and leaned closer in what seemed a conspiratorial gesture. His voice was quiet, but a light shone in his eyes.

'Seen this start? Very, very, very challenging. Millwall. They don't like me. Carlisle, Tranmere, Stevenage. All came down from League One. York, spent a lot of money. Bury, favourites for the league. And then we'll be OK. So get me to September the thirteenth when we've got Mansfield at home. I'll be a happy man if I'm still around.'

League Two football may be anachronistic in this elitist age where the Premier League has become a homogenised, globalised TV phenomenon, but it applies the law of natural selection ruthlessly, and provides an invaluable, if unfashionable, proving ground for managers of Ainsworth's obvious promise.

He would be safe, and make the most of his great escape by setting a promotion pace, but eight other managers would lose their jobs in the first five weeks of the season. The victims included men close to him, who were worthy of his gratitude and received his unequivocal respect. The Grim Reaper's scythe was razor sharp, and shone blood red.

4

Out

Bad news travels fast. The ringtone on Gary Waddock's mobile phone, the type of klaxon which once warned a submarine crew of an imminent dive, signalled another good man had gone. He hit the mute button in deference to those around him, tired-eyed men in chain-store suits who were disturbed from their murmured, faintly desperate sales pitches.

It was 10.57 a.m. on September 1, 2014. Waddock, a neat but incongruous figure in designer jeans and a dark checked workshirt, sat in a hotel lobby in High Wycombe within earshot of the M40. He had ordered a small vanilla latte, which was in immediate danger of going cold. The text message revealed Joe Dunne had been sacked by Colchester United.

The usual platitudes were trotted out in a statement timed at 10.53 a.m. Dunne was praised as 'a Colchester legend' by chairman Robbie Cowling, a recruitment specialist who made great play of his mature working relationship with a man he described as 'a remarkable servant' of the League One club. They had shared a range of books on the philosophy of leadership, including the latest counter-intuitive work by Malcolm Gladwell, which used the example of David's victory over Goliath to suggest life's underdogs had the inherent advantage of surprise and flexibility. Dunne, whose fate was sealed by five consecutive defeats, had every reason to dispute the theory.

So, too, did Waddock, who was only three days into pre-season training when he became the innocent victim of football's version of a drive-by shooting, his replacement as Oxford United manager by Michael Appleton following a sudden change of ownership. It had been a turbulent half an hour; Graham Kavanagh's sacking by Carlisle United had been announced at 10.30 a.m.

'The news flashes up and then agents and friends ring you. It's the nature of the business; it's horrible, because you are relying on other people to lose their jobs so you can have an opportunity to go back in. I know Joe and Graham. They're good people and it is very sad for them. It's cruel, but that's the way it is.

'We all get the sack, and we all have to come to terms with that. The first time it hits you hard. You think, wow, well, why me? You probably take it too personally. When it happens again you tell yourself, OK, right, this is part of the job. You have to get used to this. You accept your life expectancy as a manager is two years, if you're lucky.

'I'm quite realistic and honest with myself. When I've been sacked I've always asked, what did you learn from that? If you get another opportunity, where will that be? There's no point me looking in the Premier League or Championship. If I do get a job, it could be at Conference level, because I got Aldershot promoted, or it could be a League Two club looking to get into League One, which is what I did with Wycombe.

'Geographically, Carlisle is a long way away, but I'm very much about my career and if it means me having to move, I'll move. I'm interested. Colchester want to bring their young players through. I've had experience of that so, yeah, I'll look at that, too. Firstly, am I the type the chairman would look for? Secondly, would it be the right club for me? I'll consider that in the next day or so and maybe apply.'

Too late. The Colchester vacancy was officially filled at 5.30 p.m. that day. Regime change was clinical and suspiciously smooth; Dunne and his assistant, Mark Kinsella, were replaced respectively by Tony Humes, the club's head of youth, and Richard Hall, who was promoted from the Under 21s. A new recruitment structure and strategy were simultaneously introduced. Cowling, who had been reducing the playing budget by £300,000 each season, signalled his intention to stop putting money into the club from 2016.

Waddock, one of more than 80 applicants, would make the shortlist at Carlisle, but be overlooked in favour of Keith Curle, who had been out of work since being sacked by Notts County in February 2013. He is accustomed to the curt cruelty of the game, having been controversially excluded from the Republic of Ireland's 1990 World Cup squad by Jack Charlton. Longevity demands an ability to deflect bad news, and a willingness to disassociate from its occasional unfairness.

He knew he had 'no chance' once it became clear a restructure at Oxford would involve a new chairman and chief executive. 'They had every right to bring their own man in. It's their club. I don't take it personally. I never have done. I move on very quickly, because if you dwell on it, it could be difficult to get yourself going again. It's done. You put it to bed. These things happen.'

He felt no anger towards Appleton, whom he had met only once previously, while working as Karl Robinson's first-team coach at MK Dons. There was no point in making contact to exchange empty platitudes since all he cared about was speaking to the players and staff he had assembled over the summer. They, at least, had the security of short-term contracts. His most poignant duty was to apologise to those players who were suddenly vulnerable, since they were on trial that week. Some had rejected opportunities to go elsewhere, because they believed in him. They trusted in his track record, especially in straitened circumstances at

Wycombe, where Gareth Ainsworth still referred to him as 'Gaffer'.

Football subtly closes ranks around its own in times of stress. Waddock had worked for the Premier League, overseeing academy standards at Fulham, West Ham, Tottenham and Chelsea, after being sacked by Wycombe. He took advantage of an immediate offer to return to West Ham, to put on occasional sessions for the older age groups. He agreed to assist Martin Allen, his old QPR teammate, on an *ad hoc* basis at Barnet. Gestures of empathy and respect were appreciated.

'Take David Pleat. I've known him because I've played under him. He rang me and asked if I was OK. For somebody like him to think of me, and pick up the phone, was just brilliant. People don't see that side of the game. I have the utmost respect for him. There's so much knowledge there. I listen to him, and know I'm going to be a better manager and a better person for it.

'I will work. I want to work. Whenever I've been sacked I've put myself out there. I've spoken to a number of chairmen and they liked that, because I didn't just sit on my backside. I hate the uncertainty of this period. How many guys are like me, just waiting? It is getting harder. The silly season usually starts around October, but it is earlier than ever.

'I've never spoken to anybody about the sack. I think you stay clear of that. I've never asked people, "What did you do when you were out?" You take it for granted that you get out there, to see and be seen. I won't attend a game where I feel the manager is under pressure. I know some guys do that, but I wouldn't be comfortable with myself sitting there.

'If I knew I was getting a job in six months' time, I could really enjoy this time, go to games, build up my information on players. But this could last a day, or last for ever. You just don't know. That is the worrying thing, because you know what you want to do, but you might not get the opportunity to do it.'

Fate had randomly bonded him with Dunne. Aged 52 and 41, they were products of different football generations, but linked by the threads of allegiance, resilience and availability. Waddock's first managerial role, at QPR, was traumatic; he succeeded Ian Holloway as a caretaker in 2006, but lasted for only two months once he had been given the job on a permanent basis.

He had made 21 full appearances for the Republic of Ireland, as a dynamic midfield player, over a decade from 1980, while Dunne won a solitary Under 21 cap. The younger man's playing career, as an assertive defender, was ended at 29 by hip problems, while Waddock, a protégé of Terry Venables, rehabilitated himself in Belgium after being encouraged to retire due to knee damage.

They were united by a sobering set of statistics: it takes a sacked manager 18 months, on average, to find another job. Fifty-eight per cent of first-time managers never get back into work when they are discarded. Around 35 per cent of dismissals are the result of a breakdown in the relationship between manager and chairman, or club owner.

Dunne was told to stay strong by Tony Pulis, a family friend. He was invited to observe England's age group players by Aidy Boothroyd. Brendan Rodgers offered him the chance to study Liverpool's Champions League preparations. Karl Robinson shared coping strategies. Yet, psychologically, he remained an outsider. His public profile was low, and did scant justice to the sharpness of his intelligence.

He had spent 18 years at Colchester, as player, youth coach, assistant manager, caretaker manager and, finally, first-team manager. Inevitably and unfairly derided as a cheap option when he succeeded John Ward on September 27, 2012, he survived for nearly two years through painfully acquired self-sufficiency.

Dunne had been forced to grow up fast on the terraced streets of Inchicore, a Dublin suburb developed from a marshland village known in Gaelic as Sheep Island. It has always been a place of fluidity and commerce, from the boom of the late 18th century, fuelled by the trading route of Ireland's Grand Canal, to its expansion as an engineering hub, a century later.

He was a self-reliant boy, who became the man of the house at 13, when his father died. He had yearned to be a football manager from the age of nine, when, as a Liverpool fan, he stood in front of the bedroom mirror and conducted imaginary television interviews in character, as Bob Paisley and Joe Fagan. His school friends eulogised Kenny Dalglish, the player; he preferred to analyse Kenny Dalglish, the player-manager.

His life in what he acknowledged as 'a rough area' was rapidly shaped by his independence of spirit and ferocity of ambition. He became comfortable with big decisions; when he was 15 he consulted a map, and left home for a trial at Gillingham, a town of which he had only vaguely heard. He was offered an apprenticeship after a fortnight, and accepted without telling his mother. His first manager, Damien Richardson, became a surrogate father.

'I left my mum by herself but when I got there I had this sense of I've got away. Damien was really inspirational. I looked at how he organised people, brought out the best in them. He had humour, he was hard, and you wanted to be guided by him. I just felt, I want to do that. Almost as soon as I was in England he let me coach the kids in the car park at the back of the stadium.

'I'm a teacher. Management these days is teaching. Coaching is teaching. You can't just coach technically or tactically, you've got to coach sensitively and holistic-ally. People were too quick to tell me what I couldn't do. Tell people that too often, and they lose confidence.

My approach comes from my time as a youth coach, because that was when I was teaching life skills.

'One of the first things I did was to read a wonderful book called *Imagine*. There's a story in it about a child going to the fridge for the first time. They come into your room with a big glass of apple juice, so what's the first thing you say to them? "Don't spill that." And what do they do? Spill it. They came in proudly, thinking, look at me, I've done it for myself, but a careless word and it is, "Oh! Sorry, Daddy. Sorry Mummy."

'I tell young players the biggest crime is not fulfilling their potential, not just in football, but in life. Study for something, learn languages. I was in charge of their education, making sure they got their grades. I saw influencing a kid's life as the great reward. Young players are a blank canvas, and sometimes you miss that as a manager, when it becomes results-orientated. I try to treat people with humanity. I don't believe in conflict. Conflict leads to aggression, aggression leads to frustration, frustration leads to a lack of ideas. You just end up shouting at each other.

'To get the best out of a player you need to understand the person. Obviously there will be times when he chooses not to engage, and that's when you have to be upfront, and talk through why he's not in the team, or why he may or may not have to leave. I tell the truth, because I've been lied to as a player. Everyone has been fed a story now and again. When that happens, you lose trust.

'The human side of the game is so important. I lost my father very early. He was ill for four years, never in the house, always in hospital. So I know what being brought up by a single parent is like. In football we go to the inner cities, the sprawl, to look for talented players, so we need to empathise with their circumstances.

'Everybody wants to be judged by their status. Who's got the best house, best car, best clothes. Who's got the best watch, the best phone. Who's got more hits on Facebook, more followers on Twitter. If your life is based on the guy in the music video sat in the front of a Bugatti with six naked women around him, we have a problem. Do we need to be so shallow? We have a responsibility in the football industry to help the young men within it.'

I had spent five hours speaking with Dunne at Colchester's training ground, ten days before he was sacked. Florence Park was Cowling's pride and joy, modern yet welcoming; the ambition of measured progress through the development of young players had literally been set in stone. As we lingered on a balcony overlooking four pitches which backed on to neatly tended gardens, the manager's reflections had uncanny prescience.

'I remember my early days, before we came here,

when we had to train on pitches where you had to pick up needles before sessions. There would be broken bottles. Junkies would be knocking around. There was dog shit, all that kind of stuff. We've come from that, so we know what it's like to have nothing.

'We trained in the army garrison for a while. That was very uncomfortable. You would have players training and thirty, forty yards away soldiers were packing their rucksacks to go to Afghanistan. Then you heard about 3 Para losing people, and it was just horrible. You've got footballers whooping and hollering and you see army cadets looking at them, thinking you fucking pricks. We had to get out of there.

'We're an evolving club, and I know the point will come where that's it. When I go, and I will, the chairman and I have agreed in writing that the next manager has to follow the cycles. So nothing changes. What I have to do is keep on learning and hope that at some stage what I've done will get me another opportunity, irrespective of where it is in the game.'

His pride in his philosophy was tangible as he showed me around a dressing room which he intended to be a monument to his inclusivity. Instead of decorating the walls with the usual motivational posters, he had asked his squad to define themselves as a group, and present their expectations of their coaches.

Their value judgements were printed on sheets of A4 paper, placed above the pegs on which clothes were expected to be hung neatly: 'This is not a holiday camp . . . Respect for each other . . . Consistency of emotions . . . Don't take it to heart . . . Continuity . . . Communication . . . Professionalism . . . Positivity . . . We look after ourselves.'

They were meaningful words, thoughtful sentiments, devalued so comprehensively by results that they were barely worth the paper on which they were written. Since Dunne had gone, and a new manager was setting the tone, the messages were historical curiosities, hieroglyphics on a Pharaoh's tomb. He retained his principles, but had lost his platform.

'I can't think about the "what ifs". The biggest thing about fear is that it creates things which actually don't exist. You catastrophise events. I can see how people fall into despair. People give you good advice when you have a difficult time but we're all consumed by our job. We all share the same fears, the same dread.

'When you're a first-time manager it is where do I go from here? I have no problem talking about that. It has taken me ten years to get a philosophy together. Then you see it start to fall apart in front of your eyes. You think, I've worked so hard for this. I'll keep on working, but it's getting away from me. Everything I've worked my whole life for, everything I believe in, is now judged on a run of results.

'It's about the dimensions of your comfort zone. You either want to stay in it or you don't. No one can really understand what it is like to be a manager until they have done it. It's like standing on an iceberg. You look around and you're drifting, and everyone else is on the shoreline. You're on your own. That's how I feel every time I step out there, into the technical area.

'There's roughly a ten-metre strip. It feels about ten miles from safety. People will help you as best they can, but you're on your own. You just don't realise, before you do it, how incredible an experience it is. Your mind becomes your friend and your enemy. You're bollixed if you let fear in. You learn about the power of the three words to which no one admits: I don't know.

'You must be aware of the impact of your mindset, how you come in in the morning, how you speak to the players. You have to judge your body language. And as much as you try, sometimes you are going to be pissed off. I admire people with energy and a passion to self-improve, but also a desire to help others. Some people are just in it for themselves. They're horrible people who have the self-drive, but don't give a fuck about anybody else.'

He spoke with an orphan's haunting eloquence. His eyes, a delicate blend of grey and green, blazed. He swept his hand through a high, slightly thinning hairline flecked with the first frosts of silver. It was almost as if he was inspired by the intimacy of his reflections.

'Sometimes, as a manager, you almost get snow blindness. You watch a match with such intensity, and with so much happening, that you almost black out. Your brain is processing all the information and it can't compute. For a split second, it shuts off. It reactivates, but generally I have to walk back to the dugout.

'That's my coping strategy, my trigger to get back into the moment. When I have recomputed, got my head back in the game, I walk back into the technical area. Can you explain that? Is it natural? I try to drink a lot of water, out of habit mainly, but I also remember being told that dehydration causes stress. I'm not particularly educated as some people claim to be, but I think I have a good eye and an ability to retain knowledge.

'The first eighteen months you just forget about your family. I had moved back to Kent, and used to stay in a hotel three nights a week. I did my coaching, worked from nine in the morning until nine at night. When we moved back to Colchester we bought a house near where the stadium was being built. I watched it go up, so when it was open I stayed there longer, because it was convenient.

'Everything just builds up and up. I had a two-, three-minute drive home, but when we lost a home game, I swear to God I would get in my car and drive for an hour. I'd drive down the A12 and back up the A12. I'd go off into the countryside, stop the car, and not know where I was. Now a psychologist would probably tell you, "You've got issues there," but that's how it was.

'I'm thinking, how can I fix things? Next minute, I'll

come up to a traffic light. I don't know if I'm going left or right. Where am I? Seriously. You think something's got to change here. When I get home the missus'll go, "Where have you been?" And I'm like, "I don't fucking know. But I'll tell you what I do know. I know my team for Tuesday night. And I know what I'm doing in training next week."

'I can see why people go off the scale with it, but that's management. If you want to do it, I don't care who you are or what you do, you're going to feel those emotions. You're going to have self-doubt. You're going to have fear. You're going to put your health at risk through long hours and not eating properly. You'll have the meal deal, sandwich, crisps and a fizzy drink . . .'

The hierarchical structure of football invites a culture of bullying and casual contempt. Dunne has never forgotten arriving, as a young coach, to find his personal effects in a cardboard box, thrown into a corridor without explanation or apology because a staff member, aligned to a new manager, commandeered his office. The contrast with Boothroyd's maturity, when he became Colchester's manager, was marked.

'I was caretaker manager when Aidy got the job. He impressed me straight away with his knowledge of the players, the staff and everything else to do with the club. He does his homework. He taught me about thoroughness of preparation, and helped me cope with my anger. Basically, he worked me out.

'I owe him a lot. He challenged me to believe in myself, and changed me, in a football sense, by sending me to study the systems at Ajax and Anderlecht. That's when I realised I was miles behind. I thought I was a coach, but needed to do so much more work to justify that title.

'I watched how they were forceful with their players, but gave them leeway to think for themselves. Their coaches only step in if the point they are trying to make doesn't come across. Afterwards they go and have a beer. It's very relaxed, jeans, T-shirts, players and coaches talking about football. There's trust and respect.

'The more I looked into the European side of the game the more I started to see a completely different aspect of football. It changed my way of thinking. We attach too much importance to tradition in this country. There's no definitive way of playing; what can we learn from other nations? How and why are they progressing?

'The one thing I've worked really hard on is that emotional outpouring. I was an emotional player who showed passion and commitment, but as a manager and a coach you've got to lead by a different example. There are times you feel the frustration of a fan, when that shot just misses, or a chance is lost, but the approach needs to be more intelligent, because the environment is changing.

'I played in a promotion-winning team at Colchester in 1998. It was a group of driven individuals, who developed a real camaraderie. But what I could never comprehend as a player was why I would always have a headache after playing against a Premier League team, even in pre-season.

'I'm sure the lower down you go, a player can only process one movement, one sequence of play. Top players process three or four. They see it quicker, think quicker, and that's why they are where they are. To maintain that level of processing information, you're going to have to train your brain. That's what Brendan is doing at Liverpool.'

To prove the point, Rodgers had just overseen the appointment of Pepijn Lijnders as Liverpool's Under 16 coach. It was a low-key move, which merited a two-line profile on the club website, but signalled a shift in player development policies. Dunne had come away from the Dutchman's session at a coaching conference in Wales that summer convinced he had seen the future. His eclectic range of influences testified to an enquiring mind.

'I want to improve, further educate myself. Pepijn was at Porto at the time, but his mannerisms, how he brought the best out of the young players in his session, told me there is another way. He put his theories into practice with such passion, but also with such intelligence. The drills were high intensity, and player-specific. I just thought, wow, that's wonderful.

'I also watched Roberto Martínez put on a couple of

sessions. He taught me that the key to bringing out knowledge is how you interact with people. He was authoritative with his information, but imparted his knowledge with such enthusiasm. You can't be mono-tone these days.

'I was a player at Gillingham when Tony Pulis came in. We were struggling and he brought in eleven new players. Straight away you knew this was different, that this guy was ruthless and would get his way. He was very good to me, even though I left because I wasn't in his team. He changed the personality of the club, but brought success without destroying lives.

'I was at an LMA meeting not long ago, when Ian Holloway spoke brilliantly about his beliefs, and how we should never stop learning. I will always remember as a player drawing two–two with Bristol Rovers when he was their manager; he was ranting and raving at the referee, but still gave us the respect of standing outside our dressing room, shaking our hands as we went in.

'Aidy was clever in the way he consciously used emotion. Before one game, against Millwall, he put the flip chart in a certain place in the dressing room. He told me, "When I come in make sure you're stood out of the way, because I'm going to boot it across the room." Sure enough, he did. It helped him get a point across.

'I'm trying to take the emotion out of it as much as I can, and I'm conscious of being constructive after a game, but sometimes, at half-time, you need to let them have it. At Crawley last year I smashed the tactics board, and told them the second half was about guts and desire. They were excellent after that. It was the same at Rotherham, where I punched one of the lockers.

'It's old school, what we grew up with, motivation through passion. There's a lot of talk about the hair-dryer, but I've come to the conclusion that the biggest thing is a player's self-worth. If you can convince him he's worth something, and explain how he can make himself better, he generally tries to do what you've asked him. It is character-driven.

'Top managers adapt and move. I like to think I'm a forward-thinking young manager, but some people, in their ignorance, will argue I can't be because I've oper-ated in the bottom half of League One. We have to get them to open their minds a bit more. Don't judge people based on who or what they are, or where they've been.

'We've got pundits who have played at the highest level. They've got great knowledge of the game, and can speak from experience about what a player needs to do at a particular point in a game. But they can never be in the mind of a manager. They can only assume what the managers they worked under would have done.'

Being sacked for the first time is a rite of passage. When it happened to Waddock, he was counselled by Bobby Campbell, the former Fulham, Portsmouth and Chelsea manager, who is a trusted member of Roman

Abramovich's inner circle. Dunne drew upon the advice of Pulis, but was still coming to terms with the chasm which separates idealism and pragmatism.

'Harry Redknapp asked me how many first-team games I'd done. I told him just over a hundred. He went, "Well done. If you pass seventy-five then you're probably going to stick in the game." I told him he'd made my day. I magpie bits and pieces from all the top managers, but the best piece of advice I've received is not to model myself on one individual. I try to be myself.

'We work our bollocks off down the leagues, to progress through the system, and people tell me to be more selfish, to think of myself more. They think I'm mad when I say there is more to the game than winning. You are judged continually as an individual, and loss of status is massive. You're told, "Get to the top. Just try and get to the top."

'Be careful what you wish for. I see people ripping the heart out of a club for their own ends and it does my head in. I suppose I'm trying to be rational in modern society, where rationality doesn't exist. It's mental. You're a manager and you ask about the long-term goal. It's "Just fucking get promoted. That's what we want." OK, I'll get you promoted, but eventually it is still "See you later."'

Waddock was not around to share Dunne's swirling emotions, but he had captured the subtext of the conversation: 'We're all the same, when the ball is rolled for the first game of the season. We're all going to get promoted. We're all going to be successful and progress our careers. We're all going to get the sack eventually.'

Neither knew it at the time, but their paths would cross again.

5

Ollie's Flying Circus

The poster above Ian Holloway's head merged images of a blazing-eyed boy and a snarling lion. The slogan 'Stronger Together' was incongruous, since the figurehead of the accompanying promotional campaign was an unapologetic individualist who had marched defiantly to his own drumbeat during 19 seasons as a football manager.

Holloway is a one-off, a tsunami of unregulated emotion, surreal metaphors, rose-tinted reminiscences and florid common sense. He was seeking redemption of sorts at Millwall, home of the ultimate reality check. He had just moved house for the 32nd time in a career shaped by adversity and defined by achievement at unfashionable clubs, but retained a familiar air of restlessness.

They are used to the howl of the underdog at the Den, and identify with a survivor's cunning. Holloway had been received rather more warmly than his predecessor, Steve Lomas, whose appointment was greeted by a bedsheet banner strung across the main gate. It instructed him to 'Fuck Off' before he had even taken a training session.

Holloway had saved Millwall from relegation the previous season, when they were bottom of the Championship with nine games remaining. They had begun decently, taking ten points from five league games in August, a sequence started by the tribal rite of victory over Leeds United, their northern *doppelgänger*.

He was saying the right things – 'We know the world is waiting for us to fuck up but anyone who writes us off is as thick as a canteen cup' – without being measured for a saviour's silks. A small group of dissident fans, mobilised by stuttering form in September, had already christened him 'Hollowords'.

Serenity was never a realistic prospect, despite Holloway being unveiled as Millwall's 'Plan A, B and C'. He understood the club's mentality since he was an outsider by instinct and inclination. His personal and professional challenges had ranged from malevolent club owners to his wife's lymphatic cancer, and he was eager to prove himself after being overwhelmed, physically and psychologically, by the task of keeping Crystal Palace in the Premier League.

He resented being judged according to stereotypes

created by bizarre social media montages which implant immodest images in the brain, such as Cristiano Ronaldo being 'hung like a hamster'. Over the course of a three-hour conversation, which at times had the dissonance of a primal scream, a much more calculated and complicated individual emerged.

He deserves your full attention, and I will only interrupt when necessary. To set the scene: he speaks quickly, in a Bristolian burr which has never lost its marmalade tang. He veers from engaging to vulnerable, from profound to puzzling. His face is small, expressive, childlike when relaxed, but mournful in repose. He is in a tiny, white-walled office. To borrow an old tabloid masthead, all human life is there.

'I'm a very emotional person. I have been all my life. I'm too much like my mum. She'll cry at a kitten not having a drink. It's unbelievable. I was the youngest of three; my brother is nine years older than me, my sister six years. I had to go to school in my brother's clothes. I can remember my dad saying, "Oh yeah, you were a mistake," but my mum shot back, "I'm happy I made that mistake." He was always teasing me, but I think you're moulded by those sorts of things.

'I had the lucky scenario in that I was the youngest, so I knew I had Mum's full attention. I was always her baby. I wanted my dad's attention, so I'd play football and win for him. The big gap in ages used to annoy me. I'd have to go to bed earlier, have less pocket money, and it really used to get to me. I've had this thing about fairness all my life. I can't shut up. I've got to have an opinion, if there's something I don't think is right.

'Judge people by what comes out of them. That was my dad's motto. He was in the navy. He was an able seaman, with working-class values. He went in at eighteen, met my mum, and she made him come out, because her dad was in the navy and she didn't really know who he was, because he was away for two or three years at a time.

'Dad was a good amateur footballer, but he never made it. He was on my case. Believe it or not, when I was twenty I had to be in at half eight at night. Dad used to say, "You've got to go to bed early if you want to be a professional. If you live in my house, then that's what you do if you expect to be a footballer. If you don't make it, son, let it be for lack of ability rather than lack of effort."

'I used to tell him I wanted it more than him. I wouldn't have gone away at eighteen. But, and here's the thing, he did so because he didn't know who his dad was. When he got to fourteen, he found out who he thought was his dad was actually his stepdad. His father was a bandleader who played saxophone. He was blown up during the war. Dad never knew what his real name was. He wanted me to know he was happy as Bill Holloway, and wanted me to be proud of who I was.

'He told me always to go through the front door in

life. Never the side door, or the back door. You might get thrown out, but if you land on your back you get up, dust yourself down, and go again. If you see something happening that is wrong, don't turn a blind eye. Help a stranger, because you will get it back, threefold. Dad was a man of simple, wonderful logic.

'The best football managers are not just great tacticians or geniuses when it comes to seeing something in a game. They're fantastic with people. They sell them the strength which comes from self-belief. I was thirty-three when I started as a manager, and came from an era in which you were expected to have respect for authority figures.

'We were brought up as footballers by senior pros. We were brought up as men by our fathers. If you disrespected a teacher at school, good God, you were scared stiff to go home. If you even dreamed of a copper stopping you, you would be terrified. When I left Bristol Rovers for the first time, to go to play for Wimbledon, it was the biggest learning curve of my life.

'I bowled in there, the most naive person in the world, at twenty-three. I couldn't cope with it, couldn't handle it. I couldn't understand why the Wimbledon lot would cut someone's pockets out of their trousers, why they thought that was funny, why they might have a fight, why they might not trust their teammates, why they might tease them. I was like, woah. I died, mate.

'It wasn't until I went back to Rovers and I played

for Gerry Francis that I found a real influence. He could see behind my eyes, behind my bravado. He became my father, really, when my dad died. Gerry knew he was ill when he asked me to come back. I was twenty-five when I lost my dad, and it absolutely killed me. I love my mum to bits, but it's just your dad, isn't it? We used to fall out, because I was carrying his fears as well as my own, but I felt so lonely, because I couldn't ask his advice.

'My old man said to me a long time ago, "Son, I was never anybody so you ain't got it tough. Life's tough when you've got to walk in a great man's shoes. Always walk in your own. Make that mark because someone might talk very nicely about you one day. Be proud of how you do things. You have to be who you are, and you have to do it your way."

'It still hurts me that my kids didn't know my dad. He was only fifty-nine, and passed away before they were born. I would have loved to have had a word with him about all those issues which crop up as kids grow up. It's only when you've held your own son that you know why your dad kept on at you.'

His wife, Kim, whom he had met at 14, on the school bus, had been told she was almost certainly infertile, following chemotherapy treatment. Their son, William, was born ten months after their marriage, in May 1987. Identical twins, Eve and Chloe, were born profoundly deaf two years later. Their third daughter, Harriet, was also born deaf, despite assurances this was unlikely. The positivity of his response to disability borders on the lyrical.

'I've been told that my wife has a one-in-three chance of living. I've been told I won't be able to have kids. I've got four. Has being deaf affected my daughters? No. I'm proud of them. They're well-educated, brilliant people. One has got eight GCSEs and three A levels. She's a little star because we had a system running when she came into our family.

'We were signing to her right from the off, because of our experience with her sisters, so she's missed no information. The girls have taught me about the biggest skill in the world, communication. You do it all your life, and it is just a beautiful thing. Words are like Baileys, poured over some ice. The ice is melting, you've got a fire going in the room, and it's just gorgeous.

'As a football manager, you adapt to the knowledge that every one of us is different. We might mean the same thing, but say it in a different way. We might study the same painting, and see different things within it. The girls taught me that we even hear in a different way. Those electrical signals, which we know as sounds, are sent from your cochlea, your inner ear, to your brain. It is up to you how you interpret them.

'My twins had the same loss, but one of them can speak and the other can't. It doesn't make sense, does it? One of them relies on BSL, British Sign Language, the other uses signed supported English. How marvellous is that? We all learn in different ways. My daughters changed my life. We knew they couldn't hear so we taught them a visual language.

'When they couldn't get information they needed encouragement. Say, for example, we showed them a ball. We had to tell them two hundred times what a ball was, rather than them hearing the word and remembering it. What's the lip pattern to that word? If you don't get the timing right, they won't even look. If you do it when they're not looking, they won't get it. So you have to wait for them to look, and I'm not a patient man.

'If I don't get what I want I'm a horrible bastard. But with my daughters, I have to be patient. I used to raise my voice to my daughters when they were misbehaving, and they thought it was funny. We'd steal upstairs when they'd been sent to their rooms, and find them laughing. I need to be so much more aware of speech and how lucky I am with it.

'I didn't understand the power of the word because I was so visual with my daughters. They rely on seeing things. I now look at football as a visual experience. I'm standing there, on that line, and I see the game as this choreographed dance, with people moving in rhythm. It's weird, like a sea of pictures. When it works, when the figures are in sync and they are where you want them to be, it is so cool.

'I think to myself, how do footballers do it? If they have thoughts, how do they come? How does Wayne Rooney have a quick glance into space, receive the ball, and respond to the movement around him? It is all a bit *Good Will Hunting*, unconscious genius. The best footballers' brains are wired totally differently. They might not be able to solve a mathematical problem, but they are very clever.

'Think of David Beckham, of how his skill is ingrained. He has practised enough, so that his brain can compute exactly how hard he needs to hit the ball to put it on that postage stamp, time after time. He will never be like a snooker player and attain perfection, his one four seven, because he has variables to consider – the wind, the sun, the movement of the other players. He is a genius, though, at defining visual patterns.

'I played in the QPR team which finished fifth, as London's top club, in the first season of the Premier League. I was cracking on a bit, and got dropped for Ray Wilkins. I was fuming, because I knew I had been playing well. Ray was brilliant with me. "Come on, old man," he said, "what's wrong with you?" I told him it was not his fault, but I was going to kick him all over the place in training.

'On my life, he said, "Please do." So the challenge was down. I was going to rattle him. I wasn't a dirty player but I could run, boy could I run, so he knew I was coming. We played on a hockey pitch at the old

QPR training ground in Acton. It was magnificent. I tell you what, I didn't get anywhere near him. We collapsed afterwards, and cracked up laughing.

'He said, "That was brilliant. I didn't have to think about anything but passing quickly and moving into position to receive the return ball early, because I knew you were going to be up my arse, trying to kick me. I was four or five passes ahead of you, because I had to be." He saw the angles and outcome in his head. I never forgot that lesson.

'As a manager, I'm now four or five passes ahead of what I need my team to do. That is all because Ray taught me how to think like a top player. Some of them, like Suàrez and Sturridge, Yorke and Cole, don't even know they're doing it. Managers have to have a sense of how their players' brains work. There's not one on the planet worth his corn who can't do that.'

Holloway is a man of contradiction and impulse. He took up painting after attending anger management classes. He tried self-sufficiency, with a smallholding which offered freedom to ducks, chickens, turkeys and, unfortunately for mortality rates, foxes. His latest preoccupation was the creation of an organic football club, a risky business since the bucolic idealism of *The Good Life* is not exactly an asset on the assault course of the Championship.

'I've decided that, screw the results, I'm going to play in a way in which I believe. I'll look for the performance

I'd pay to watch myself. That will eventually get me results and, in the meantime, I'm going to teach everyone around me the things I've found interesting, the way I think the game's evolving.

'I'll concentrate on possession and look at the transition into defending. Can you get higher up the pitch? Can you put pressure on? Can you then get back to your shape and be solid and hold it? There are four different elements and I'm talking about them all the time. It's so exciting for me, trying to solve problems, where I used to think, oh my God, we've got to win, win, win.

'When I was out of work for a year Gary Penrice, my mate, said, "Ollie, go and be inspirational. Go and look beyond your back garden fence. You're an artistic fellow, and to be honest, watching your teams, I'm bored shit-less." I went to France, watched the Spanish national team, saw Swansea five or six times. I literally drew up how I wanted to play on a sketchpad.

'When the ball's there, where do I want my centre half? What if he's getting closed down? I'll get a midfield player to drop off there. What happens to your full back? He pushes up there. What happens to these other two midfield players? They're there. What happens to your front three? I drew up a little graph. When it goes here, you've got to do that. How do we get support there? We work the switch there. Where's the space? He's got to pull in there.

'So, I've gone away, and made up some sessions to make it all work. I don't like transfer windows, I don't like adding new players. I've done that. After games I will look at the coaching points of why we didn't win, and get out there on the training ground. I want to try to make them better people first and then make them better players. Every one of us, in our lives, should be allowed to make a mistake. But we should never make the same mistake twice.

'I'm going back to English and British values. Am I the big boss? No, I'm not. I haven't got a big cigar or a fancy desk. I'm the foreman. That's how I see it. I've got my CEO, who is close to the big boss so I get all the workers, the players, to work for them. If my big boss gets a phone call from one of my workers who ain't happy because I ain't picking him and he says, "Hang on, I want him to play," then what's the point of me being there?

'What I'm trying to say is that I've come full circle in my career. I just want to work for people who when we sit down, we talk, and decide what we want to do. I like to know where I'm going because results are so transient, aren't they? They come and they go. You can have a good group of players, and get three injuries at the wrong time when the window is closed. The kids aren't ready. You lose a couple of strikers and you're knackered. I don't care who you are.

'I honestly believe that some managers are lucky

enough not to worry about it. They know why it's happened. They're so secure in themselves they know they can go out and coach and get a different result. The ones who worry are the ones who have got a bit of a dodgy chairman. It's terrible because they go home and it is all oh my God, what could I have done about that? I could lose my job.

'Do I care? Of course I do. I woke up yesterday morning after we'd lost and felt awful. I had a choice to feel so sorry for myself that I'd ruin my wife's day. I don't do that any more, but I told my lads today why it hurt so much. I got a little compilation together and put it on fast forward, which I've never done before. It showed them that so much of what we'd done, our shape and ideas, was good.

'They're brilliant lads but I said, "Fuck me, you've got to have some positive energy. We've lost, and we might lose again. If you can't see how well you're playing and if you can't allow yourself to make a mistake, knowing I'm not going to cane you, then what are you doing this for? A win isn't so great that you can walk around like some mad-assed biker. Defeat shouldn't be so bad that you're cowering in the corner like you're some little mouse."

'If you take the emotion out of me, I'd be wasting my time. That's part of my management, part of what my players are buying into. But emotion cannot drive what you're doing. When I've been at my best, in play-off finals with Blackpool and Palace, I've been absolutely rock solid. That's when you learn about yourself, because if you are a little bit gone, it can't be seen. The truth is, that's where you want to be.

'We all have an inherent ability to shine. When we're in that pure zone, where we're not inhibited by thought, we just do it. You can't explain it, it just happens. You have to have that inner trust. Personality can fill a void. I was so calm in those matches I put a different message out there. It was I'm going to do this, not I want to do this. It was a conscious effort, to tell them we are going to be in the Premier League.'

His demeanour suggested he had walked through the back of the wardrobe and was taking the air in Narnia. The world was a place of infinite possibility and hidden danger. Time and again, he returned to the example of his guardian angel, Bill Holloway, the father who told him never to believe in the afterlife.

'If you look at it logically, my dad wanted me to be good but he didn't know whether I was. All that worrying about me, watching me all the time didn't make me any better. It just made me nervous. If he'd have said, "I know you're going to be good, I trust you," it would have made a huge difference to me as a human being. However he did it, he made me want to please him.

'As a manager you can do your job in so many ways. You can scream at them, be a bully. You can have a calm structure and talk them through it. You can be one of the lads, or be aloof. You can do it by über-planning, or by no planning. You can just say, "Come on, lads, let's go and enjoy ourselves." You have to create your own universe.

'In my universe I want people to say, "I want to pay money to go and watch that team. What a wonderful way of playing. They lost but I enjoyed that." That excites me. I don't get excited about a one–nil away win. I don't get excited about a five–nil defeat. I just don't. I know I can win, lose or draw the next game. It's how we do that that matters to me. It's about how you go about teaching a group to become better people.

'Sometimes you have to pick the battles you win, to end up winning the war. I work with the CEO and the chairman to try and guide them, to show how the football club should grow, to have a long-term future. I'm not going to put all my chips on black and then say, oh, you've got to put all yours on red next time. Some managers do that. Others might as well talk out of the window to their chairmen, who just do what they want. I'm not political. I'm just straightforward.

'Football epitomises my life, because it gives you hope, dreams, the chance to be somebody. The little man can beat the big man every now and again. It has made me feel all right about myself because I fitted into a team, and my team trusted me. It has given me values as a gift to be used in other areas of my life. I've earned money from it. I can't see anything better.

'It can be such a great game because it teaches you how to really become part of something, how to share your energy. But it's changing because of foreign owners with different expectations. The agents are running the show. It has become a cattle market. We're losing the little man, aren't we? My dad made me understand the importance of putting in a shift, but the attitude of some players stinks.

'They come here because this is where the money is. They don't understand what football means to someone who works hard, but now has to pay forty quid to see them play instead of twenty. Work for them, you son of a bitch. You read about people throwing money out of a car window, thinking it's funny. Ignorant shits. If you want to do something good with it then pull over and give a load of it to a homeless bloke. What message are you giving?'

Holloway's problems have been most acute when he has failed to manage upwards, to self-possessed chairmen like Milan Mandarić at Leicester City, Karl Oyston at Blackpool and Steve Parish at Palace. He was eventually sacked by the quixotic Gianni Paladini at Queens Park Rangers, but had the compensation of marshalling fleeting defiance, before being replaced by Gary Waddock.

'Gerry Francis told Chris Wright, who was then the

owner, I was what Rangers needed at the time; someone who would never give up, who wasn't a poncy fancy Dan. The Rangers fans love an arty-farty genius, but the club needed a muck-and-nettles man. We weren't famous any more. We had nothing left. Gerry told me it was likely we'd go into administration, but I didn't give a shit. This was huge for me, a boy from Bristol.

'I got them promoted on a budget of five point six million. We were relegated, crashed into administration, haemorrhaging money, but I got them back into the Premier League two years later on half the budget, two point eight million, with virtually the same group of players. Paladini didn't want me. The boys used to call him "El Zorro". When he came into the dressing room they'd say, "Oi, Zorro. Why don't you fuck off?" We had nothing, and that suited me. When my back's against the wall, that's when I'm best.

'When I needed my lads, people like Marc Bircham, Danny Shittu, Clarke Carlisle, Gareth Ainsworth, what did they do for me? They won seven games in a row. We were two–nil down in four of them, and won three-two. That was because they knew I'd been there for them. That's why all this "get the bird in a taxi" shit on YouTube gets to me. It all came about because I was trying to protect Clarke.

'I was worried about him, because I thought, this kid's had it. The police were going to get him. He's a drinker, in a mess, doing all sorts. He was in my fucking team one Saturday and he hadn't turned up. We won three-nil against Chesterfield, but the first question I get is about Clarke. I knew by that time we'd found him, pissed.

'I just said, "He's got personal issues, I don't want to talk about it." They still wanted to know what happened, so I told them to mind their own business. I didn't give a fuck about what they'd heard. That's when they tried to get round me by saying how brilliant we were. We were shit, so I was fuming. I'm thinking are you serious? And that's when it gets dangerous.

'When I'm bored with all the questions I go off on a tangent. I should have stuck to the script and been serious about football, but instead I came up with all this stuff about us not being our best but we've pulled an old dog. I meant no offence, but it has left me looking an arse. People don't realise it was all to protect someone. I was under pressure and I dealt with it the only way I know, to try and minimise it by making a joke of it.'

Ollie's Flying Circus includes references to mating badgers, copulating mermaids, preening burglars, computer literate chimpanzees and central defenders with broken noses who can smell around corners. He compares himself to 'a bad rash, not easily curable'. Yet he cries when he listens to Bill Shankly speeches, as he mourns lost innocence and simplicity of purpose.

'I would have died for that man because of how he

said things, and what he did because he wanted others to have a better life. I mean, goodness gracious me, how great is that? I'd just fall over for people who want to do something inspirational. As managers, we all know you're only really appreciated in football after you've gone.

'When Liverpool were in the Second Division Shankly actually started talking about how they were going to win the European Cup. How did he believe that? Yet all of a sudden his energy expands within that football club. Look what he did for them. Yet they sacked him. By the end of his life he was being treated better by Everton. For God's sake, how can that be? I'll bet someone told him, "That's life mate, that's football."

'Do you know what I see football as? Yes, Mr Blatter, no, Mr Blatter. Do you know what? Fuck you, Mr Blatter. You've got no clothes on. That bloke who has told the emperor he's naked? That'll be me. There are no half measures in my life. When it all gets a bit too intense I don't like who I become.

'I need the humour, because that serious side of me can be too fucking serious. I have to see the funny side of things to balance my life because, to be fair, how much of this world is right up its own arse? Don't just take what's out there. Make a difference. As my mum tells me, every day, "Look for the good bits, son . . ."'

6

The Helicopter View

The human body is considered to be at its lowest ebb between 3 and 4 a.m. That is when Shaun Derry can invariably be found inscribing his deepest thoughts, private fears and random insights into the black book he cherishes, as a child treasures a favourite teddy bear. He carries it everywhere, as a reminder of the addictiveness of his ambition.

'It's a mixed book of everything. If we were to open it together it wouldn't make much sense to you. But it does to me. It's all my thoughts, all my queries. It's got notes, lists, scribbles, ideas, things I've seen or done, and I know I can always refer back to it for ten or fifteen minutes in the afternoon, and find something of value.

'I wish I'd started keeping the book earlier, because you forget how intense the experience of professional football can be. There are some key things that have happened, not just in my career but in other people's

101

careers, that should have been written down while they were fresh. I suppose it is only when you reach a certain age that you feel the need to start picking the bones out of it.

'Every manager will tell you that when they wake their first thoughts are about football. I used to sleep great as a player. Now I don't sleep so well. I'll probably have four or five hours, and then I'm awake. As my mum used to say, things seem worse in the middle of the night. I can't say I'm enjoying this job, but it is just something that I have to do.'

He is on the third edition of his black book, in two years. He would be on his 30th had he chosen to record every absurdity, betrayal, fleeting triumph and egregious insult of his time at Queens Park Rangers, where the souring of a lifetime's ambition, reaching the Premier League, became the driving force behind his move into management.

Derry was one of the cavalrymen who followed Neil Warnock's headlong charge towards promotion from the Championship, only to be reduced to cannon fodder when Mark Hughes assembled what remains one of the most dysfunctional groups of multi-millionaire footballers ever seen in the English game.

'One story sums it up. You've got to remember, I'd been changing alongside the likes of Luke Young, Clint Hill, Bradley Orr and Jamie Mackie for a couple of years. Such good lads, such great pros. In comes Júlio

César, Brazil's goalkeeper. A lovely guy, I have to say. Now, I used to have to travel round the motorway to get to QPR. Some days it would take me an hour and twenty, other days it would take me two hours.

'I prided myself on never being late for training, apart from this one day where I'd had an absolute nightmare and every single decision I made, ducking and diving to avoid the traffic, was wrong. Júlio saw me and said, "Where do you live?" And I said, "Kent." "Where's Kent?" And I explained where Kent was. He went, "Why don't you get a helicopter?" I said, "That's not a bad one, Júlio. I'll have a think about that one, Júlio."

'By this point Luke Young had moved further down the dressing room and I called out to him, "Hey, Youngy, how much are helicopters these days?" He'd heard what was going on, and he put his hands over his ears. Júlio thought I was being serious. He said, "You can get one for a hundred and fifty grand." One hundred and fifty grand! I drove to training in a VW Golf! It was ridiculous, absolutely ridiculous. As far away from reality as you can be.

'We had elevated ourselves into the Premier League with a stereotypical, honest, hard-working, appreciative group. Clint and I had been roomies for four years. We'd shared a lot of Friday night chats. We chewed the cud, talked about what we would do if we were in charge. When Neil lost his job, the spectrum of players changed. You could tell their only intention was to earn as much money as they possibly could.

'I was offended. Throughout my career, from eighteen all the way through to thirty-five, I never forgot it was a privilege to be a footballer. I played with like-minded people who had the common ground of wanting to be the best they could possibly be. I loved it, absolutely loved it. But the last two years at QPR were my worst. I thought, well, this can't be right. I'm playing at the top of my profession, I've fought every single inch of the way to get here, but I'm not enjoying it. How can that be?

'The club had lost its identity, almost overnight. When you're at a bottom-rung Premier League club and you're seeing people arriving in huge super cars, with a different watch every other week and clothes that cost three, four, five, six thousand pounds apiece, there's something very wrong somewhere. I've never forgotten what Harry Redknapp said to me about Frank Lampard.

'He said he deserves every penny he earns from the game because he works harder than anybody. And that was all he said. Not the best player. Not the most gifted, technically. Not the nicest man off the field. He works harder than anyone has seen a pro work. That's why Frank Lampard deserves the plaudits he gets. I was bitter because all these lads we'd brought in on multi-million-pound contracts didn't care about the club.

'But here's something. Fast forward a few months,

and I walk into this environment, at Notts County. The characters, albeit on a lesser wage, were very similar. The lack of appreciation for the football club was the same. That's why I did it my way, using old school values.

'All those Friday nights with Clint, when we talked about how to deal with difficult situations, were put to good use. So, after everything, I was thankful for my time at QPR, because it showed me how not to manage people, and how to look at the character of players, first and foremost.'

He worked on the wrong side of the Trent for the comparison to be entirely accurate, but there were flashes of the young Brian Clough as he went about his work at Notts County. He holds trenchant views, but doesn't particularly mind who he upsets because he believes his principles are sound. His temper can be short and his tongue savage, but he is capable of instinctive kindness and possesses the common touch.

He is 36, but football age doesn't necessarily equate to biological age. Spiritually, he is a throwback to an era in which defenders left their foot in, had a pint with their adversaries, and fired up the Quattro before disappearing into the night. He is a sheepskin man, though he tries to get away with wearing skinny jeans. He has been here before.

Greg Abbott, the former Carlisle manager, plays the Peter Taylor role to his Clough. He featured in a scrawled shortlist of potential assistants in the black book, and agreed to join Derry while the recruitment process was under way. It is worth recording in detail, because it offers an insight into the power of personality, and the remedies required for a moribund club seeking salvation.

Derry was on a coaching course for his UEFA A licence when he received a text from a friend, informing him that Chris Kiwomya had just been sacked, after a 34-match run as manager. The club was five points adrift at the bottom of League One, and looking for their 14th manager in ten years. Derry wanted the job, so he simply asked for it.

'I still felt I had something to offer as a player, but I just knew it was something I had to go for. I picked up the phone to Jim Rodwell, the chief executive, that night. My first words to him were: "Hello, Jim, you're talking to your wild card." The conversation escalated from there. I met him on the Tuesday, at the George Hotel in Stamford. Jim was with the chairman, Ray Trew, and his wife, Aileen, and their son.

'We sat around a big table and I just said, "This is who I am. I can't tell you what I am as a coach, or as a manager, because I've not been one before, but these are my beliefs as a person." I explained the situation I had at QPR and that I envisaged they had similar problems. I explained how I would deal with them.

'I would expect everybody first and foremost to be

on time. I'd got the impression it was a little bit of a free for all. I didn't want players going to the hierarchy behind my back, because I knew that was happening as well. I said that we would be organised, me and Greg, and the training would be harder. We wouldn't just run them, but we'd do a lot of football-related work on shape to make it more organised.

'I just wanted to bring people together. I knew what the fans here wanted because I've got friends who are fans and family who live in Nottingham. I'm not saying that my way's going to last, but I knew for that time, that situation, the club needed my type.'

He represented a gamble, but he was one of their own. He had been away from his birthplace for 15 years, playing for Sheffield United, Portsmouth, Crystal Palace, Leeds United and QPR, but his voice still carried an East Midlands inflection, the ghost of a dialect which had Nordic and Anglo-Saxon influences.

He cared, all right. The club had a history of periodic upheaval, but it represented a thread which ran through his life. He spoke vividly about himself as an awestruck boy who played for them for the first time on his tenth birthday, representing Notts County Intermediates in the Leicestershire League.

His father, John, a season ticket holder who regularly telephoned the club to complain about abject performances, used to take him to training on a rubberised five-a-side court behind the ground on Monday and

Thursday evenings. It was a military operation. Home from work as a lorry driver at 4.15 p.m. In the car at 4.30. Ready to train at five o'clock.

Shaun recalled another formative influence, almost as if it were a bereavement. He was at the start of his second year as a YTS trainee, and played up front in a pre-season friendly, away to Oakham. Manager Colin Murphy and Steve Thompson, his assistant, were sweet on his attacking partner, Tim Wilkes.

They called Derry over that night, told him he was wasting his time and could leave. The boy then found the man inside. He told them he would crack on. He would get his head down and keep coming. Never say never. He would prove them wrong.

Derry was fascinated by Jimmy Sirrel, who had three spells as manager between 1969 and 1987. He was a distinctive figure, with a deeply furrowed brow and an uneven set of teeth which resembled the broken keyboard of an old piano. His Glaswegian accent was impenetrable, and his frugal management style took County to the old First Division.

All the YTS boys loved to watch him arrive at the club in the mornings, not out of a sense of reverence or duty, but to see how many times his battered car would hit the wall outside the main entrance. He was hopelessly short-sighted, easily distracted and had a one-track mind, focused on football. The horse chestnut tree just inside the main gate was another seemingly unavoidable obstacle.

Derry's favourite story involved a chance meeting, when he was doing his chores: 'It was my turn to clean the dressing room after training, and as I walked in I saw Jimmy on his own in the big old-fashioned bath we used to have. That was one of his little rituals, so I thought nothing of it. Then I saw his eyes were closed. There was blood in the water. Christ, he's dead, I thought. I panicked. What should I do? Who should I run and tell? I decided I needed to take a closer look to make sure. I'm right beside the bath when he opens one eye and says, "What the fuck are yae doing, young 'un?" Turns out he had nicked his lip badly when he was trying to have a shave in the bath.'

Abbott's name was in the black book, on a wish list compiled after a conversation with a good friend, the former Notts County player Andy Hughes, a development coach at Bolton Wanderers. Derry had known him for eight years, having first met him when Abbott was youth team coach at Leeds.

'We'd kept in contact. He wasn't a friend as such, but he was somebody I respected and knew as a very good coach who had delivered at Carlisle under huge financial restrictions. Geography had been against him because being so far north meant only a certain amount of players would want to go there. My chance coincided with him being sacked, and I knew I couldn't do this on my own.

'If I'd walked into the football club with a young

number two, the players would have turned around and said, "Hang on a minute, we'll have him." They'd have taken their chances with me. But with Greg it was different. He's an experienced number one, a number two in name only. I give him the power to do and say whatever he wants, because I trust him. After that meeting I had a feeling my life would change, and it did.'

His first day in charge demonstrated the scorpion dance which occurs when any new manager walks into the dressing room for the first time. Derry had prepared by calling a 9.30 a.m. meeting of existing support staff, who worked in a warren of tiny, low-ceilinged rooms beneath the main stand. He assured them he would reciprocate their loyalty and laid down the ground rules.

'We are the blue shirts,' he said, referring to the colour of the club's training kit. 'The players are the black shirts. The blue shirts are the ones in power. Don't ever let the black shirts feel they can run this club because they can't. That's all I've seen for three years at QPR and I didn't like it.

'This is a profession like no other. One of the major words flying around at the minute is "networking", but it is about more than that. It is all about trust and respect, dealing with people on a personal level. That's something I was never party to as a player. You need to be selfish in football, but make it work in a group situation.'

The team meeting was called for 10.30 a.m., and the malcontents duly played into his hands. 'Whenever I say there's a meeting, I don't go in two minutes early. I go in on that dot. As you can imagine there were loads of eyes staring at me, and I thought, this had better be a good speech. I was so happy when I realised two players hadn't turned up. That gave me the perfect opportunity to state my authority and say, this is who I am. You will conform, otherwise our relationship stops here. I got rid of one of the players at the end of the season. The other one, a lad named Yoann Arquin, who seemed to be quite a big character within the dressing room, only played two games for me before he was shipped out to Ross County.

'He turned up forty-five minutes late, so I asked him to come and see me immediately after the meeting. He had a baseball cap set to one side, and a lollipop in his mouth. I told him to take his hat off, get rid of the lollipop, and told him that we would fall out. And we did, during our first training session when he didn't try a leg.

'At the end of the session we had a nine v nine, and two other big characters, Andre Boucaud and Joss Labadie, clashed. The way they spoke to each other was a disgrace. It was, from both sides, incredibly disrespectful to a teammate and fellow professional. That's when I stepped in and explained I would never accept that as a manager.

'I would have preferred it had they started hitting each other, because that gets it over and done with, but such head-to-head verbals linger, and always rear their ugly head again.' In such a context, the term 'big characters' wasn't exactly intended as a compliment. Labadie's contract was quickly cancelled. Boucaud was among 17 players discarded in the summer of 2014. Bizarrely, they started the new season as teammates at Dagenham & Redbridge.

Derry was obliged to build on the apparently impossible, County having escaped relegation to League Two by winning six of their last nine matches and surviving due to the minimum requirement, a draw against Oldham, on the final day. A negative mentality was being addressed, although there was missionary work to do closer to home.

'I'm in about my seventh or eighth match in charge, and I'm on the touchline. There were only about three thousand there and all I can hear is my dad, sitting at the top of the stand, slaughtering the team. I go back home afterwards and there he is. "Dad," I say. "Shut the fuck up, please. You're not a normal fan any more." He grins and Mum starts laughing. What do you do?'

He was sharing a house with Abbott, who was 15 years older but had the same adolescent humour. They made his curries last four days at a time, answered to the nickname of 'Mr & Mrs', but had the easy air of brothers. Similarities between Derry and another former Notts County manager, Neil Warnock, were not entirely coincidental.

'Neil has a knack of getting five, six or seven lads in to run a dressing room his way. They're people he trusts, who have an appreciation for the club first and foremost. They're steady players, who are consistent, not just on a Saturday afternoon, but from Monday to Friday. Where Neil is different from others I've played under is that he comes alive on game day.

'He gets an extra ten per cent from you. His man management on the opening day, when we lost four–nil at home to Bolton in our first match back in the Premier League, was so good it was scary. The lads were despondent, feeling sorry for themselves. He came into the dressing room, shut the door, and started clapping his hands and smiling.

'I knew what was coming, but one or two of the lads couldn't understand what was going on. He went, "Isn't it good to lose four–nil at home? I'd fucking rather lose four–nil at home in the Premier League than win two–one at home in the Championship." All that anger, worry and upset had gone within one sentence. We went to Goodison Park the next week and beat Everton one–nil.

'I can tell, even at this junior stage of my management career, when the lads are going to perform. I can see it in their eyes. I'm learning about different personalities. I've got a player, Gary Jones, who's the best. I know when Gaz is on his game, because he gets angry, itchy, and he can't sit still. He's stretching, moving around the dressing room, and is going to be all right. On the flip side I've got Liam Noble. If he's chirpy and relaxed I know he's all right.

'I was a hard player to manage, very opinionated. I expected everyone to match my standards. I kept myself to myself because I was comfortable with who I was. What I'm starting to understand now is that you need to build relationships, and your barrier needs to come down at certain times so that you can take people with you.

'When I go to a game now, to scout a team or an individual, I'm very conscious I'm a rookie in a new job. I had respect as Shaun Derry the player, now I need to gain respect as Shaun Derry the manager. That can only be earned by my actions. I remember Graham Rix, my manager at Portsmouth, telling me he had to treat the kit man exactly the same as his best player. The principle of common respect is paramount.'

I studied Derry closely during two home matches in the opening phase of the season, to get a flavour of him and the club he was attempting to reinvent. He had a squad of limited quality, which was clearly over-achieving, as if driven forward by the force of his personality.

He was sent to the stands after an angry clash with the fourth official during a 2–1 win over Colchester

United in one of Joe Dunne's last matches as manager. County ended the game with nine men; he took a seat in the stand, and used Alan Smith, his player-coach, to ferry messages to Abbott in the technical area.

Meadow Lane, bathed in late-evening sunlight which shone at an angle of 45 degrees across the pitch, was a place of small shrines and minor achievements. Flags flew at half-mast to commemorate a supporter who had recently passed away. A brick on the external wall of the main stand paid tribute to 'Kate and Jim Mullen. Devoted. Together Forever'.

The stadium was dark and silent when we lingered on the touchline after the match. Derry paused to say goodnight to the groundsman, who had locked up. 'To be honest, that was coming,' he said, his voice sandpapered by strain. 'I've felt on the edge of being sent off for a few games.' He gestured over his left shoulder, towards the pitch. 'They just don't realise there are lives on the line out there.'

He had been championing the cause of his support staff, whose three-month contracts were 'not worth the paper they are written on'. Ceiron Keane, a promising Irish full back, had been sent off on his debut. He was one of four players in the match-day squad earning £150 a week. 'Our budget is less than last year, so the pound notes mean more to the lads.'

The second match, four weeks later, should really have been staged on Tyburn Hill. It had the feel of a public execution. Russell Slade, Derry's first youth team manager as a County trainee, was being ritually humiliated by Leyton Orient's new owners. I sat directly behind the away dugout among home fans who would not have been out of place in an Alan Bennett monologue.

Grown men addressed me as 'mi duck' (it apparently derives from 'Duka', a respectful Anglo-Saxon term, rather than a waterfowl) and offered mint imperials. A man behind enquired of my new friend: 'How's your daughter? Still living in Skegness?' The reply – 'No, Liverpool' – was strangled by a defensive error which inspired the quaint admonition 'bloomin' 'eck'.

Slade was in an impossible position. He had been told, in front of his players, he would be sacked if Orient lost. Self-styled president Francesco Becchetti, who had made his fortune in the waste management and renewable energy industries, was using the club to launch a reality show for his Italian TV channel. He sat in judgement, like a Roman emperor, on the directors' balcony over the halfway line.

The County fans tried to incite Slade – 'You'll be stacking shelves in Poundland soon' – but their hearts clearly were not in it. He won them over by turning to face them, removing his baseball cap to reveal the bald head celebrated in song by 331 travelling fans, and bowing low. He conducted himself with immense dignity after a 1–1 draw, but had no idea whether he still had a job.

Derry, leaning against the wall leading to the dressing rooms so he was a safe distance from reporters assembled at the mouth of the tunnel, was incandescent. 'Who the fuck do these people think they are?' he said, quietly but venomously. 'Where is the game going when a proper manager like Russ, who has done the right things ever since he started here, is treated like that? It's an absolute scandal, and something needs to be done about it.'

Slade eventually escaped from a club so dysfunctional that the senior players ended up conducting their own pre-match team talks. Few of the Italian staff spoke English, and morale plummeted accordingly. Slade was recommended to Vincent Tan by the Thai partner of one of Barry Hearn's closest colleagues, and joined Cardiff City on October 6, but the fit did not seem to be comfortable. He was soon under pressure from fans and a sceptical local media.

Derry admitted a conversation with MK Dons manager Karl Robinson, about making a conscious attempt not to take the result home with him, resonated uncomfortably. He and his wife, Jolene, had undergone IVF treatment which led to the birth of their daughter, Lilly-Marie. The realisation she'd had 14 bedrooms in the first seven years of her life prompted them to retain the family home.

Shaun, who also has a son, Jesse, was racked with guilt: 'I found myself being a bystander in my own life last year, looking into my family from the outside. I was spending an awful lot of time in Nottingham, and on my days off in Kent I was only there in body, not in mind. I'm now trying to park the football club in Nottingham.

'I work such long days because on a day off, on Wednesday, I can enjoy the kids, and share family life properly. I miss them dreadfully. It's tough when you want to see your kids grow up, but I can't do anything else. I've known for years that this is what I wanted to do. This is the natural progression. I'm not a footballer any more. I'm a manager.

'Am I in a position where financially I can be out of work? Yes, for a short amount of time. Am I willing to put management to bed if I'm out of work for long? That's something we've spoken about as a family. There's a plan B, which would be a complete lifestyle change in another country. That's me being as open as I possibly can be about the situation.

'The buzz isn't the same as being a player. I used to love coming home after a game, ninety-five minutes, legs absolutely killing me. I used to love that feeling of being thin, of having worked the edge off my body. I used to love Sunday when I was sore and struggling to walk around the park with the kids. I felt like I'd earned my money, win, lose or draw.

'As a manager the buzz only lasts for half an hour to an hour after a game. Then I'm looking forward, trying to prepare for the next opponents. Greg's helping me with that. He keeps saying enjoy it, but I can't because I'm eager to keep progressing individually and as a team. I want to do well for the club and I've openly said eventually I want to move to a bigger club, because I have always set my sights high.

'I'd love to manage in the Premier League, but so would so many other people. I'm aware there are some mightily good managers out of a job. I'm not making any demands, and whether I get to the Premier League remains to be seen. I've got to earn the chance. Like I said, I'm a junior in this role. But I have a goal.'

Those ambitions are annotated in that black book. It also contains the case for the prosecution concerning Mark Hughes. It was time to decamp to the Potteries, to hear the case for the defence.

7

The Case for the Defence

It seemed somehow appropriate that Mark Hughes had the assiduous air of a county solicitor, taking instructions on the last will and testament of a valued client. He leaned forward attentively, listened with respect, and was clear and concise in his professional judgement. Here was a man of stature, conscious of his rank.

Instead of sinking into the soft folds of a low-slung sofa, he chose the former footballer's option of sitting on a straight-backed office chair, looking out through a picture window on to the main pitch at Stoke City's training ground. His iPad, used constantly for research purposes, was placed on the coffee table. A blue ring-bound folder, on a neat and tidy desk in the corner, contained statistical data and session plans from his morning's work.

Football management is a hall of mirrors, which can

flatter or distort, and it was difficult to resolve the contradiction between the assured figure who had found a niche at an unashamedly blue-collar club and his previous incarnation, as someone who oversaw strategic and spiritual chaos at Queens Park Rangers for ten months in 2012. It was best to cut to the chase, and ask for an explanation for the aberration.

'I think at the time I was hard done by. I knew a lot of people thought I'd do very well to get back after that, certainly at Premier League level. I felt I was getting judged on twelve games at the beginning of one season where I'd managed three hundred odd games in the Premier League, so I was sustained by the hope people would look beyond that.

'The first few weeks after being sacked are hard to take because there is a sense of frustration. You feel people aren't given the real facts because there's a lot of shit that follows a manager out the door. I've never really gone in to protect my own position or reputation, wrongly probably. When I came out of QPR I didn't say a thing, again probably to my detriment.

'I've never been bitter, because the only person you hurt in that circumstance is yourself. It's initially difficult, probably more difficult for your family and friends because they feel really upset about your situation. They know how hard you have worked to really make it happen. So you feel for them and have to indulge them to a certain extent. I've always taken the view that you just park it, move on and look for the next opportunity. If you do that, then you won't get damaged by it.

'At the end of the first season at QPR it was great. We stayed in the Premier League, but I knew that group of players wasn't good enough to keep us there. There was a huge turnover. I brought in nine, ten players that summer, which I've seen happen this year with certain clubs. You make decisions and bring in better quality. Of the lads that went out of the club, not one of them got a Premier League contract, which tells you that maybe they weren't quite good enough at that level.

'The dynamic of the group is the key to it all. If it doesn't gel quickly, it becomes really difficult. We had guys coming in from a higher level. We had guys coming from abroad who were good quality but it was their first season in the Premier League. We had other guys who were conscious that maybe I was looking to move them out.

'There was a lack of trust on all sides. From my point of view there was a lack of trust in the group. They probably had a lack of trust in me because they could see me bringing other players in. The owner and the CEO had no experience of the Premier League. The factors for a stable base weren't in place. We were trying to address the bigger picture, but we were also trying to address the dressing room. I just got spread a little bit thinly and lost my focus in terms of the players. We tried to get them on board and working in the right direction but it was too fragmented.

'I'm now at a good club, with good people. They have been in the Premier League for six years, so guys who come up through the Championship but can't sustain you long-term are natural wastage. It's been more measured and people have left at the right time, whereas at QPR we were trying to irritate people to make them go because, to be fair, it was probably in their best interests. They'd say, "Well, if you want us to go you'll have to pay us," so it was a car crash.'

At the risk of getting ahead of ourselves, something was immediately apparent. Hughes seems suited temperamentally to a more structured, relatively stable working environment. When he found that as a player, at Manchester United and then at Chelsea and Blackburn Rovers, he was successful. He excelled at Blackburn as a manager, and is subtly reshaping Stoke, a club popularly defined by the muscularity and diligence of the Tony Pulis era, out of what he admits, significantly, is a sense of gratitude.

When that supportive ethos is conspicuous by its absence, as it was in the politically febrile atmosphere when he managed Manchester City and QPR, problems arise. I found myself recalling another age, 1986, when I first met him. Terry Venables, then Barcelona manager, smuggled me into Albania, a closed country emerging from the dictatorship of Enver Hoxha, as his translator for a third-round UEFA Cup tie against Flamurtari Vlorë.

Gary Lineker, the striker Hughes was brought in to partner at Barcelona, had more acute political antennae and sharper social skills. He was attuned to the scale of a club still a generation away from selling their sporting prestige and cultural purity to Qatar. Hughes was more reserved, better suited to the tranquillity and intro-spection of North Wales, where he had been brought up by his mother and grandmother. He preferred to observe.

That trait should never be confused with weakness since, when he returned for a pivotal second spell at Old Trafford, following single seasons at Barcelona and Bayern Munich, a formidable collection of alpha males deferred to his quiet strength. He didn't say much, but when he did so he was listened to intently. A singular leadership style was being developed, almost subconsciously.

'It was a strong dressing room. Brucie and Gary Pallister used to shout all the time but it just used to be noise. It was important noise, if you know what I mean, because it got people's attention. It was noise at the right time, which can be a positive. My voice wasn't the strongest, but I had views. Everybody's different, and to a certain extent you have to know yourself.

'My personality is one of an introvert. That's just me. Sometimes people have said, "Well, maybe that's not the right type for a manager." I think it has actually helped me because when I have to make a point, forcefully or strongly, it has more resonance because it's a surprise. You're not the life and soul of the party but you can have more impact.'

His coaching ambitions coalesced through exposure to a different type of character, and a more intense form of respect, when he moved to Chelsea in 1995. Here was a club in a chrysalis state, long before it became the golden butterfly of the Mourinho/Abramovich era. Hughes began to change its nature, with other imports such as Ruud Gullit, Gianfranco Zola and Gianluca Vialli.

'I was part of the furniture at United, really. It wasn't the case that people came to me for advice because others were more ready to impart that advice. But when I went to Chelsea they were just a mid-table team. Whenever I spoke in the dressing room about what I'd done, just in conversation, I sensed that the younger players sat up and noticed. I thought that maybe I could affect them in a positive way.

'Playing was still my focus, but that was around the time I started doing my coaching badges so an idea was ready to germinate. I learned a lot from the culture of the Italian lads, rather than the British mentality. I saw their self-discipline, how they prepared properly. I looked at Luca, who sometimes felt he wasn't getting what he needed to be the player he was in Italy.

'He struggled initially because the game was refereed differently. He was expecting to be given free kicks, so he'd go down a bit too easily. It took him about twelve months to understand that he needed to resist and stay on his feet, and then the crowd would be with him and he'd have a more positive experience.

'I know for a fact he worked right through the summer that second year to get physically stronger to cope with the demands. If, after training sessions, he found he'd not had enough he'd do it himself, because he knew what he needed to be the best. His success was no coincidence.

'I was fortunate enough to have a round of golf with Corey Pavin at Celtic Manor before the Ryder Cup there. He wanted to have a look at the course and took me in with him. He was hitting these balls, drivers off fairways and stuff, and I said, "How do you do that so consistently? That's brilliant, that." And he said, "Well, I train more than you. I practise more than you." And you think, well, of course you do. There's a reason why you're good at it. So the likes of Zola, Vialli, Beckham, Cantona, they just stay out longer than the rest.'

There's an element of the stork, dropping babies down chimneys, to most managerial careers. Fate plays a disconcerting role in determining an individual's direction. Hughes had no real thoughts of starting out as Wales manager in 1999, but had little choice when, in between matches against Italy and Denmark, Bobby Gould resigned.

'Bobby, bless him in his wisdom, recommended

myself and Neville Southall to do it, so we were really chucked in at the deep end. I'd done my badges, but because I was still playing I hadn't really thought too much about where it was going to take me. It was one of those situations where an opportunity presents itself and you've got to grab it.

'I made the conscious decision that I was going to be the manager of Wales and be a player with my club, Everton at the time, and then Blackburn. I didn't want to muddy the lines. I didn't have a clue what I was doing to be perfectly honest. It was as simple as that. I was given the chance because I was an international player who had been around for a long time.

'All of a sudden I was getting knocks on my door at half past eight, nine o'clock in the morning, with people saying, "Right, boss, what are we doing?" I had to learn quickly, but if you walk into a situation where people want you to do well, then you've got half a chance. That was certainly the case here at Stoke, and certainly with Wales.

'We'd had a period where it hadn't gone great so, for want of a better phrase, anything different was going to be better than what was there before. Sometimes it works well when you go into it blind and a little bit naive. I didn't have the skill set or experience to pre-empt problems, so I needed good staff who could point me in the right direction and allow me to find my way as a manager.

'There's no right or wrong way. You can be autocratic, or a bit more empathetic. As you evolve as a manager and as a coach you get an understanding of what works for you and your personality type. Players can smell if you're trying to be something you're not, so you have to be honest with yourself, and with them. I was honest in terms of saying, listen, I'm trying to find my way here, I'm trying to do things better than they were done before.

'That gave me a little bit of leeway. My standing in the game meant I was allowed some slack, if that's the right word. There's always a point that comes quite quickly where you have to stand and tell them things so they think, actually, that's good information. It doesn't matter what your standing is as a player. If you start as a manager and you're talking bollocks then you quickly lose whatever reputation you had.

'You've a couple of games. Straight away, most players are trying to work you out, decide what you can give them and whether you can help them to be successful. If you start on the right foot you've got an opportunity. As you get older, and you've had more positions, you have a better understanding of what's required. I think the key is that you have to know your subject.'

The influence of Sir Alex Ferguson is not as strong as is popularly assumed, although Hughes did seek his advice in how to rehabilitate himself after the QPR farrago. He is more self-taught, a student of other sports and a surfer of TED talks, an online source of more than 1,900 lectures on a range of issues. Some are, to be charitable, obtuse ('Why you should care about whale poo' . . . 'Better toilets, better life') but others ('Five ways of listening' . . . 'The power of believing that you can improve') can be distilled until they become relevant to his work. The eagerness with which he used his iPad to show me the diversity of subjects on offer was surprising and, frankly, endearing.

'I'm always being asked about formative influences. There are markers I'll revert back to. I'll go back and remember something that happened to me as a player, and use that knowledge to hopefully make the right decision as a manager. It's an amalgamation of things. I'm forever trying to get the best bits of information that will help me do my job. It doesn't matter where they come from or whether they're from my past or somebody else's past.

'The All Blacks' leadership philosophy is really good. Some think if you allow people to develop and become leaders they become a threat, but actually it makes them better at what they do. The higher you go, the more players have self-responsibility about what they want to achieve. You have to have an understanding of who those individuals are in the group you're working with.

'It's about recognising the right moments to give the group a bit of insight and context. Most of the time they hear me droning on about playing this way or that way, or formations and the like, but if I start telling different stories, talking about something outside of football, it might get their attention. It depends on the individual. It's really important to understand what works for one player works differently for another, because the same information is registered in a different way. You have to be careful, because sometimes what you think you're saying to people isn't what they're hearing.

'There's a balance to be struck, especially when you are at a new club. You're trying to work your group out, in terms of what they can give you, but they're doing the same. They're looking at you and thinking, can you make me better, are we going to be successful with you, or are you crap? And there's always that bottom line: are you going to help me get a new contract?'

Hughes spent four years as Wales manager before he took his first club job, at Blackburn in 2004. It was a seamless transition from a playing career in which he won two Premier League titles, four FA Cups, three League Cups and two European Cup Winners' Cups.

'When I got the opportunity I had a philosophy, clear ideas about how I expected my team to play, perform and behave. When you're a player and you go straight into management, you don't usually have that. If you were a right back you might know everything about being a right back, but you don't know how it relates to centre halves or midfield players, or the striker, so you have to re-educate yourself in terms of what football is all about.

'It doesn't matter how long you played, you've just got a little bubble of understanding. When I took the Wales job I knew how to play up front and score goals. I knew exactly what my role was in the team. But if I was honest with myself, did I really know what I did and how that affected someone else? Not really. It takes time to change your mindset and be more intelligent at football really. I wish I was playing now. I'd be a great player because I know a lot more and have a better understanding of everybody's needs. Trouble is I can't run . . .'

And he cannot hide. Managing Blackburn, in essence another four-year apprenticeship, was a positive experience. He developed a broader understanding of the complexities of running a Premier League club from John Williams, the sort of quietly efficient chief executive he could have done with at Manchester City, where he was saddled with a rhinestone cowboy named Garry Cook.

'City was an unbelievable experience. I moved from Blackburn because I thought it was a step up, bigger crowds, bigger stadium, just a bigger club. The reality was that it wasn't bigger, in terms of what was underpinning the club and the quality of the people who were there. It's easy to forget it was a mid-table club. There were a lot of changes to manage, even before the perception changed overnight, with the new owners.

'It was, OK, the owners want us to be this type of club. How do we get there? It was difficult, really difficult, because you are conscious that people expect you to go in the market and buy the best players because you have all this money. So we'd have these conversations – "Well, we'll go after Kaka" – but we couldn't even get in the room with them. It didn't matter how much money we had. It was a joke.

'It wasn't the Manchester City of today, a world power, but we had to try and find a way. It's not what we thought it was, I have to say, on a lot of levels. But in terms of the learning experience and understanding how people react it was invaluable. OK, results didn't go particularly well so I was at risk, but there were a lot of power bases. You'd see people thinking, uh oh, I've got to protect myself here.

'Football magnifies human behaviour. It's a unique sport and there's so much focus on it. It's ridiculous. The only way you can keep things level and stable is by winning football matches and there's only really the top five or six clubs that can consistently win week in, week out. The rest of us need good owners, good CEOs who understand the game, like I've got here.

'If you're in position and a new owner comes in, it's pretty much a given that you'll leave, because you're not their guy. It was always only a matter of time before

I was going to be replaced at City. They allowed me to go into the second year but I think I was probably sacked two or three times. The decision was officially taken after the Hull game, which we drew.

'Khaldoon, the chairman, flew in for the Chelsea game because the expectation was we were going to get beat, and he could sack me. We won, so he had to fly back out. He flew back in for the fifth-round FA Cup match against Arsenal, and we beat them, so he had to fly back out again. Eventually, we beat Sunderland, four–three, but he'd made his mind up, so I was toast.'

That match was a PR disaster for City, a club with a cunningly disguised culture of corporate artifice. Hughes's fate was common knowledge as the game played out. Aware of the visceral emotional impact of his touchline vigil, which had the metaphorical power of a condemned man standing on the scaffold, he milked the moment. Though reserved, he had never been afraid of retaliation.

He learned to ski during a six-month break, began to keep a reflective diary, but made a series of errors which hinted at an underlying confusion. He caused mortal offence by leaving Fulham to find a club which matched his supposed ambition, and walked blindly into the man trap at Loftus Road. His loyalty to his friend and adviser Kia Joorabchian, a controversial figure who exposed Hughes to accusations of vested interests, was admirable, in its way, but reckless.

His predecessor at Stoke, Tony Pulis, was underlining his reputation as one of the shrewdest politicians in the game. His departure from Crystal Palace on the eve of the start of the season was a surgical strike, since he knew his value as a survival specialist would increase in exile. He maintained his profile as a media pundit, refused to enlarge on the circumstances which led to him leaving Palace by 'mutual consent', and watched the stakes rise. He would join West Bromwich Albion almost as soon as his gardening leave ended.

His influence at Stoke, testament to the personal bond he had established with owner Peter Coates, extended into every crevice of the Britannia Stadium, yet it represented little threat to Hughes, since he and the club were comfortable in their own skin. Change wouldn't be radical, and it would be respectful, but he had the power to shape his own destiny.

'I think when I came here the club were ready to do things in a different way on a lot of levels. I could be honest. Nobody's right, nobody's wrong. You're only right if you win football matches, so that helped my situation. I think everyone wanted me and my staff to succeed because they were ready for change.

'I understood the club's demographic. I'm in tune with that anyway, because I came from a council estate. You think council estates are great when you're a kid, but your mother's thinking, Christ, I've got to get him out of here, you know? So I've got an understanding of my responsibilities. The area is low-income and people have this football club right within their midst. So much focus is on the game at the weekend.

'There's a danger if football ignores that, because it's a potential consequence of the amount of money coming into the game. We need a lot of football people at the top level whose upbringing gives them an under-standing of how difficult life is and the value of a pound. Football is basically a working-class game.

'I didn't really have a father figure. We were a one-parent family but I never really saw the difference between friends of mine who had a mum and dad in terms of the clothes I was wearing. My mum was working, so when she wasn't there my gran was there. I had to stand on my own two feet, because sometimes Mum was gone before I woke up, and I had to get myself ready for school. You're shaped by your experiences, I'm sure.'

The largely unearned wealth of the game has changed its dynamics, because the workforce is increasingly cosmopolitan. Hughes's team has evolved, in terms of patience and retention of possession, but remains yeoman-like in outlook, despite the bold colours applied by such Barcelona graduates as Marc Muniesa and Bojan Krkić. Like all leading managers, Hughes has had to develop discretion, due to the diversity of his dressing room.

'Ours is more British-based, I'd suggest, so you can

dig people out on occasion. You have to be more conscious that different nationalities can't deal with being confronted in front of people. You have to pull them out individually, or you lose them totally. You still give them the same message but it's done away from the confines of the dressing room.'

Recruitment at Stoke, a notable success, is a modern, collegiate process involving a technical director, who accepts Hughes has the final say in any transfer. Preparation is scientific and, judging by his eagerness to share the secrets of his loose-leaf folder, a source of some pride. He has immediate access to historic coaching plans, and real-time data on players' heart rates and training intensity.

'Every session I've done since I've been a manager is in here. This is last year's. Every session is logged, so when we have a similar phase of games, I can refer back to them. We work on load and intensity but also on freshness. Logic tells you if they're not fresh at the weekend they're not going to perform, so the quality of work has to be right and the quantity accurate.

'We'll taper it down and do movement patterns on a Friday, very light, but as the year progresses we keep pushing them on physically. Science tells you that by increasing the workload every week they should be getting stronger, but still as fresh at the end as they were at the beginning. Some teams peak, get to Christmas, and fall off the edge of the cliff. My teams don't usually do that.

'The sports science guys have a voice, and that's why it works. As long as the theory is right, and they convince me we need to do something, then we go with it. There are occasions where you have to override that process, when it's just gut feeling, because sport is emotional. Maybe there'll be something on a scan and you ask the player and he says he's OK, so you go with him.

'I do this because it's the next best thing to playing. It will never replace it, because once you finish it has gone for ever. When I see them going out before games I tell them they're lucky bastards. I still feel the emotions I had as a player, but in different degrees and different amounts. When you get it right as a manager it is undoubtedly as fulfilling as scoring a winning goal because the responsibility lies with you.

'I think I can achieve things here. We are in a league where there is a huge amount of financial strength, which we haven't got, so we have to achieve in a different way. But at a top club, you're just keeping them where they have always been. Come here and be successful, and people will remember you for ever.'

Case dismissed, Mr Derry. QPR was an instance of the right man in the wrong club at the wrong time. The flaming torches of the protest march are casting an ominous shadow across the North East, and there is another case of perceived injustice to investigate.

8

A Self-made Man

Autumn announced itself through the musty scent of fallen leaves and intermittent rain, driven by a northerly wind which sliced across the railway track adjoining the training ground. Alan Pardew was quick to seize on my schoolboy error of not having worn an appropriate coat. 'Well hard, eh?' he chuckled good-naturedly.

He was in his element, tutoring Ayoze Pérez, a young forward of rich promise, scouted in Spain's Segunda División and signed for relative peanuts, €2 million. The language barrier was overcome by the universality of football technique. Pardew was animated, tactile. He manipulated the player's shoulders so that his muscle memory registered the body shape required to take the ball naturally and fluidly on the half-turn.

John Carver and Steve Stone supervised sprints, plyo-metric exercises and a five v two possession drill. After

40 minutes, the first team group gravitated towards the main pitch, in front of a pavilion where, barely believably, two palm trees stood sentinel. In the brief lull in the multilingual babble, while drinks were taken before a pattern of play session, the senses were assaulted by a jackhammer being used in an adjacent builders' yard.

Pardew blew a whistle and brought his players to order. He was seeking to ingrain a high-intensity pressing game, and his consequent commentary during an intra-squad practice match was a stream of consciousness: 'Sometimes you have to go "bang" . . . I'm going to go . . . no half measures . . . wait for the loose pass . . . good possession . . . ready to go, ready to go . . . fuck it, we're trying to get a goal here . . . don't switch off . . . we need ten regains . . . don't let them think quicker than us . . . I'm telling you, step off, let them play, and we're in trouble.'

This was life in the bubble. The loyalists remained at the gate, a familiar mixture of the retired, the unemployed and schoolboys who had evidently slipped out of classes after taking the precaution of attending roll call. They peered into any car which arrived as if it contained the secret of eternal life. When Rémy Cabella, a putative folk hero, arrived in his white Porsche Cayenne with Montpellier plates, he was confronted by a human roadblock.

It was business as usual at Newcastle United, in more ways than one. Despite the devotion of those who sought scribbled autographs and snatched selfies, the club was in turmoil. Journalists were banned for doing their jobs, fans were increasingly militant, and staff and players alike still seethed at the pettiness of owner Mike Ashley, who had restricted their ticket allocations.

Pardew was the lightning rod, the sacrificial victim being fitted for a mock coffin. The gentlest criticism he received was to be lampooned as a Sports Direct version of George Clooney, common and revealingly cheap. The most virulent sought to portray him as a traitor to the cause, a quisling. An online campaign calling for his sacking had gone viral.

Sue Banks, a kindly lady who acted as PA to Pardew and the previous eight Newcastle managers, confided, 'It has been awful at times for Alan', but he made light of the abuse. 'I've had worse,' he said, though he admitted he no longer liked his family to attend home games 'because they hear everything'.

He had agreed to allow me to witness a day's work, despite a blanket ban on media at the training ground, and I had arrived with an open mind. He was unaware I knew of his private acts of solidarity, such as telephoning Aidy Boothroyd during the last weeks of his tenure at Northampton with an offer to oversee the loan of any of Newcastle's development squad players he required. He was quietly supportive of Martin Ling's attempts to rehabilitate himself.

It was easy to see why Pardew alienates so many. He had the traits of the dominant male: he was composed and excessively comfortable with himself. He spoke slowly, as though sifting diamonds and in a mime of teenaged thoughtlessness, he had tossed his tracksuit trousers across a room dominated by a portrait of Sir Bobby Robson.

His sentences occasionally trailed off, a sign of a man conscious of the impact of his words. Yet there were clues of sensitivity and substance, a poem dedicated to 'My Father' and, alongside the autobiographies of Michael Jordan, Pelé and Jackie Stewart, the book *Talent Is Overrated: What Really Separates World-Class Performers from Everybody Else.*

That was apposite, since it dwelled on the principle of so-called 'deliberate practice' and attempted to cast new light on the age-old debate about the relative merits of innate talent. Its central conclusion, that world-class performance in sport, business or the arts is more the product of calculated diligence, tallied with Pardew's own experience.

There was a cultural element to his case. Were he a coach in a mainstream North American sport, such as baseball, American football or college basketball, his success in thriving despite not entering professional football until the age of 26 would be deemed worthy of the full soft-focus treatment, complete with lachrymose soundbites.

Here, instead of being celebrated as a working-class warrior, he is resented for the ferocity of his ambition. He is still fighting, figuratively and occasionally literally, the battle which crystallised his character, on the building sites of London in the late 1970s and early 80s. He was immediately engaged when, by way of introduction, I voiced my suspicion that his knowledge of working life outside football fundamentally shaped his personality.

'Yeah, that's true. My formative years are quite simple really. I was not good enough at school to land a professional football club, so at sixteen I went straight into non-league football, into men's football. I was a very slight boy, and a lot of the guys scouting in those days made their choices on physical size, so I ended up playing senior football in a boy's body.

'I was slightly better technically than the others, but was kicked from pillar to post. I got to understand that side of the game, where you come in for a bit of attention, and people are trying to intimidate you physically. I worked my way through the non-league ranks back into the midfield from a striking position.

'The money (six pounds basic, one pound win bonus) was insignificant, really. It was classed by some of the lads as beer tokens the wife didn't really know about. As a single lad it was my Saturday-night-out money. I was typical of a time where, if you didn't grasp a good education, you followed your father. He played a big part in where you ended up. Mine worked in a glazing company, so my work there went in tandem with the football.

'Building sites are tough. With some trades, like glazing, you're in their way and you've got to stand your ground, otherwise you're going to get bullied and you can't get your work done. I was one of the ones who stood up to that kind of provocation. I didn't really like bullies, so I used to get myself into trouble. I wasn't a particularly great fighter but I wouldn't back down too much.'

He laughed, lost in the reverie. He helped build London landmarks such as the NatWest Tower in the City, and Sea Containers House, an ocean liner of a building on the south bank of the Thames. He knew what it was like to be on the scaffolding as dawn broke on winter mornings. He developed a quick, caustic humour as a defence mechanism.

Playing for clubs like Whyteleafe, Epsom & Ewell, Corinthian Casuals and Dulwich Hamlet was a release. On Sundays he even turned out for the Surrey amateur side Morden Nomads.

'Ah, the football. I loved football, and would work really hard to get out early. In those days I did piece-work, where you were literally paid for what you did on the building site. It wasn't guaranteed earnings, like a day's money. I had to put a certain number of windows in to get paid, so I used to go in at seven when people were still having breakfast, making sure I could finish by three.

'They were big windows, on like a balcony system. I had to do three of those balconies in a day, so that would consist of a pair of doors, five windows, and a couple of little windows. Then I'd get off, get home, try and get my kit, beat the traffic so that I could get to training or to a game. Later on in my career, when I was playing for Yeovil, I was doing the Sea Containers House in Blackfriars. I put all the windows in that, I did, and still walk past with a bit of pride.

'I'd get in my car for a couple of hours and drive down the A303 or whatever it was to Yeovil, and get there just in time to put my kit on, to train or play a game. I'd drive all the way back, get in bed about half one, two, get up and go to work to start at seven. That's work. That's a proper day's work. Well, that's more than a day's work, and I did that for about fourteen months.'

He had given up football for six months, while he worked in the Middle East, and was faced with taking a pay cut when Crystal Palace offered a professional contract on £400 a week. He was on 'good money' on the sites, and earning around £160 a week for Yeovil, who were desperate to get out of the Isthmian League and return to the Conference. His transfer fee was £4,000.

'Palace were flying with a new young manager, young players, but were being held together by buttons really.

I was buttons. Ron Noades, the chairman, did the deal and managed to talk me into taking a pay cut of a hundred and fifty pounds or so, which I wasn't particularly pleased about. He was an expert at that. It was "you'll get your rewards, son" and all that. To be fair to him, he did reward me as I went along, not in a grand way, but I ended up in a team that was very aggressive in its play. It was the Wimbledon, John Beck, long ball game. Steve Coppell's management was based on not putting the ball at risk.

'I find myself looking back at that time, as a manager myself, and know, for sure, that it hindered the development of our footballers. It was the whole POMO bit, position of maximum opportunity. Reaches, and the pitch being longer in the corners and all that. I mean, my job at Crystal Palace in midfield was to win the ball back, have two touches and put it in the corner.

'There really wasn't much else I needed to do, and if I could nick a goal that would be good. It made you look not very attractive as a footballer, and it took me a while to adjust to that, because at Yeovil I used to mess about with the ball and quite enjoy it. It was a successful period, though, because we had two great strikers, played with two wingers, and the two central midfielders had to cover a lot of ground. I could do that, and was competent enough to hit a decent pass now and again.'

The ease with which the story is told, the underlying

message that hard work is the ultimate football philosophy, whatever blueprints are sent from the coaching hub at the FA's grandiloquent palace just outside Burton, suggests, correctly, that it is part of Pardew's welcome brochure.

'I think it's an important message that I've always carried with me, and I can carry it with credibility. I sometimes see managers who have been in the bubble, as you put it, talk about it on the telly, but they can't talk about it like me, because they've not done it. They can talk about the fans, and what it means to the fans. They can gauge it, but they don't know it.

'I was the fan. I was the bloke buying the *Sun* on the building site, who couldn't believe how badly that team had played or that individual had done. I couldn't understand why I watched someone at Chelsea or Fulham and they hadn't tried a leg, when I had paid my money to go in. Even though I was a non-league player, I used to love going to watch games. I still do.

'So I know. I can register that to the young players here and try to bring it home to them. It doesn't mean to say they take it on board, because a big percentage of the players really and truly don't get it. They'll never get it. They don't need to. They're good enough to play professional football. They're good enough to earn their rewards.

'Acknowledgement of the normal world just bypasses them, as it does with rock stars and people who earn vast amounts of money. They become somewhat immune to the realities of what work actually is. There is a balance to be struck, though, because expectation gets the average footballer all tense. He takes on too much.

'I think if a player here knew what it meant to one of our hardened fans I don't think he'd be able to play. Without being slightly detached, could he play, knowing how the club is embroidered in people's lives? Bless those two boys, John and Liam, who got a cheap flight to New Zealand via Amsterdam and ended up losing their lives to go and see us play on a pre-season tour.

'They were background faces we knew well, always at the stadium in my time here. It brought things home, in no uncertain manner. That affected the club and affected me. That could have been my daughter. So we can't ignore conflict in the Ukraine, and we can't ignore what goes on in Iraq, Syria and Libya. We can't ignore politics because actually it will impact on you at some point through the random nature of life . . .'

He paused, aware he was straying from the point. The thought struck me that here was a man who was too often complicit in the complication of his own life. He has had a consistent struggle to be accepted – West Ham fans, for instance, refused to sing his name for two seasons when he managed them – and has had an adversarial, some would say cynical, relationship with the media.

Football teaches its own to mistrust public shows of emotion, save for kissing the badge with the passion of an android, or choreographed collective gratitude at the end of the match. If fans heard Pardew speaking like this more often, in a manner which would appal sociologists but enthral the phone-in philosophers, he would be more likely to be accepted as one of their own.

It was no surprise to discover that when he began his coaching career at Barnet in 1995 he was doing the Knowledge, in anticipation of becoming a London cabbie. He would have been typecast as the Wittgenstein of the Westway or the Bertrand Russell of the bus lanes.

'Players in the modern game have changed. They're softer now, they're not as battle-hardened, and I think that's because life is easier across society. You know, 'we've never had it so good' and all those other quotes we keep hearing about these days. I'm not saying owning a property is as easy as it was ten years ago – it's not. But generally, in Great Britain, you can have a life where bread is on the table, and small luxuries come into the house at the lowest levels.

'A lot of these players are working-class players. This is a working-class club. We have players from France and from Holland, whose families are working class. They have a good work ethic. Young people are always going to want a sparkly something – a car, shoes, what-ever. That doesn't necessarily mean, though, that when they go out there on a Saturday they don't have that will to win.

'I'd pick out Jack Wilshire as somebody who has had some bad press for some of the things he does. I don't think anyone can say he doesn't care, that he doesn't give everything of himself to win. That's a trait of British players, but they are softer and here is the reason for that.

'Something like eighty-five per cent of kids in our academy are from one-parent families. We worked out that sixty-seven per cent of those kids had a mother bringing them up and therefore they are slightly softer than they would be having Dad as a threat. I'm not saying that Dad would come round and slap the kid, but certainly the look, the threat, the warning, toughens kids up.

'My dad was like that. I was proper scared of my dad. He never touched me but I was in awe of him. It was a lot tougher at school, more disciplined. It's a lot softer now, guidance and development. One of our characteristics, one of our strengths as a nation, was our strength of character. The danger is that it is being diluted a little bit with the social system we have now, particularly with one-parent families.

'That's a concern, something we talk about at the club. That's why discipline in the academies is very, very important. We run on very similar lines to the army here at Newcastle, making sure that the boys get the discipline, and understand how important it is that they do their work.'

Pardew has spent time with the armed forces, seeking a fresh perspective to hone his management skills, just as he has visited Formula One teams to glean an insight into the principles of teamwork, applied under intense time pressure and immense global scrutiny.

I have friends who have served in Special Forces, the SAS and SBS. Such elite groups base their recruitment strategy on a candidate's capacity for self-development. Toughness is not an overt characteristic; they seek those whose strength is modulated and carefully controlled. Someone with Pardew's history of bristling, starkly public aggression would be an unlikely recruit.

The charge sheet is well known: Arsène Wenger has twice pushed him following eyeball-to-eyeball touchline confrontations, in 2006 and 2014. Pardew pushed a linesman during a game against Spurs in 2012, and was caught on camera calling Manchester City manager Manuel Pellegrini a 'fucking old cunt'. Pardew's most inglorious moment was his instinctive decision to head-butt Hull City's David Meyler in another touchline squabble.

'Of course, you've got to be honest with yourself when you get it wrong. As you get older, I think that gets a little bit easier. I've made many mistakes in my career, on and off the pitch, and by the side of the pitch. You've got to grow, got to understand that you need to be able to control your emotions. My incidents on the touchline last year made it very, very clear to me it needed to be addressed.

'At the time, against Hull, I actually didn't think it was as bad as when I saw it on TV later. You're involved in the incident, so you don't anticipate what people have seen. You watch a replay of it as a second body, if you know what I mean. I'm watching myself as somebody else, as others see it. When I did so I was shocked, deeply embarrassed for my fans, my family, my team.

'You really just want to go and hide in a hole, but I couldn't hide. Immediately after the game I went to see the chief exec, and we agreed we should do something straight away. He came out with a figure [a £100,000 fine] and, to be honest, I didn't argue, even though a couple of days later, I thought it was a little high. It sent out the right message that I needed to have a period of reflection.'

He consulted Keith Peacock, the former Gillingham and Maidstone manager, who had worked with him at West Ham. He sought the counsel of Lee Richardson, one of his closest friends, an architect who had played with him for Whyteleafe and scouted for him at Charlton.

He also benefited from the LMA's mentoring programme, which offered access to professional advice on self-control and defusing tension in the workplace. He valued the insight of former England limited-overs cricketer Jeremy Snape, a mental-conditioning coach who was helping Sri Lanka prepare for cricket's World Cup.

'I want to win trophies, but I've got to be employed to win trophies so I can't be doing stuff like that any more. My ultimate ambition, as an Englishman, is to manage the England team, so I have to show over the next two or three years that I'm not only a good coach and manager but also that I can control my emotions on and off the pitch. Simple.

'The strange thing about that time is that I didn't feel under a great deal of pressure. I reacted to a threat and a sense of injustice, if I'm honest. That's probably my trigger point, that I have to watch out for now. I'm not an eighteen-year-old glazier having a go at a chippie: "Get off my back so I can put my windows in!"

'I've never really instigated a situation, in my view. I don't like mentioning the Pellegrini one, but he accused me of something. Wenger came on to me, but he said something very important at the Premier League managers' meeting at the start of this season.

'He complained of having a camera, a remote TV camera, permanently on him with a microphone, two yards from him. He asked for it to be removed, because it was intrusive and he couldn't do any work, because they were just looking for one sullen moment. We've all been there. The photographers just zoom in on you, waiting for that reaction shot.'

There are 5,136 million reasons why such scrutiny will

intensify in the coming years. That's how much, in sterling, the new Premier League TV deal is worth. Broadcasters demand a megaton of flesh in return for such obscene sums. Their focus on the technical area has turned managers into matadors who play lead roles in the armchair theatre.

Throw into the mix Pardew's toxic relationship with the Newcastle fans, as another mediocre season is laced with anger and frustration, and the volatility of the situation requires no overstatement. He identifies the keyboard crusaders, usually anonymous adolescents, as an ever-present threat.

'You have to be really resilient, as a player, coach or manager, in the Premier League at the moment, because of social media. I don't think we get offered a lot of protection and I think it's a sad slant on society that it's like that.

'Let's for example say one of my players dallies on the ball. It's nil–nil, he gets robbed and the opposition score. You're not just getting the press the next day saying, "You made an error in midfield, what were you thinking?" You get it replayed Saturday night, Sunday afternoon, Sunday night, Monday, maybe even through to Wednesday on *Sky Sports News*. You've got social media calling you and your family all sorts of obscenities. We can't even police that.

'As a manager you are affected, more and more, not just by the result but by the sales and marketing team, by a player who has for whatever reason got himself into a situation that's not related to football. I meet managers and coaches who get bitter about the media in particular, and the game in general. They're worried about the owners.

'I've had some tricky ones, and I'm not saying that this one [Ashley] is not particularly great or good, but you have to understand they are coming from a different place. Therefore they have different issues and problems from you. My owner, here, has a particular way he wants to sign players and we have a small window in which to operate. That makes it a lot more difficult.

'But we all have our own agendas. It's different for Brendan, my mate at Liverpool. It's different for Van Gaal, who, let's be honest, has got to come at least second and get a cup this year. We have to be shrewd, clever. Not only that, we've got to improve and get near the top four. Do I want to end that dream, and come out at my Friday press conference and say, "Listen, guys, we're the eighth best team. If we can finish eighth it'll be great?" No.

'I've had tricky periods before. Everyone thinks I went to Reading and it was all great. Well, it wasn't. It was very tricky with West Ham in the Championship, and certainly near the end with Tevez, Mascherano and the takeover business. I had a pretty comfortable season at Southampton in terms of the team but not in the background. The chairman was very difficult. You must have principles in what you do, and you must be strong with those principles, because they get tested big time.

'When the critics come for you, and the results are poor, you must keep setting the right tone. There are millions of clichés about what to do when the hard times come, but the most important thing, as a manager, is that you're honest with your players, and you're fair with your staff. I won't let it affect me, and maybe my background has something to do with that.'

Pardew excused himself, to pop in to see the squad complete their post-lunch conditioning work in the gym. Earlier, he had taken some time on his own, to meet with the enigmatic French winger Gabriel Obertan. I took the opportunity to linger with John Carver, his assistant, in the dining room.

He was engaging company, regaling the table with tales of his time at Luton Town, where the kit man slept on the premises. He spoke poignantly about a missed opportunity, managing Toronto in Major League Soccer, an experience overshadowed by the ill-health of both his parents. He spoke with unwitting prescience about the lure of being a football manager. 'I'll be a manager again,' he said. 'It gets inside of you. I've worked with Sir Bob, and Alan is one of the best.'

Sir Bobby Robson is the patron saint of Newcastle United, the friendly ghost of St James' Park. No one has ever bettered his reflections on the humanity which should underpin any football club worthy of the name:

'What is a club in any case? Not the buildings or the directors or the people who are paid to represent it. It's not the television contracts, get-out clauses, marketing departments or executive boxes. It's the noise, the passion, the feeling of belonging, the pride in your city. It's a small boy clambering up stadium steps for the very first time, gripping his father's hand, gawping at that hallowed stretch of turf beneath him and, without being able to do a thing about it, falling in love.'

A thought occurs to me: Alan Pardew is still on piece-work. He would move to Crystal Palace in the New Year in the same way he moved building sites, from the NatWest Tower to Sea Containers House. For others, such as his friend Brendan Rodgers, tradition was a little more tangible.

9

Wear the Crown

Brendan Rodgers strides forward purposefully, right arm extended in greeting. His eyes are locked on to his guest with the accuracy of a Star Fleet phaser. His fulsome smile frames a face flushed by recent exertion, a brisk three-mile jog in the early afternoon. His body language is word perfect.

'I love to run on the streets around here,' the Liverpool manager says, with the ease of a politician circulating at a cocktail party. 'I love seeing the people going about their business. These are our people. I love running late in the afternoon, when the doors are open and the dinners are on, and you can smell the mince cooking . . .'

Stop. Right. There. Please.

A lot of British coaches need you to succeed, Brendan. As current LMA Manager of the Year, you are too important an asset to sell yourself short with what sounds to me like the sort of whimsy which died with The Waltons. Reverence for tradition is one thing, an unnecessary threat to your authority is entirely another. Don't give snide whispers about your superficiality substance. Deny the snipers a stationary target.

Results, in the immediate post-Luis Suárez era, might be patchy. Your team is a work in progress. Offer reassurance, rather than additional ammunition for critics who have suddenly, predictably, become emboldened. Give an insight into the authenticity of your work, a reason for more Premier League owners to employ organic, home-grown leaders like you.

Let's start this chapter again . . .

Brendan Rodgers ushers his guest towards a flip chart situated behind the long sofa on which they had been seated, briefly. The pad is thick, evidently well used, and the edges of the pages are crumpled. The eye is drawn to the front page, which contains four words. The first letter of each word is written in red felt tip pen. The rest are in black.

Commitment
Organisation
Responsibility
Excellence

There is a calculation on the right-hand corner, which looks to have been written in a hurry: 17 x 12 = 204. Further up, on the same side, there is a childlike drawing of a stick man with a jagged crown on his head. Rodgers, a copious note-taker on the sidelines during matches, explains he likes to 'think in ink'. This is his version of the 'Liverpool Way'.

'I go through this with every player. First and foremost it's about a vision, an understanding where you as a player are going. I need to know where you want to go with the club and with the team. Have a clear vision, a clear philosophy of how you work, and then have an inherent belief in it. From that, I work on what I call the core. Every player I meet, every one I speak to, goes through this, OK?

'I first need them to understand the commitment of what it takes to work every day. I don't need players motivated, because some days you get up and you're not motivated. But if you're a life-saving surgeon, you work on commitment. If you do five operations a day and save people's lives, you might be motivated for the first four, but the fifth guy needs you like the first one. So you need to commit to your work. No matter how you feel, it's about being committed.

'What we'll then do is organise a system to enable you to be your best. No matter how old you are or how young you are, you want to be the best that you can be. I will help with the infrastructure here, to make a plan for you to maximise your potential. From that moment on, I make it very clear it's your responsibility.

'What I say to players is this: "The crown is on your head, my friend. You are the king of your destiny. Don't come crying to me. I will put everything in place for you. I will be open with my communication. I won't waste my life telling you something in six months' time that I can tell you now. So you take the responsibility to be the best you can be, and do all the things that we ask. Commit to our play. You will have a greater chance of excellence. You may not always be at your best, but the responsibility is with you."'

TV viewers are familiar with Rodgers' eloquence, even if he is occasionally prone to the stilted language of coach-speak. Most managers have an aptitude for saying a lot in public, while revealing little. Yet in this environment, on a one-to-one basis, there is compelling intensity to his delivery. His voice has a richness of tone, so that he echoes a priest reading a favourite passage of Scripture. He goes on to explain the context of the calculation in the corner.

'Here's a boy I had in here this morning. He's eighteen. So I am saying to him: "You've got seventeen years left in the game, if you're a really successful player, you look after yourself and you're lucky with injuries. You will play until you're thirty-five years of age, right? So, look, seventeen years, multiplied by twelve, two hundred and four. You've got two hundred and four pay packets left in your lifetime as a player. And see, at the end of this month, that becomes two hundred and three. And all those wage packets you've had when you're thirty-five must keep you for a lifetime, until you're eighty. That's money to look after your mum, your dad, your kids, your family. So take that responsibility to develop this core, because once this is done, this is done. Maximise yourself. Remember, this is your life. So don't wait on it, create it.'"

It is tempting to see modern football as *FIFA 15* made flesh, vivid and instant entertainment. But players in a computer simulation game are inanimate objects. Rodgers, and his peers, must deal with fêted, flawed young men. The struggle of Mario Balotelli to establish himself at Anfield, following a £16 million transfer from AC Milan in August 2014, was a case in point.

Rodgers was counselled by some colleagues that such a volatile character represented an untenable risk. Yet his need for a striker was urgent, following the loss of Daniel Sturridge. His belief in the power of the mind, established at Swansea, where he employed a neurologist, had been reaffirmed by Liverpool's recruitment of Dr Steve Peters, the clinical psychiatrist famed for his work with Olympic athletes.

'You have to recognise where your players are in their career, their life. So, for example, Balotelli, and the life he has had. His starting point is totally different from most others'. Not too many kids were born into a family of four and were the only one given away. So you can't treat him like everybody else. You can't treat him like the guy who has grown up in a secure family. As a manager you look to the human-needs element of the player first, before any professional or coaching aspect.

'I had Balotelli in here for three and a half hours. I talked him through the CORE principles. I said, "Listen. You're a fantastic talent. You're a good guy. I've done my homework on you. You're a clever boy. People try and make you out to be stupid but you're a clever boy. But I need you committed here."

'I know how hard he is trying. This is a kid who wants to succeed so much. I see him as like many kids I worked with at Chelsea, boys who were written off, given no hope, boys from the street, inner-city kids. They're told they're this, they're that, they can't do this, can't do that. When I lost Suárez, I lost a wee bit of what I've had all my life, people who were written off, and I felt I needed something like that, for me.

'I had a great group here. The boys would do exactly what I said. Everything. Don't get me wrong, the biggest boys in the group have the edge. They're no choirboys, but they're shaped well. I loved Suárez because he challenged me. Not in a negative way, but just having to think about him. I had to think every press conference: what's going to come to me? It was always about Suárez. I'd pull him in here: "What are you doing, my friend? What *are* you doing?" But I'd also speak to him about other issues, to do with his life. That's why Balotelli and I speak every day.'

His explanation had an air of authenticity, especially since it contained a tacit admission of a finely developed ego. Very few football managers are altruistic; their starting point is selfishness, or, at the very least, acute self-awareness. Endgames vary, from mere survival in an insanely competitive profession to opportunistic advancement at almost any cost.

Without values, however, they are lost. There was a revealing edge to Rodgers' voice when he considered his inheritance, which included a number of players on high wages who were content to coast. Rodgers seemed affronted, not as a football man, but as an individual whose upbringing in the village of Carnlough in County Antrim highlighted the importance of frugality.

'Stealing a living, I call it. You know, you have an obligation to a wonderful football club; the money is in your bank every month. This is one of the few countries in the world where you can be guaranteed that. At the very least you have an obligation to be professional. I have a profile, in my mind, of the sort of player I want around me.

'First and foremost he needs to have talent, the personality to play at a club with this pressure. He must have the capacity to learn. Mentally, he has got to be hungry. That's got nothing to do with age. It's to do with desire and ambition, no matter how much you earn. To meet the demands we set, the speed at which we ask players to play, you need to be technically strong. Mentally you have to be able to work.

'As a manager, as you grow at a place, you become a facilitator. If we're talking about leadership I've been through three phases here. I was very dogmatic at the beginning, not in a bad way but "This is my philosophy. This is how I work. Boom. Andy Carroll, I'm going to let you go. British transfer fee record? It's about how you are on the field and off the field."

'Once the methods are in place and up and running I become more pragmatic. And then, as players start to understand how I work, it becomes more educational. I'm now at the stage where I'm more multifunctional really. It goes back to my background in development.

'My rule has never changed. You see, for me, how I've worked with Liverpool is no different from how I worked with the under tens at Reading. No different. I don't see myself as a coach, or as a manager. I see myself as a welfare officer. I look after the needs of the player, and the group. So, I understand that that is technically, tactically, physically, mentally, but also lifestyle, socially. I work with these kids like they are my own. I give them advice like I was giving advice to my son.

'I try to go beyond "OK, this is what the club can offer you." I've studied coaching, but the first and last things I look at are the human needs. Somewhere along the line football misses the point that these boys are talented, but they are no different from the guys on the street. They're just very fortunate that they aren't having to do the jobs that most people have to do. So I take on that role as a supporter of their welfare.

'My philosophy is still very clear on how we work, the demands of every day, the work ethic, the intensity. And like I said, it all revolves around this core, because I always refer back to that. I had a player in here once. I told him, "If you're not committed, then go to Sunderland. There's other great clubs in this country. Go to Aston Villa. But at Liverpool it's a different commitment, a totally different commitment."'

Bold words, brave words, noble words. They are delivered, once more, with a passion which softens his Ulster accent. But theories, by definition, offer no guarantees. In the rough and tumble of a Premier League season, it is tempting to extemporise, to sacrifice aspects of a once-sacred philosophy to expedience.

Rodgers' philosophy is not that of a romantic poet, skipping through meadows with a sonnet on the tip of his tongue; it is tangible, in the form of a 180-page document entitled 'One Vision, One Club' that is his life's work. Yet, if there was any time for panic, the late autumn of 2014 seemed as good as any.

Managers are first in the firing line when signings are questioned, and the chorus of disapproval at the lack of instant return on a summer investment of £120 million in a transitional squad acquired uncomfortable volume as winter edged ever closer. The irony is that, at a club like Liverpool, which has an analytical approach to recruitment, traditional power bases are eroded.

Rodgers insists he has final say on signings, but was vulnerable since he was bound by the conventions of collective responsibility to a so-called transfer committee, featuring chief executive Ian Ayre, head of recruitment Dave Fallows, director of technical performance Michael Edwards, chief scout Barry Hunter and Fenway Sports Group's Mike Gordon.

When points on the board are deemed more important than personal and professional instincts, a manager has a choice: fight or flight. Rodgers' response reminded me of Phil Jackson, the fabled US basketball coach, who speaks about 'leading from the inside out'. He is not afraid to challenge his athletes by sharing deeply personal thoughts and beliefs, such as Zen Buddhism.

The aim is to promote a mutual sense of understanding, which in turn develops mutual respect. As a coach, he seeks to get his players thinking about the way they perform and lead their own lives. Dressing rooms can be cold cynical places in professional sport, but Rodgers is unashamedly open about the importance of his own background.

He still bore the scars of the loss of his mother, Christina, to a sudden heart attack, and his father, Malachy, to throat cancer. They were 52 and 59 respectively, no age in an era when the traditional allotment of three score years and ten is being revised by medical advancement and improvements in quality of life. He spoke of them with such warmth and pride, their enduring influence was obvious.

'They brought me up on a council estate in Northern Ireland. We weren't affected directly by the Troubles, but they were a part of life every day. What affected me was the work of my father and mother. Dad was a painter and decorator. He had no trade behind him, but he could do anything. He was brilliant with his hands. To get money and survive he became a maintenance guy for this guy who recognised how clever he was. He ended up being a really good friend to this guy for twenty years, a trusted ally.

'When I was a young lad, going through the trials for the international team, I saw what he had to do to get me to Belfast. When I think back on it, my father was dependent on being paid on a Friday, by this guy who had a load of money, but who didn't probably give a shit about him. My poor dad was reliant on that cash to take me to football, to feed his family. That shaped me. I would never wait and rely on anyone else. I would create it myself.

'My parents gave me values in terms of work. Dad would come in at night, have his dinner and my mum would look after us all, five boys. He'd be straight into building a kitchen, an extension, right through until the early hours of the morning. Bang. Up again in the morning and away. Yet he still had time to do things for us. He was my hero as a child. He took me everywhere. I wanted to be like my father.

'An amazing man. My mum equally so, in a different way. She was a volunteer for an Irish charity who travelled the world raising thousands and thousands of pounds for children for over twenty years. She showed me the caring side, the importance of principles. Early on in my life the seeds were sown that I'd rely on no one but myself.'

This is not a serene look through the rear-view mirror. It is a statement of faith. Rodgers negotiates his own contracts. He is multilingual for a reason, since it extends his professional reach. He has ensured a long-held, long-term ambition to work in La Liga has reached the ears of influential Spanish journalists. He regards football as 'a circus at this level' and insists 'you have to leave room for normality'. Critics who accused him of narcissism reckoned without his inner steel.

'I've been through probably the most traumatic four years of my life since 2010. I lost my mum. I lost my dad. I split up from the woman I loved for twenty-three years. I had a court case, two Old Bailey trials over six weeks with my son, who was charged with sexual assault, which was an absolute disgrace. Yet professionally, here and at Swansea, these have been the best four years of my life.

'Something has to come from within. You have to put the professional and personal to each side. It's about being happy of course, but the owners have paid me to do a job, so I will do the job. I know you've seen Shaun Derry at Notts County. There's a story about Jimmy Sirrel there which has stuck with me since I was a young coach.

'His wife, Cathy, died late on the Friday night, but he came in on the Saturday. Nothing was said. He got on with his job, he did his job. Team played the game, won the game. Normally after every game, him and his wife would sit at a little table and have a glass. Then they'd go. This Saturday night he quickly popped into the bar. Someone asked about his wife, and he said, "She died last night." He'd lost the woman of his life, his right hand, but he still came in and did his job. Makes you think, doesn't it?'

His career is one of calculated progression and occasional rejection, and an ability to compartmentalise his life was essential at Liverpool, a club of emotional extremes. His eagerness to respond to the culture of club and city left him open to accusations of manipulation of tradition, and, at times, he seemed to genuflect before the legend of Bill Shankly a little too extravagantly.

'It was the reason I came,' he said simply, making sure eye contact was sustained. 'For me it wasn't just about a club. It was about the right club. I went to Watford, my first job, because I felt the chairman gave young managers a chance. But I went also because it was a great family club. When I went to Reading as manager, I'd done nearly fourteen years as a coach and as a young player there. I felt I knew the club, as a family club.

'Then I was out of work. I would have coached an under fourteens team as opposed to taking the wrong club, but I ended up going to Swansea, because of the values, the ethics and how they worked. I knew when I left there I could only go to a club that would fit into my way of working and my ethos. That was the reason for coming here. Liverpool: working class, hard honest graft. You do things in a certain way.

'There's still a nostalgic feel to this place. I get supporters coming in here with a flag that's been signed by every Liverpool manager. I look and see that that's actually Bill Shankly's signature, and Bob Paisley's. It's surreal. I'm seized by the feeling of how lucky I am, but also by a fear. I look at where I've come from and look at what I've got to live up to.'

His responsibility is not confined to his club; Rodgers is a status symbol for British coaching. He finds himself in a fashion industry, where there is an increasing tendency for Premier League clubs to recruit from the catwalks of La Liga and Serie A. The Bundesliga will probably supply their supermodels, Pep Guardiola and Jürgen Klopp, sooner rather than later.

'For years I've heard British coaches were behind the times, about passion rather than tactics. I studied the game in Spain and Holland, travelled around the world for fifteen years. My teams are flexible tactically. They might say of me, "Well, he knows a little bit about what he's doing," but I'll never be regarded as a master-class manager. I would be if I was a foreign manager.

'If you're a British coach, stood on the side and not shouting and screaming, then you don't have the passion. Behave like that if you are foreign, and you're thoughtful, educated. I've had to create a brand for myself around my philosophy, because I was never a big player. I know people are looking at me and accept that.

'There are some fantastic British coaches out there who have never been given a chance, but the simplicity of it is there are also those who aren't good enough. You can't tell me that, down the years, England haven't had technical, tactically aware players. But they're not asked to play an aggressive game. They're always made to feel inferior. You know, playing wide midfield, you can come off the line, but watch that hole there, you've got to get back . . .

'There's a guy I really respect in the coaching fraternity in youth development. He was delighted when I moved from that area into management at Watford, but when I got the sack at Reading I could see the pain in his face. He looked at me and went, "We all really wanted you to succeed." It was as if he was hurt for himself and the modern breed of coaches who are coming through.

'I never got the time. I took it badly, but it gave me extra motivation. I went away for ten days. I wrote about ten pages on things that I'd done well and obviously things for the next time. You know: I need to be more clinical. I need to get to the decision quicker because this isn't development now. This is what can happen – you can lose your job.

'So now, instead of giving them ten games, as you would in youth development, I might only give them two or three if they're not performing. Players are being well paid to perform. If they don't, I'll help them, support them in other ways, but they may have to come out. That was the difference. I became more clinical, in terms of the decision, in terms of the team.

'I was sacked in the December. Mum died, and she died quickly, on February 3rd. That knocked me for six. For three months or so I was the pillar for my family. I'm the oldest of five boys, and I can see my brothers suffering. I've got to go again because I'm now representing them. So I get back on my feet again, get the job at Swansea in the July, and then my father passes away. He was young as well. I'd had enough time to reflect. I knew what I needed to do.'

There it is again, that mixture of self-absorption, the acknowledgement of his 'brand', aligned to a willingness to test the strength of broad shoulders. Five years studying neuro-linguistic programming, where, to use a favourite phrase of his, 'the quality of your life is the quality of your communication', had not been wasted.

Liverpool chews managers up and spits them out. Gérard Houllier and Rafa Benítez became overtly sensitive to criticism when their stature was challenged. Roy Hodgson's famed erudition failed him when confronted by high-profile failure at Anfield. Rodgers is acknowledged as a brilliant coach, but to become a dynastic manager he might just have to get down with the kids.

His background in youth development has already seen him have a strategic influence at academy level. He has extended the season of all age group teams from May until July, when schools break up, to give them more time for tactical training in better climatic conditions. He believes the pressing game is suited to the mentality of the young British players he seeks to advance.

He radiates justifiable pride in the acceleration of Raheem Sterling's career, which may ultimately be matched by that of Jordon Ibe, who was recalled to his first-team squad after completing his education on loan with Steve McClaren at Derby County. Rodgers has seen Jordan Henderson mature from 'someone who is told you can't do this, you can't do that, you can't run' to 'a natural leader'. Such strategic investment in youth is fraught with surprises.

'When I speak to young coaches I say, "Listen. You're

entering into a life where you will grow old but the timeline of the players you will be working with will stay the same, from sixteen to thirty-five, more or less. You must stay modern, and you must stay young, without being a dick. It is important that as you grow away from that age band, you stay in touch with it."

'I'm forty-one now and I think, Christ, how old am I getting? OK. Some of the kids have to Google Ricky Villa to see who he is, and what he did for Tottenham in the early eighties. But Mike Tyson? I've got young players who have never heard of him! But if I don't speak with them, if I don't understand their social lives, how can I manage them?'

He, too, was growing up. His relationship with José Mourinho had lost its warmth, as it evolved from mentorship to rivalry. Almost before he knew it, his most significant rite of passage was upon him. On November 4, he left Steven Gerrard out of Liverpool's starting line-up against Real Madrid, in a Champions League tie in the Bernabéu.

His selection of a virtual reserve team was an admission of his failure to come to terms with the demands of European football, despite many hours in his office attempting to work out optimal squad rotation. He had used another flip chart, each page of which featured 12 football pitches, to trace out his teams for an extended series of games, injury permitting.

This gave him an idea of the balance of his squad,

and showcased emerging strengths and weaknesses, but was incidental, given the furore created by Gerrard's marginalisation from the sort of marquee match which was central to his legend. Hanging juries were formed in an instant. Rodgers was accused of having sullied a legend, having spat in the face of an icon whose loyalty and humility were seared into the soul of every Liverpool supporter.

Gerrard's managed departure would dominate Liverpool's season and help to define Rodgers' career. Before that drama played out, and things went from bad to worse in December, the manager rummaged on the floor of his office for another flip chart. He found a page and, for dramatic effect, knocked hard on a convenient coffee table.

'Steven knocks on the door. "Can you see me, boss?" He's thirty-two. England captain. It's not really happening for him at the time. He's talking about his body language, the number of goals he's scoring, the angles he's making, the penetration he wants to bring into his game. "Boss," he says, "I need to improve."

'We write all this down. This is Steven Gerrard, remember. If I don't have confidence in what I'm doing, if I don't believe what I'm telling him is right, I fluff my lines. I tell him that he is a pillar of this group. We are representing millions of people, so you've got to get your chest out. Wear the crown. You're the king of your own destiny.'

10

The Lollipop Man

Across Stanley Park, Roberto Martínez was dealing with similar problems of transition, tradition and exaggerated expectation. He and Brendan Rodgers are the Siamese twins of the Premier League, products of the same club culture at Swansea City, and arbiters of the same fashion for inclusive, emotionally intelligent football managers.

Each was discovering the limitations of lofty ideals. Everton and Liverpool were not going to match their previous season's positions, fifth and second respectively. In Everton's case hipsters were stroking their goatees and making comparisons with Newcastle United, who failed to build on fifth place, and Alan Pardew's installation as Manager of the Year, in 2012.

Martínez and Rodgers occupied adjoining cages in football's human zoo. Martínez was 46 days younger than his neighbour, but had by far the better playing career, even if much of it was spent in the trailer parks of the lower divisions. Each was an adventurer by instinct. They lived and worked in foreign cultures to improve themselves, and it does not take the greatest leap of faith to envisage their rivalry being resumed one day, as managers of clubs in La Liga.

Garry Monk played for them both. As Swansea's current manager, a young coach of similar mindset and ambition, he values their counsel. He had yet to succeed Michael Laudrup when, in an interview in the *Guardian* in November 2013, he provided the most authoritative comparison between the pair.

Monk identified their similarities: the clarity of their vision, the purity of their passion and the intensity of their tactical aggression. They were hands-on coaches, who devised and delivered stimulating sessions in which a player touched the ball between 600 and 700 times. Both were calm in the dressing room, and used their eyes, rather than their voice, to communicate displeasure.

He felt Martínez had a tendency to leave his teams a little too open, whereas Rodgers 'took us mentally, physically and tactically beyond the levels we had been at before'. Each was an exceptional man manager; Martínez paid him gratifying respect by naming him captain, while Rodgers invited him into his house so they could plan his coaching career.

Pay your money, take your choice. Either could have been responsible for the following reflection on the nature of their calling, and the raw material with which they are obliged to work: 'I don't see this as a job. It's just a way of living. I help to create a person. You share aspirations and emotions, adversity and problems. I get on better with human beings than footballers. A footballer is just a term for someone over a specific period of time. He turns up on match day. I work with human beings the other five or six days a week.

'The footballer is just a consequence of a game, a game we play with our feet. The footballer can be risky, ambitious, sometimes thick. It's always a game of errors, and how he reacts to those errors helps you understand the human being. Different personalities react in different manners. Sometimes it's hard to understand the things they do on the pitch and how they react.'

The pop psychology is delivered in the clipped, cadenced tones of a Catalan teetotaller who appreciates the power of his reputation as one of the nicest men in professional football. He is the Lollipop Man of Goodison Park, smiling, helpful and reassuring. His diligence and sheer decency inevitably shape perceptions.

He had been reluctant to allow me to observe his training sessions. I didn't reveal his identity to Martínez at the time, but I had been told by his former roommate Gareth Ainsworth of his penchant for punishing any player who lost possession in a ball retention session by obliging him to drop to the ground and deliver a set of press-ups.

It was an innocent enquiry, which received an interesting response. 'Who told you that?' Martínez said when I asked for confirmation, his smile failing to prevent a sudden impression of alarm that an insubstantial secret had been shared. He suggested the ritual had a positive aspect, since he only penalised purveyors of sloppy passes, but maybe there is more to him than meets the eye.

He has wanted to be a manager since the age of nine, when he shared the dugout with his father, also Roberto, at CF Balaguer, his home-town club. The boy was already a veteran, since his first conscious memory is of being the team's mascot, at the age of two.

Martínez's dark eyes softened, as he made a conscious effort to recall the feelings of that day: 'It's so early in my life to remember but it's like that flash when you see a picture, it just appears. Balaguer was playing at home and the match was even. The pitch was sand at the time. Then it became grass. Now it is Astroturf.'

He had a gentle upbringing, in a town of 15,000 souls, situated between Zaragoza and Barcelona. His father, who had played in the third tier of the Spanish game with Algeciras, on the Bay of Gibraltar, managed part-time, and ran the family shoe shop after acquiescing to his wife's desire for security.

'My mum wanted a little more stability, but my dad was always manager material. His professionalism, the way he saw the game, was as good as you would get anywhere. We were always discussing teams and formations and ways of playing, so my education was with him, really. All I wanted to do was to play football, become a manager, and own a shoe shop, because that's what I felt was me.

'My dad set huge standards in how you should be committed to the game if you wanted to be a part of it. It should be a passion; it should never be a job. I was very fortunate because we just loved sharing football together. It could be from watching a game, and asking him why he was picking this particular team, to going to practise and play together.

'From that moment on he probably made me a very curious person from a football point of view. I followed big managers like Johan Cruyff when he arrived at Barcelona and changed the ideology of a big football club. I studied Arrigo Sacchi when he was at Milan and John Benjamin Toshack when he took on Real Sociedad for the first time. I wanted to know why certain big managers did certain things in a certain way.'

The influences endure, as does the cultural gesture of implied respect in using Toshack's full name. Cruyff bent a Catalan institution, a global footballing power, to his will. Sacchi was a crusader against *catenaccio*; he employed a sweeper and man-markers, and trusted in the technical and tactical intelligence of a creative number 10. Martínez left the family home at 16, to take up a professional contract at Real Zaragoza.

'That was the biggest decision. Even now, my mum and dad still remember that moment. They were losing their son. It was tough, but my dad knew that was the price of football. You have to be prepared to lose your environment and your home comfort. My mum found it a lot harder, but I was lucky I had been able to do what I loved from a really early age.'

He played only one game in La Liga, as a second-half substitute in a 2–2 draw with Atlético Madrid in the last game of the 1992–93 season, but impressed consistently in the B team as a resilient, technically able midfield player. That led to the most unlikely of expeditionary forces being assembled in July 1995, when Dave Whelan persuaded Martínez, Jesús Seba and Isidro Díaz to sign for Wigan, then a humble club in the old Third Division.

They were inevitably introduced as the 'Three Amigos'. No stereotype was too lazy; they posed in sombreros (the photographer failed to realise they were Mexican in style rather than authentically Spanish) and crashed the club's Ford Escort because they drove the wrong way around a roundabout. They had their pre-match meal at Asda and invited fans in for tea at the semi detached house they shared.

Martínez scored in their debut, an FA Cup tie at non-league Runcorn, and forged a new life. The others lasted two seasons in exile; Seba is now one of Martínez's most trusted scouts, while Díaz works in northern

Spain, in an internet business. Where would Martínez be had Whelan not come calling? Would he be selling stout brogues and replicating his father's lifestyle?

'Ooof, that's an impossible question. I always believed life should be lived by trying new challenges, constantly, and by being curious. I've never been guided by finances, or the easy choice. I've never done what people would expect me to do, and that's why I've ended up how I've ended up. I'm not saying my life would not have been very different, but I'm sure my approach would have been the same. Even in Spain, I would be trying things that maybe people hadn't tried before.

'When we came to Wigan in 1995 it was just so new. Who would leave Spain, where you've got the weather and the lifestyle? It wasn't normal to think of playing in the British game. I do feel that we are all products of our own experiences and some things shocked me, especially in the dressing room.

'I was analysing games and sometimes we won, but we were lucky. The manager would come in and he would be wearing the happiest smile on earth. And that wasn't sitting well with me. In the same way, another day we would be very unfortunate to lose because we were the better side. It happens. And the manager would lose the plot and put that act on . . .

'I have lost my temper, but not as an act. When I do it, it's because of a feeling of disappointment, more than anything. I feel a manager should help his players to win games, so the moment we do things that are not up to the standard, I feel let down. I can accept and understand any kind of mistake, as long as the approach is right. But if someone drops their standards or takes their position for granted, that angers me.

'But it's never an act. I've never bought into that kind of management. Maybe that stuff gets some players going, in a certain kind of environment, but I would just rather be honest. If you have to come in after you've won a game and say, "Look, we were very lucky and I think we need to work harder on what we do," that's fine. In the same way, if you lose a game and you play so well, what's wrong with that?

'That's a cultural difference, possibly, and I've been very fortunate in the experiences that I've had as a player. They allowed me to understand a dressing room really well, so I think my relationship with players is full of information. The way I like to manage is through aspiration. I'm not a manager who believes in being on top of people.

'I've been a young man in a foreign dressing room, having to earn my place with no language whatsoever. I had to be effective for the manager when I was a very different type of player, who probably wasn't fitting into the team's way of playing.

'I've been involved in a dressing room at a club with administration problems. At Motherwell we all got released, had our contracts terminated. Our lives changed from one day to another. I've been in another dressing room, at Walsall, where the only way to survive was a multicultural approach. We had Brazilians, New Zealanders, Spanish, English, Scottish and Irish players.

'We had to understand every culture, respect each other even though everyone reacted differently towards adversity. I've also been involved in a dressing room at Swansea where, as a foreign player, I was captain of a team fighting to stay at the professional level in the last game of the season.

'Of course, players have changed over the last twenty years. Society has changed. Football has gone to a more professional level. I think we've got rid of the ones who work hard and party hard. They shaped the way the game was played in the mid-nineties. Being a footballer now brings clear sacrifices. You can't do what other people at your age are doing, and for some that is a big price to pay. The lifestyle of a footballer has changed immensely.

'The finances, with the new television deals, have changed everything. In most cases it has been a real positive. Obviously you could talk about the lack of loyalty of the players, but we have to be realistic and say the markets have opened a lot. We've moved away from the time a player found his club and stayed for ten or fifteen years. The game is updating to the times that we live in.'

So what endures? What are the values he cherishes, beyond the inevitability of submission to market forces and fashionable indulgence in a culture of marginal gains through the effective application of sports science at the highest level? What defines him as a human being rather than a footballer?

'It's a great question because I know what the values are but I've never sat down and tried to collate them all. I believe in human relationships, and I think that a manager and the owner or chairman of the board need to have a human relationship to be able to give stability, good strategy and a good plan for the future.'

So he manages upwards?

'Yes . . . oh, no, not really. You don't manage upwards, you manage through the same way of thinking. It's not trying to manage people, it's trying to understand there is a direction and a plan. Human values become footballing values, the honesty, discipline, bravery, the arrogance. There is a happy balance where you allow the player to express himself, allow him to think and make decisions. But give him too much and that leads to a lack of clarity. He becomes an individual in a team sport.

'It is important to work with people who reflect your values. There are many angles to look at when you assemble a squad. You don't get successful teams by having everyone fitting the same role. You can use the hunger and enthusiasm of young talent to give the group an unknown quantity. You need experienced players, good characters, and a mixture of cultures to have the right balance.

'I'm not the sort of manager who wants to win the game on Saturday and see what happens after that. I prefer a long-term project. I like to build things, make decisions that may not be rewarded for another five or six years down the line. I don't think you can work in any other way.

'It's making decisions I know are right for the football club, not for an individual, which could be me in my position, a player, or even the team at a specific moment in time. As a manager you're a custodian of an incredible history. That relationship with thousands of families must be taken into consideration.

'The fans knew me at Swansea. We had a very strong bond because we went through critical moments when we were fighting relegation. As a player I dropped from the Championship to join them in League Two. They saw it as a strange move, but appreciated it.

'Brian Flynn was the manager at that time. He said to me, "I want to get out of this by playing football." You can play good football in the lower leagues and achieve your aims. That has always been my point to prove, as a technical midfield player.

'I couldn't go in to tackles or fifty-fifty balls. I wanted to play the game by defending with the ball and having more possession than you. That, in the lower leagues, was unheard of. As stupid as it sounds, they never stopped telling me, "You can't play like that and be successful."

'Looking back now, I started thinking as a manager from the day I arrived at Wigan in 95, because I had to find a way to fit into the way of playing in Division Three. I had to work constantly in a tactical way, to be effective. That gave me so much insight into what works, what doesn't work, and how you can fit a basic belief into the British game.'

It all seems very reasonable, and he is. Yet he is in a job where careers depend on disputed decisions. Kenny Jackett admired him as a man, when he took charge of Swansea in 2004, but felt he lacked the durability to compete. His legs had gone, to be blunt. Martínez fought his way back into the team after being dropped, savoured promotion, but was still released at the end of his contract.

'Kenny felt that I was probably at the end of my career. We respected each other a lot but I didn't understand it at the time because I felt I could help the team. He always treated me with real honesty, but the truth is the way I played is very different to the way he wanted the game to be played, and that's very much acceptable. That's what you get in football, different opinions. If you don't fit, you leave. I hope I never let him down in terms of effort and giving everything, but those things happen.'

The self-imposed diplomatic code denies us confirmation, but I'd wager a shiny shilling that Martínez took special satisfaction from beating Jackett's Millwall in the semi-final on the way to his signature achievement, winning the FA Cup in 2013. A brief indulgence in *schadenfreude* doesn't make him a bad person.

'I was in a very unusual situation in League Two, enjoying my football with Chester. I've got a two-year contract and then I get a phone call. I never applied, but I get the manager's job at Swansea. When I got the opportunity, I knew there were three things that would be in my favour.

'One, I knew the fans would give me time, because we had a strong bond. Second, I knew every single player in that dressing room. I knew where they were going when they were having a party. I knew what they were thinking when they were losing a game. I knew what aspirations they had. I'm sure when I turned up they were going, "No, no!"

'Third, I was so touched by Huw Jenkins, the young chairman of a League One club, giving the job to a young manager who was playing in League Two. That was so unusual, and, again, I am driven by unusual things. I get excited by people who have good football vision, good life vision. Swansea is unique. It's a micro-country, a bubble, and it's very intense.

'You need to understand the fans have a huge ownership of the football club in terms of what it represents in their lives. They feel they have a big say in what's going on. The area is phenomenal, because they make you feel like a Premier League player even when you're playing in League Two. The downside is that you have to win every game. It's their club.'

It's never a bad idea to praise the boss, and it is striking that Martínez's career has been characterised by the close, empathetic nature of the relationship he has developed with his club principals: Jenkins, Whelan and Bill Kenwright at Everton. The association appears to verge on bromance.

'The reason I sign for a club, or not, is whether I can rely on that relationship. I learned very quickly that I don't want to be the sort of manager who does what people expect you to do. I'm quite different in my approach. I want to work on visions. It's a bit romantic, if you want, but to get there you have to have a real understanding of the person alongside you, the chairman.

'Huw, Dave and Bill are in very different stages of their lives and careers. They are very different personalities, but they share that sense of dream. They can feel I've got the right intention. They can trust me, and they are going to support me through the difficulties. They see I am working for the club, not just for myself. That creates a big relationship.

'Huw and Dave embraced all we were trying to do.

With Bill, it is exactly the same. He is an incredible human being. I never met anyone so crazy about their football club, for the right reasons. I judge a lot on gut feelings. When I first met Bill, at a game at Goodison Park, we just said, "hi." It just felt right, really, really natural.

'Then when we, Wigan, beat Everton in the quarter-final of the FA Cup at Goodison, there was an incredible feeling in the crowd towards me. We beat them three–nil, but it wasn't hostile or anything. There was just respect, an understanding it was something that was meant to happen. It was a strange feeling, hard to describe.

'When I met Bill for the first time, I knew he was genuine. I knew we could work together and chase a dream. Remember, when I went to Swansea, the first thing I said was our aim is Premier League football. They could have locked me away for going to a club in League One and saying that. But slowly people began to think about it. We got promoted to the Championship and started playing in a certain way, and they saw it was possible.

'That's why it was such a dramatic rupture when I left. The fans felt that everything that had been built was going to collapse. You cannot imagine the reaction. It went from love to hate. I got a lot of letters from people, really hurt and asking for an explanation. You're not in a position to come out and say, "Look, we've grown too quickly. I need to go, to let the club settle a little bit. Get some breathing space and go again."

'If I'd stayed they would never have accepted that. But we didn't have the finances to keep going at that rate. We had players on loan we couldn't replace. They had to go back. I couldn't come out and say that because it would have put a lot of pressure on other people. But now they understand. We've gone back to how we were before.

'At Wigan, we did everything in five years. We were in the Premier League, so we said, OK, we need to play in Europe. People thought we were crazy, but we ended up there, through winning the FA Cup. So when I came to Everton I needed to speak about challenging for the Champions League. Again, they tell me we're crazy.

'Everyone knows what we are fighting for, as a club. If you haven't got a really strong relationship with your chairman, a real understanding of each other, it's impossible to achieve in the modern game because, today, you lose three games and you're out. That's where I have always been very careful. I had opportunities to leave Wigan every year. As a manager you know when it's the right time to leave, for the good of the football club.

'Financially you've got six clubs, City, United, Chelsea, Arsenal, Liverpool and Spurs, who are working with budgets at incredible levels. The rest of us, you can get a good generation, a bad generation. Seventh position is realistically open to Everton, Newcastle, Southampton. Let's see what happens in February, March, when teams start to fall away.'

The second half of Everton's season pivoted on Martínez's ability to adjust in adversity. He had revamped David Moyes' renowned scouting system, and pledged to be 'clever and creative' in team development, yet the team was laboured and one-paced. The power of positive thinking has its limitations, and murmurs of discontent were being amplified.

'The fans are our football club. They remember the glory days, the sixties, the eighties, the trips to Wembley. My ambition as a manager is to please them, so they can feel the School of Science is back and that we can aspire to win titles. There is a real soul here. It tells you good things have happened here in the past.

'It has its own story, and that's why it is such a beautiful place to play. When you get the fans screaming and shouting and getting behind the team it gives you warmth and energy. I don't think we'll ever lose that, but it's also not easy to play in front of a Goodison crowd when things are not going well and you need to get on the ball. It's not easy at all.'

Martínez may very well be a dream weaver who works with 'incredible' human beings. He is undoubtedly a hugely talented coach, acute, brave, principled and incisive. But football isn't a tour of Hollywood studios, complete with gushing commentary and saccharine sentiment.

Let us recognise Roberto Martínez for what he is: an undercover pragmatist. His instincts may be sound, but he added the insurance of a Spanish physiotherapy degree and a postgraduate diploma in business management from Manchester Metropolitan University to underpin his football philosophy. His career has been rather more than a happy accident.

Swansea City are a modern club, built in his image. He moved from Wigan at a time of maximum opportunity, when the FA Cup had been won. He can commune with Everton's ghosts and celebrate the club's spirit, but he is in a cruel, results-driven business. As Christmas approached, Rodgers was making his move to recalibrate, instituting a 3–4–3 system.

Could Martínez respond similarly? Was his reputation threatened by the emergence of Garry Monk at Swansea as a manager of the highest quality? If the Lollipop Man stepped out carelessly into oncoming traffic on the road which winds around Stanley Park, he risked being run down.

11

The Making of a Manager

The questions were starting to multiply. What are the base metals turned into gold by the best football managers? Do bloodlines have a bearing on success? Are club cultures self-perpetuating? What is the difference between a self-promoted philosophy and a slickly presented confidence trick? Where will a new managerial model evolve? The search for answers led to a training complex hidden in the hollows of the Gower peninsula.

Garry Monk defied appearances on a dull, cold winter's day. Pink-tinged saddlebags hung beneath tired, watery eyes. He was fighting a throat infection, and sounded as if he had gargled with iron filings. By his own admission, he was finding it difficult to delegate and impossible to switch off. Life at home, with three children under three, was emotionally fulfilling but physically draining.

The pale, angular features of the Premier League's youngest manager gave him a resemblance to a post-adolescent Draco Malfoy, one of the enduring characters in the Harry Potter saga. Clues to the source of his wellspring of natural energy lay in his age, 36, and the proclamation in the stairwell leading to his first-floor office, which was no bigger than a box bedroom: 'This is the team that makes no excuses.'

That is taken from Monk's blueprint for Swansea City, a document programmed into the iPad given to each player on his first day at the club. It outlines a collective vision, incorporating tactical strategies, performance goals, personal standards and an explanation of the culture of the city they represent. 'Living the values' may be a corporate cliché, but Monk's approach to learning on the job lent the phrase unaccustomed substance.

'It sounds silly, but it is not. The whole point of everything I've done, and it's still in its infancy because I've got a lot to do, is to take as many excuses away from them as possible. You know the stuff players come up with: "The grass is soft today, we didn't know what we were going to do, the instructions weren't clear."

'I've seen and heard it too many times. I've trained with players who think they can nick half a yard on you, or nick an off day, take it easy. If they look at the manager and reckon he doesn't care, he won't notice, they take liberties. Take all of that away, and they think, shit, the onus is on me, I can't fuck around, I haven't got an excuse today.

'This is an opportunity of a lifetime for me. That's why I'll do whatever it takes, work every hour of every day until I get to what I feel is the right way of doing it. I don't know whether you ever achieve what you really want, but if I can get as close to it as possible then that's good enough for me. It is all-consuming, but that is the only way you can do it.'

It had already been a productive day. Monk had just completed a deceptively low-key meeting with Swansea chairman Huw Jenkins which confirmed Wilfried Bony's agreement to sign a one-year contract extension. This would enable the club to strike a more favourable deal in January, when the Ivory Coast striker was sold to Manchester City for £28 million.

Training had been principally devoted to one-on-one defending techniques. All sessions are filmed; Monk wears a radio microphone so he can check the clarity of his communication, especially the pace at which he delivers instructions. He provides players with three bullet points to consider, and one definitive message to digest.

He assesses the subtleties of his body language with psychologist Ian Mitchell, an important sounding board who, unusually, works proactively with him on the training pitch. They drill down into the detail of a high-performance environment, developing trigger points so players can think faster and with greater acuity.

Halfway through his first full season in charge, he was carrying out a stock check. His players were unaware he was already mentally making decisions as to those he would discard the following summer. He sought a new breed, technically adept and intellectually capable in a football rather than an academic sense.

'I'm using this season to get a way of working. I'm trying to weed out the ones who can't think. They stand out like a sore thumb in the sort of training we do. You're doing a passing and movement drill, a shooting drill, or whatever, and you see the ones that get it straight away; bang, and they're into it. They're the thinkers. I need more of them.

'On the other hand, you get the ones that go back to the wrong station. They're stood there waiting, unsure what they are supposed to be doing. They're looking at you, asking again and again. Imagine what they're going to be like on the pitch, in the pressurised circumstances of a game. They won't have time to ask what to do. I'll help them, of course I will, but every second counts, and you need ones who can think on their feet.'

Monk's self-reliance was forged in an obscure League Two match on August 8, 2006, a 2–2 draw at Scunthorpe on a mild Tuesday evening. It was the second game of the season, and his leadership qualities from centre half had been recognised by Kenny Jackett, who made him Swansea captain at the expense of Roberto Martínez.

His perspective changed in the 29th minute in an apparently innocuous challenge on home striker Andy Keogh. He snapped his hamstring tendon, severely damaged his anterior cruciate ligament and sustained significant nerve damage. He saw Jonathan Webb, the former England rugby international who has become a prominent orthopaedic surgeon, in his Bristol clinic 36 hours later.

'Within a minute he said, "I've got to get you in this afternoon," so I thought, this must be really bad. Then he said to me, "I have to warn you, there is a chance that your career could be over." Shit. What am I going to do? I'm twenty-six. Football is all I've ever done. I'm not prepared for anything else. I'm scared. I'm emotional. I'm going to lose my career.

'I was with Richie Evans, our physio at the time, in the hospital room, waiting to go down to theatre. They gave me ten minutes on my own because they could see I was upset. I prayed that when I came round the surgeon would say, oh, it's all brilliant. He didn't quite say it like that, but the operation went well. Then it was about rehabilitation.

'I was out for a season. I can empathise with players who have long-term injuries. I know how it feels when they're doing the hard, solitary days, when it is dark and the boys have been and gone, because I did it, more than did it. They had to rein me in because I was doing too much, so I can relate to what they are going through on a mental and physical level. That helps.

'Equally, I can tell when somebody is trying to pull the wool over my eyes. A lot of it is body language, a front. You can just tell whether they are being honest with you. You know which characters will give you everything every single day, and those who will cut corners. They tend to be the best players, ones who have that little touch of genius about them. As long as you let them know you've clocked it, and you realise what they're up to, they usually think twice.

'That injury was a defining moment for me. Don't get me wrong, I know about the world and I'm quite a clever lad. I'm very streetwise and I know my stuff, but I realised football was all I really had. I started taking my badges, paying really close attention to detail in training sessions. I'd log what managers would say, and how they said it, not just to me but to other players.

'I analysed why the manager asked me to do certain things, or play in a certain position. I weighed up the benefits of a particular session. I paid special attention at team meetings, to see how the information was delivered. You take the bits that work, but also the things you don't necessarily agree with. I noticed when the manager didn't handle situations well, or when he didn't speak as effectively as he should have done at half-time.

'In general, though, I've been very lucky with the range of managers I've played for, from my days with Glenn [Hoddle] at Southampton. Brendan was the most complete, and his man management was brilliant. Everyone talks about Roberto and the philosophy he brought to the club, which was great, but Kenny was the one who gave us a winning mentality. He projected his values – hard work, perseverance, a determination never to be beaten – on to us.

'I've played the typical British way, up and at them, give it to the front man and all that, but I've also played the continental way, in the football we play now. I can see the benefits of both. That stands me in good stead. People doubt you all the time in this game but I like to prove people wrong. That's what drives me.

'When I did my knee, for instance, everyone thought, oh, that's him done now, he's finished. When we got promotion in my first season back people said I couldn't play in a higher league. They said the same thing, all the way up the divisions. Even now, I understand the position I'm in. The club captain taking over and then getting offered the job full-time wouldn't happen at any other Premier League club. People expected me to fail, I'm very clear on that, but for me it's a source of motivation.'

Opportunity presented itself in messy circumstances on February 4, 2014, another fateful Tuesday. Michael Laudrup claimed he was sacked by email, after being assured his job was safe. He threatened legal action, but eventually reached a financial settlement, on May 23 of that year. Suddenly, Monk's horizons stretched far beyond planning an internet venture with his brother and preparing to coach at academy level.

He gave the two most important speeches of his life. The first, infinitely the most intimate, was to his wife, Lexy, who was eight and a half months pregnant with twin sons; it was part apology, part job application. The second address was to staff and players, after Jenkins had informed them of Laudrup's abrupt departure.

'I didn't have to, but after the chairman had spoken, I talked about what had happened around the club. I just spoke from the heart, about how I would do things. I knew what I wanted to put in place, a way of working, of dealing with each other, which was different to what had gone before. That wasn't a slight on anyone; different managers choose different ways with their group, don't they?

'I realised the importance of what was coming up, with the Cardiff game that weekend. The rivalry is unbelievable and I have experienced it. They had already beaten us once that season. Nobody had ever done the double, so I spoke about what the club stands for. I wanted them to know how we'd got to where we were, and why we'd achieved what we'd achieved.

'Our biggest strength had always been the group being

so tight and together, but I felt we were a bit too divided. That's not to say they were bad lads or anything like that, but when you play for a team you should understand what that team is built upon. I talked about what wearing that shirt really means to people brought up from babies to support Swansea. I wanted the players to think, he's not mucking around here.'

He played unashamedly on emotion, giving players and staff a DVD which detailed the club's rise from the brink of relegation to the Conference through the eyes of their supporters. Victory gave him a springboard; he was determined to prove old school values, drilled into him as an apprentice at Torquay, where he cleaned boots and swept the dressing rooms, could coexist with new age training techniques.

Each player has an individualised programme, set in pre-season but subject to revision. Monthly planners identify major team meetings, at which the game plan is introduced and discussed. Meetings before each training session identify the aims and responsibilities of the day. They are illustrated by in-game video packages, to give them a competitive relevance.

'I know it sounds a cliché, but the first thing I say to the players before we start training is "hard work". When they come through the gate I ask them to give everything they've got, every single day. I want them to think about what they are doing, not just get a sweat on for a couple of hours and go home. I realise they're not all going to be thinking about football for twenty-four hours a day – they're not managers – but I'm looking for them to challenge themselves.

'They have to understand why they train, and what they are doing, so that when they're out there, on their own, they realise you have given them the tools to solve a problem. I was always an organiser as a player, responding to things which were happening around me. I was the communicator, getting players in the right position, relaying what the manager wanted and what I was seeing.

'If you can get better players than I was to do that, or at least recognise what they should be doing, you've more chance of being successful than not. I talk about game management with them a lot. Everyone wants us to play great attacking football, but when that doesn't work, what do you do? What should we all be doing? I've made sure that every single one of them has a responsibility that is clear, with and without the ball.

'There can be no grey area. It's about repetition, repetition, repetition. For instance, it's taken them four months to fully understand our defensive system, without the ball. They still make mistakes but the key is they understand them. They know, "Shit, that was down to me." Or, "He shouldn't have been there." I allow them to use their imagination, play off the cuff, but ask any one of them what the others should be doing in a particular situation and they'll know. It's that clear for them.

'I spoke to them about Bayern Munich, when they played Barcelona in that Champions League final. They were the best team I'd ever seen. They rotated positions so intelligently it was second nature. I remember Thomas Müller ended up at centre half for five minutes. He knew exactly what he was doing, where he should be. A player ends up in all sorts of positions in a game. It might only be for a second or two, but he needs to know what he's doing.'

Monk leaned forward and pushed his laptop across the desk to show me a software package which gives players access to match footage, individualised tuition and position-specific drills. He spoke eagerly of his ultimate fulfilment, seeing a player react positively and intuitively, despite the pace and physicality of his working environment.

'The most satisfying bit about management is seeing someone doing something you've trained them for, almost without thinking. You have a share in their success. If you get it right often enough, which we've done this season, it allows you to compete. It is a delicate process, because mistakes happen, and players hate accountability, especially in front of each other. They find that very hard to deal with.

'So, rather than emphasise the individual, we work with units within the team, smaller groups. It then becomes a collective process. When we show them mistakes, they can question each other. We can then go out to train, where we will show them how to correct the error. They all have their sessions, group, unit or individual, on their iPads.

'Take, as an example, all the defensive work we've done this season. They look beyond the obvious. Say we concede, ostensibly because someone didn't stop the cross. Now they know enough about how they work to look back three or four passages. Then they'll see someone else fucked up.

'At this point they're really engaged: "We did this here . . . we didn't defend this right . . . here's what we could and should have done". It's about setting a standard, and then giving them ownership of it. They have to feel part of the process, appreciate that supposedly little things are important. It's like when we go training: they all have to come out of the changing room together. If we are going to implement the plan properly, I can't have them walking out in ones and twos.

'You have to make the game plan so simple and really clear. This is how we do it. Unless we have to really chase it, or we have to consolidate, we believe in it, and we stick to it. We give them individual profiles of direct opponents, information on how they operate as a group, in and out of possession. They obviously find it beneficial, because I see them take five minutes to recap in the changing room before a game. They read the team sheets to confirm who they're up against, and take a last look at individual clips.

'The word I always use when I walk into a changing room, especially at half-time, is balance. When I'm angry my players know it, but you don't have to go absolutely mental. If I spend five or six of my ten minutes just bollocking someone, I haven't really helped him, or the group. If I've just gone nuts, I haven't given him the information to make him better.

'Put yourself in his position. Number one, you probably don't know what you've done wrong. Number two, you probably don't know how to correct it. Number three, you go out there, pissed off, thinking I'm a twat. You'll probably end up trying harder, but still making the same mistakes.

'It's far better for me, as manager, to concentrate on the next half. I give them three points defensively, three points offensively, as a group, so they have clear information. What's done is done at that point. I can show them what was wrong next day in the post-match reflections. That's when accountability kicks in, because there's no hiding place.

'I always question myself. Did I give enough information? Did I deliver the right sort of information? I've seen too many yes men in this game over the years, who will just agree with everything the boss says. I want our coaching group to question me. That doesn't involve an argument. It is more, "Did we get what we wanted? Could we have done that better? Should have done this?" That's the only way to improve.'

His most important professional relationship, with assistant Pep Clotet, is also the most intriguing. The Spaniard, promoted from a consultancy role within the academy when Monk was confirmed as manager in May 2014, is a year older, but has held his Pro Licence since the age of 26. He is the product of a complementary culture, having excelled as a developmental coach at Màlaga, where he worked under Manuel Pellegrini. He was Roland Nilsson's assistant when Malmö won the Swedish League in 2010, and had a spell as head coach of Norwegian club Viking Stavanger.

His influences are eclectic. He is a disciple of Marcelo Bielsa, the idiosyncratic Argentine coach whose obsessive credo has inspired modern coaches as diverse as Diego Simeone and Mauricio Pochettino. He studied in Holland and Germany, but found his greatest tutors closer to home, in his native Barcelona.

Johan Cruyff, the visionary whose version of total football was dependent on the speed of ball and brain, was a formative figure in his football education. He attended 160 training sessions when Louis Van Gaal was Barcelona's head coach, in order to analyse the way he balanced his team, so it could utilise a free man when in possession.

Clotet's impact during matches is fascinating and,

in my experience, unique. He dissects games into five-minute segments, analysing patterns of play to identify latent threats or potential opportunities, and is in constant, yet discreet contact with Monk, whose instinct is to take the temperature of the game from the edge of his technical area.

The collegiate approach extends to a core leadership group of seven players, who are given free rein to comment on preparation and execution. Monk is seeking to add one more individual to the discussions each month, so that an inclusive culture develops within the dressing room, almost by osmosis.

'I don't want them to come to me with a wish list. I want them to influence those around them, by taking the initiative. That way it is not just one voice, my voice, all the time. The senior players have the most power, but I'm trying to get a couple of the younger, more responsible lads in there as well, so they can influence players of their own age.

'Nobody's told me to fuck off yet, which will come, but if it is said in the right way, or with the right intentions, then I can live with that. If it is said in a disrespectful way, not just to me but to any of my staff or even to other players, that is a different matter.

'I've been around football long enough to deal with most things, you know. People talk to me about how I'm going to attract players to the club, or deal with the transfer window, but it's not rocket science. I've got a clear plan. I analyse a player, put him forward to the chairman. If we agree he is the right player for us I'll leave it to him to do the financial side of it.

'I don't have to deal with agents. That's not my job. I'm about players, players, players. If they see me speaking passionately, truthfully about a vision of the club and how I go about things, they have a choice to make. Do they trust me, or not? Of course there is pressure, but nobody is going to put more pressure on me than me.

'I think it helps that people in Swansea understand the human side of the job. I've lived among the supporters for eleven years. They've seen me in Tesco's, at the newsagent's, out with Lexy and the kids. She is incredible. That's why I do this job, to provide for them and try to secure their future, you know? I want them to have a good life. You get nowhere without the support of your family.

'My dad is a legend. He's been through the shit, standing in the rain on muddy pitches, when my brother and I were kids. Now he can enjoy it. Someone smuggled him and Mum into the press conference at Chelsea. I had no idea they were there. I was sat, talking, and suddenly saw the smiles on their faces. We'd lost but I thought, this is special. Now I'm a father I can understand the pride they have.'

In professional terms, he was anxious to continue his education. Clotet was seeking to arrange an audience with Bielsa, who once responded to an observation by the Swansea assistant by dismissing him with the curt instruction to come back to him when he had analysed 10,000 matches. The following passage from a press conference at Marseilles in March 2015, which dwells on the ultimate reality of management, gives Monk an idea of the masterclass which awaits:

> "What I try to do in times of adversity is to reinforce my convictions, and not to act foolishly, denying realities which have to be changed. I am fully aware of the fact that in bad times everyone abandons you, the media, the fans and the players. That's a part of our human condition.
>
> We approach something that smells nice – success always improves the smell of the person doing the work – and we move away from something that smells bad. Defeat makes you stink. This is not an act of victimisation, or an accusation. It is a description of something I have been living with for 30 years, and that happens in every human activity. No one accompanies you to help you win, and everyone accompanies you when you've won. It is the law of life."

Monk sought to augment such advice by studying other high-performance programmes in the off season. Kris O'Leary, Swansea's Under 21 coach, was using his contacts to secure a study visit to the All Blacks' training camp. I helped out in a small way, linking him with British Cycling's elite performance programme.

Yet he had also to look after himself. His fitness levels had dropped, inevitably, since he lacked the time to train at the level he had sustained for two decades. He sought a balance by attempting to isolate an hour in his day, to run, swim, cycle or complete a circuit in the gym, but it was not easy.

He was far from the finished article. The base metals with which he worked were pride, honesty and application. The bloodlines which linked him most closely to Rodgers and Jackett were strong without strangling his initiative. He suited Swansea's culture of measured self-reliance and, in time, will develop his own model. When I asked him how he saw himself at 50, his reticence was significant.

'I don't talk about things like that. I don't like predictions. I don't worry about the outcome, I worry about the process. I could say to you, "I want us to get to Europe. I want us to do this, and that." But I've heard so many managers say that, and I've thought to myself as they were saying it, he's a dickhead, a politician. I don't want to be seen as that.

'This is the best place for me, at this level, to develop my management. It's unique. I know a lot of people think I'm lucky, and I am, but the flip side is that I put my neck on the block. If I'm going to be found out, this is where it will happen. It is unforgiving, but I knew that when I took the job.

'There is a lot of envy in football. That generally comes from those who just want to talk a good game, but don't have the balls to go for it. You know the type: "Oh, I could do that . . . I should be there . . . Why has he got that job?" The flip side is that I've had so much support as well. From people wishing me well on the street, to other coaches, other football people.

'When that Cardiff game was coming up, I didn't think, oh, I'm going to be a manager, but when we were getting towards the end of that season I started thinking. We were safe, picking up good results. I knew I couldn't go back into the changing room as a player. Imagine me going to another club; that wouldn't happen because, as someone who has managed in the Premier League, I'd probably be seen as a threat to their manager.

'I thought, well, you've made your bed. I spoke to the chairman at the end of the season, and he said, "Look, we've not even chatted to anyone else. If you want it you can have it." Obviously we went through it all, what we'd do, how I'd approach the job, but from that point I thought, this is my path now . . .'

As others had discovered before him, that path tends to be long, and circuitous.

12

Walking the Job

Micky Adams slept solidly for a week, and spent the following fortnight helping to gather in the harvest at his brother-in-law's vineyard in the Dordogne. The sun shone benevolently on the surrounding meadowland, which curled around fortified hilltop villages like a cat sleeping on a silk pillow. In the evenings, Bergerac reds washed down locally reared duck and foie gras.

So why did Adams leave the rural idyll with such indecent haste? Why is he sitting in a featureless room off a narrow corridor looking out on to the car park at Prenton Park? Why does lunch consist of a doorstop-sized cheese and onion sandwich which has spent the morning sweating in clingfilm? If you feel the need to ask such questions, you won't understand the answers.

It is why John Still needs three attempts to finish his omelette in a rain-lashed Portakabin in the garden suburbs of Luton, where a black plastic dustbin asking for donations 'for Africa' contains a solitary football boot. He has a video interview to record, a scouting schedule to confirm and a Premier League observer to tolerate.

Each manager is in his element. Still, a legendary enthusiast who discovered Dwight Gayle, a £6 million striker, playing in front of six spectators for Stansted, is seeking to elevate Luton Town from the Conference to League One in two seasons. Adams, who found England defender Wayne Bridge as a schoolboy, playing for Olivers Battery FC in a park in Winchester, is on a mercy mission to save Tranmere Rovers from the indignity of losing their Football League status.

A laminated poster in his office, a relic of a previous regime, was touching in its innocence and damning in its implication. Under a column headed 'Allies of Glory, Themes of Ambition' it listed the following leadership traits: Energising, Empowering, Inspiring, Encouraging, Challenging, Supportive, Proactive, Availability. The adjoining column, which listed 'things we turn into and do when we are losing' was rather more relevant to Merseyside's impoverished third club. The charge sheet read: Complacent, Toxic, Apathetic, Negative, Disturbed, Drained, Dramatic, Passive.

Adams became Tranmere's fourth manager in eight months on October 18, when they were bottom of the Football League. New owner Mark Palios, the former

Tranmere defender whose tenure as chief executive of the Football Association ended due to the fallout from the controversy involving Sven-Göran Eriksson and an FA secretary, Faria Alam, needed experienced support.

Palios hoped to reinvigorate the club as a community hub, dealing in education and skill development, and the provision of social housing. He planned to create a new training base through the sale of existing land, close to the ground. Yet the stigma of relegation would be hard to bear. Adams, out of work for precisely a month after resigning from Port Vale, was deemed a safe pair of hands.

'Apart from a brief spell at Sheffield United I'd been at Port Vale for five and a half years. We lost six on the spin, but I wasn't under any pressure. I was a bit tired. The game gets you mentally more than anything. I was bored with them and they were bored with me. Everyone had heard what I had to say, so I decided to leave.

'Friends in the game said, "Are you mad?" But I cleared my mind at the vineyard, and realised I'd become a bit lazy and complacent. After three weeks I was invigorated. I began to wonder where the jobs would appear. I knew my way back in would be through League Two, so I started looking at the table again. You realise quite quickly who you are and where you should be, and that's on the training ground with your players.'

Tranmere moved out of the relegation zone on December 28 with a rare 2–1 home win over Northampton, but confidence remained fragile. Failure had become a state of mind, and Adams was obliged to deal with players whose reticence was an unconscious act of self-protection. He had to combine the roles of teacher, social worker and cheerleader.

'It is a very quiet dressing room. They're looking for help, like the puppy dog who makes pleading eyes at you. Everything is safety first. They don't know they are doing it, but their actions are governed by a desperate need not to make a mistake. Mark has belief in me. I could have sat at home and ignored his call, but I am not afraid of the challenge.

'The manager sets the tone of the place. They want guidance, and they're relying on my knowledge of the division. I've been successful three times in getting teams up, so they instantly know I know what I'm talking about. I've been here before. I was ninety-first with Fulham, with no money, yet I got them promoted. I'm the same man, with the same standards, the same work ethic. It was old school management; I was fitness coach, psychologist, analyst, the lot.

'That's where I got my first taste of the nasty side of the job. Ian Branfoot taught me the ropes when he was Fulham manager, and I've never forgotten the fanzine headline he had to read before one match: "I hope you die soon". That was the sort of pressure he was under, wicked.

'You learn from your managers as a player, good and

bad. It was all very well for Billy Bremner to tell us, "We are Leeds, go out there and play," but we didn't have Giles, Lorimer, Charlton and Clarke. We needed a little bit more to go on than that. There was no grey area with Howard Wilkinson, and Dave Bassett is still a big mentor. If I have any doubts, I always run them past him.

'Chris Nicholl was my manager at Southampton. He used to go round us individually in the dressing room after a game: "Shit, shit, not bad, shit, wanker . . ." If you got a "shit" you were quite happy, a "wanker" meant you were struggling. You learn that football is not personal. It's opinion, a fashion business.

'Who is deemed sexy? Who do the fans want? A lot of chairmen spend all their time on forums and message boards. It's bollocks. They drive themselves mad. When they sack their manager they get CVs from people who are willing to work for nothing. I don't like to see anyone struggling, but I don't think that is a viable basis on which to run a football club.

'Managers call each other mates, but we are not really. I wouldn't really trust a manager or a scout. They all want to know your business. They see the greenbacks coming. It's all, "Hello, mate, seen much? Been anywhere? Anything worth a look?" We all understand each other's problems, but we are not that close.'

Adams sought to harness the few natural advantages he had at his disposal. He was watching six matches a week, and calling in favours. Palios supported his move to forge a strategic link with Everton and Liverpool, but the development process involving young players didn't sit easily. Like many managers of similar vintage, Adams viewed modern football as a Potemkin village, an elaborate façade which disguised a poverty of ambition and ideas.

'There's a lot of shotgun recruitment in the loan market. Youngsters play false football in that under twenty-one league. It drives you mad. The centre halves split, the ball is moved precisely, and everyone thinks it is wonderful. You can afford that sort of philosophy if the game isn't going to be results-driven.

'They spend fortunes on beautiful sand-based pitches but, at this level, the last thing you spend money on is the pitch. Mark played the game. He understands the game. I'm working to help him. If I look locally, there are fewer cost implications. If players live further afield than Merseyside or Manchester we'd have to put them up. I'm not having their warm-down being a ninety-minute drive home.

'First-time managers don't get out there and watch games. They take advice from their chief scout and agents. They watch DVDs. It is your responsibility to ensure what little money you have doesn't go to waste. No manager is right all the time, but you have to do your homework. I don't see the new breed doing that, and that is why they let themselves down.

'You have young managers employing young coaches, instead of embracing experience. The fear factor is massive. If you have any self-doubt you are going to be eaten alive. I see managers setting up teams not to lose. I see players expecting a lifestyle they will never earn. We're well into the season and there are still loads of unattached players.

'There are a lot of pros out there, thinking they will ease down the divisions. They go out for a run in the park and kid themselves they are keeping fit. They are no good for someone like me. Even if they have something about them, I will have to wait at least six weeks for them to be ready to play. I haven't got that time.'

He understood the ramifications of failure. This was his tenth club, though he made a point of stressing the moral strength of his decision to leave his second, Swansea City, in 1997, after 13 days in charge. 'I was taken there on false pretences,' he said, suitably indignant. 'They broke a promise that money would be invested in the team. I either stood there and swallowed it, or took a gamble I'd be OK if I walked.'

Two of those clubs, Leicester City and Port Vale, entered administration while he was in charge. The human dimension pricked the conscience, and burst the bubble in which he and his players existed. Once again, his role was to provide emotional succour at a time of need.

'When you are in administration you realise you are

the figurehead of the club. You become a sounding board, putting football to one side and spending most of your time building a rapport with staff in other departments. You're seeing people losing their jobs and you're asking them whether they've got enough to put food on the table.

'It is difficult to take when they are letting kids go to save fifty pounds a week. The expectations of fans don't change in those circumstances, but experiences like that do change you, as a person. People here have put their trust in me, and I don't intend to let them down.'

Still was also in the dreams business, despite financial restrictions. A whiteboard behind his desk detailed scouting targets, in black marker pen. It represented a gentle journey through the backwaters of non-league football, from Boston to Matlock, Heanor to Didcot, Skelmersdale to Ilkeston. More prosaic realities were summed up by an adjacent sign: 'Remember, the toes you step on today could be connected to the legs that support the arse you need to kiss tomorrow.'

Only Sir Alex Ferguson has managed in more matches; Still's 39th season in the dugout would bring him close to 1,700 games in charge of a succession of humble clubs and unheralded players. Look closely, beyond the soft, expressive face of an indulgent grandfather, and you are met by the bright eyes of the six-year-old boy who perched on his father's shoulders during a West Ham reserve match.

He cannot remember the opposition in the first game of professional football he witnessed in 1956, but can feel the fleeting dread of dropping his bag of peanuts in sheer excitement. Other freeze-frame images, such as his one and only Football League appearance as a 17-year-old defender, playing for Leyton Orient at home to Torquay United, are darker in nature, but no less vivid.

'I know it sounds strange, but I can still see it. There's this centre forward called Friar. He tries to knock a ball past me, but I'm well in control of the situation. I see him coming. I get my foot to the ball, comfortably, but he sort of stretches. As I knock the ball my heel comes off the floor and he comes right the way through. It's not a foul, but he catches the bottom of my ankle and I twist my knee.

'I played on, had treatment, but I struggled desperately. There was only one sub, and it wasn't until the end of the game I realised I'd done my cruciate. That was usually that in those days, but Theo Foley took me to Charlton. It was the everyday training that killed me, so I went and played part-time.

'My dad used to work at the power station in Canning Town. I can still hear him saying, "Well, what are you going to do? Are you going to sulk or are you going to try and play somewhere else, and get a job?" That's pretty much what I did. I was fortunate I did well, because I was still a good player. I got a job where my mum worked, making metal tubing.

'I wasn't academically good but I was streetwise bright. I knew someone who knew someone so I got a better job as a salesman at a textile rental company. We sold overalls, tunics for British Rail and British Airways, protective clothing, all of that sort of stuff. I became sales manager for the south of England, so all was good.

'I had to pack playing in, because I needed another operation, and stumbled into management. I was at Leytonstone, and the manager's wife was taken ill. The chairman asked me to look after the team for the rest of the season, and I enjoyed it. I had no ambition, and I was looking after my mates.

'The funny thing was I had no compunction in changing the team. I had one mate, Paul Massey, who'd met this Swedish girl on holiday. He eventually married her. One day, he tells me she is coming to England for a week, to watch him play. I thought, this is awkward. He's not playing well and he ain't in my team.

'I spoke to my wife about it, and she told me I had to play him. I said that if he was my mate, he'd understand how difficult it was for me not to play him. When I told him he thought I was joking, but once I said, "Mass, do you think I'm finding this easy?" he understood. He didn't play, was still my mate, and from that day on dropping people never bothered me.'

Emotional blackmail is part of a manager's stock in trade. Still has the instincts of a market trader; he is renowned for asking players to arrive early for appointments, so he can work on them without the presence of an agent to drive a better deal. He's excused such strokes because of the warmth of his personality. The spirit of Tom Miley lives on.

'Your upbringing sends you on a path, in a certain direction. I learned a lot obviously from my dad, but I also learned a lot from Tom. He was my boss and he was football mad, God rest his soul. He used to say to me, "John, find ways of getting the people who work for you onside." He used to call it "walking the job".

'He would walk around the factory, finding out what was happening through talking to people. He knew when it was someone's birthday, when their missus was having a baby, when their daughter was getting married. He'd make them feel special, sending them a card or flowers, with his regards. Little things like that meant a lot.

'I'm running this depot, and he comes to me and says, "I want the drivers to wash their vehicles every day." Now I know they ain't going to like this. They want to do their deliveries and get home as soon as possible. Tom thinks about it, and asks me to get them together at the best time for them, which was about half six in the morning, before they went out on their rounds.

'The day comes, and he tells them they are the best distribution team in the country. He wants them to make the most of their holidays. He'd arrange a rota so that three or four of them could have a day off over Christmas, when they were all supposed to be in. He told them to speak to me if their kids or grandchildren had a school play they wanted to attend. He'd be OK to cover that.

'They all said, "Thanks, Tom. That's lovely." Then he hits them: "Oh, by the way, there's just one thing I'd like from you in return. When you come back, put the vehicle through the car wash. It'll only take half an hour, and we'll all be looking smart." They couldn't say no, could they? Tom found a way of getting things done his way. That's how I deal with players.'

His staff, who shared a long narrow office, were trying to give the impression they were not listening, but couldn't supress sly smiles. They sat along one wall like overfed chicks; only goalkeeping coach Kevin Dearden, a recent refugee from the chaos at Leyton Orient, had not worked with him on a long-term basis.

Assistant manager Terry Harris, quietly going through scouting reports at the far end of the room, was the manager's soulmate, having been with Still since 1999. First team coach Hakan Hayrettin, burly and friendly, was a familiar figure in non-league circles, and fitness coach Dave Richardson was another disciple from Dagenham & Redbridge.

Still left them alone for a moment, to challenge the Premier League's assessor by asking him to explain how the micro-managed academy system would produce players 'with the bollocks to have a career'. He returned, in true Miley fashion, with a plate of home-made chocolate cakes. He liked them so much he used them in the analogy with which he picked up the conversation.

'I like to do things a little differently. You can buy a cake from Tesco's or you can make a cake. I like making them. I've got to buy ingredients, and it takes a little time, but once it's made, it tastes so much better than the other one. It's the same with football teams. Touch wood, I've always been able to make a tastier cake.

'There are players out there, if only you look. You can tell who wants it more by the way they react to disappointment, or mistakes like misplaced passes. They don't moan, but there's a drive and an energy about them. You also can't ignore natural ability, whatever we say, particularly at the lower levels.

'I saw Marlon King by chance, playing for Dulwich Hamlet reserves. I was driving past the ground and noticed the floodlights were on. It was about eight o'clock. I knew the chairman, and thought I'd pop in and have a cup of tea. I saw this black lad, learned he was in the youth team, and took him to Barnet. It was pure fluke, really. Not the nicest boy, but a good career. He was a proper centre forward; he chased after it, you know?

'There's always something to see. Gary Breen was playing centre midfield in Gillingham's reserves when I took him to Peterborough. You didn't look at him and go "cor" but he had a way about him. He could play, but was obviously a centre half. We got him for twenty grand at a tribunal and he was fantastic. He got sixty-odd caps and played at a World Cup.

'When people ask me to name my best ever signing, I say Anwar Uddin. He was a young player at West Ham. I took him to Bristol Rovers, who let him go when he had a bad injury, and then took him to Dagenham. He epitomised what a winner is all about. He wasn't the best player, but he was the biggest influence. He dragged people with him, kicking and screaming. He told them what was expected and got us up from the Conference.

'Players are missed because people are lazy, God bless them. They are influenced too easily. Say I'm talking to you at a game. You go, "He's not bad, that so-and-so. Always injured, though. He's got two birds, he's married to one, and has another on the side." When I go away, I've got your opinion, not mine.

'That's why I never listen to other people. I go anywhere in the ground I can be on my own. If I see or hear anything I do my homework. I've got my networks. Watching players on DVDs? What's that all about? Get out there, look, and if you like what you see, never be afraid to take him. Of course it is a gamble. Even Sir Alex gets it wrong, and buys a Verón, a Bebé or a Djemba-Djemba. If you think he's the right signing, then it's the right signing. If it doesn't work, unlucky.'

Still is football's Professor Emeritus. His PhD course

might appear anachronistic in an age of starburst statistics and GPS data, but it dispenses timeless wisdom. His tutors, like former West Ham manager John Lyall, were simplicity personified, and did not mind the backhanded compliment of having their best ideas stolen.

'I grew up a West Ham supporter, and lived near the training ground. I was friends with Big Frank Lampard, Roger Cross, Patsy Holland and Tony Carr. I got to know Ronnie Boyce when he was John's assistant manager, and always used to pop in to watch my mates train, or have a chat. One day I'm sitting in the office and a kid comes in. John opens his desk drawer and throws him a tennis ball. "See that cross on the wall at the end of the office, son?" he asks. "Try and hit it." So he has a couple of goes, misses, and is told to come back later and try again. These lads come in day after day, and start hitting the target. "What does that teach you?" he'd ask them. "The more you practise the better you get."

'John used to say to me, "There's two ways of improving. You come in every day, earlier than everyone else, and practise. And when everyone else has gone, you practise some more. Or you sit in this chair, and this fella comes round with a magic wand, and he touches you. You're suddenly better. The only problem is I've never fucking seen that fella. The only way we're going to get better is to work."

'I have to admit, I've used that line all my life. What

you can never foresee is people's comfort zones. For some it is when they have finished playing. They've earned all their money, done their bit, and can look after everyone. But some get to twenty-three, twenty-four, and get a shock. They are pushed out of their comfort zone.

'They've been earning six, seven, eight grand a week for a couple of years. They've got a flash car, big house, and now they can't afford them. We've had players from Premier League clubs in here, and they can't pay for any of it, because they have not worked hard enough to maintain what they had.

'It's tough, but do you know what? I've learned a lesson over the years that sometimes it's better to tell someone the truth and make them cry than tell them a lie and make them laugh. If it is their fault, that they haven't trained hard enough and their attitude hasn't been great, then I don't give a fuck. That is their responsibility, not mine.

'I will do everything I can to help those who deserve the help. I can't afford to think of the consequences of my decisions, and I can't make those decisions based on my knowledge of their circumstances. If a player has done everything he can I'll still let him go, but I will ring around, and say if you are looking for this type, he is ideal.

'It's the same with young coaches and managers. They all come here, asking how I find my players, how I work in training. I make a point of asking people I know who are out of work to come over. I tell them there is no magic formula. Your way is your way, and if you do it my way it might not be right for you.'

Before Still arrived in February 2013, after nearly 11 years at Dagenham & Redbridge, Kenilworth Road was a place of ghosts, gripes and regrets. Luton Town have been trying to move since 1955; the ground remains an eyesore, a warren of narrow corridors and caravan park corporate boxes, but its heartbeat is strong.

Linger after matches, and you will see the manager draw his team into a huddle on the edge of the penalty area closest to the walkway which leads to the tiny, claustrophobic dressing rooms. On closer inspection the huddle contains staff and supporters. In football, this is democracy gone mad. But there is beauty in daring to be different.

'I do the huddle after the game, win, lose or draw, because if you walk straight into the dressing room you sometimes talk bollocks. Now I just give a brief outline of what I think. It may have been that we were not mentally ready. We might have been nowhere near our game. I might not be happy, but I don't shout and holler. I just tell the players we will talk on Monday, and say thank you to the supporters.

'Everyone is important. If the groundsman ain't done his job, we ain't going to perform at our best. We need him to do his best for us. If the ladies who do the food don't give us it on time, or if it is wrong, we don't eat properly, and we're not prepared. They are part of our team. Supporters pay their money every week. They're part of our team.

'People write in, asking to come in the huddle. Why not? This is their football club. Their children, and their children's children, will be here long after I've got the sack or packed up. I'm not saying they have a right to a say, but they have a right to be recognised. I have a saying – the stronger the team, the stronger the team.

'Our team is people on the pitch, people behind the scenes, people on the terraces. It includes people who can't get to the game but listen to the radio. It includes people who do what are wrongly called menial jobs around the club. How strong is that? The opposition run out with eleven, we've got fourteen thousand.'

Still would become a senior citizen on April 24, 2015, the day before Luton's penultimate match of the regular season, at Southend United. Leaning back on his chair, gesticulating extravagantly, he looked 15 going on 65. The cares of a second successive season pushing for promotion melted away. He passed the cakes around, and laughed uproariously when Hayrettin, who claimed to be on a diet, took two slices.

'Football keeps me young, one hundred per cent. Working with younger people, listening to them talk, of course it does. On top of that I'm working with clowns. Have you seen who I work with? I've got to be on the ball. Seriously, all I can do is give people responsibility they can handle. It is the recipe for success.'

Tom Miley couldn't have put it better. Most managers walk the walk, after talking the talk. Very few walk the job with such aplomb. Enjoy it while it lasts.

13

The Fallacy of Failure

December 29 was nominally a day off after a torrid, joyless Christmas. Alan Irvine sat alone in his rented flat, 102 miles from the family home in Southport, watching videos of West Ham's last three matches. He had crafted his coaching session for the following morning's training, and was applying the final touches to his game plan for the visit to Upton Park on New Year's Day.

At 11 p.m. he took a call on his mobile. The body clocks of the idiotic chorus line who had taunted him at Stoke the previous day with the chant of 'You're getting sacked in the morning' were inaccurate. Irvine was informed he had been relieved of his duties as West Bromwich Albion manager, and that he would be on gardening leave until the expiry of his one-year rolling contract.

The news was released the next morning. The club's

official Twitter feed recorded 'a sombre day for staff at The Hawthorns, because we have said farewell to a man of great class and dignity'. Terry Burton, Albion's technical director, spoke of the 'dedication and diligence' of 'one of the foremost coaches in the UK'. Such was his tone he could almost have adapted Harold Macmillan's immortal response to the definitive difficulties of politics ('events, dear boy, events'). The subtext of Burton's reflection on 'unpleasant decisions' dictated by the 'imperative' of securing a sixth season in the Premier League was simple: results, dear boy, results.

Albion had won only four of Irvine's 19 League games in charge. They were one point and two places above the relegation zone. They were about to enter a theoretically more favourable run of fixtures but context, in the modern world, veers dangerously close to an excuse. Move along, people, nothing to see here.

Irvine's appointment had not been popular, but how many of the 83 per cent who condemned him in a poll of 7,000 readers of the *Express & Star*, Albion's local newspaper, really knew him beyond vague generalities and a thumbnail sketch of his CV? The process of airbrushing a manager out of history is almost designed to promote such ignorance.

Albion have a reputation as an honourable club. Unlike some, they fulfil their contractual obligations to discarded staff. Yet the mechanics of change are dehumanising; Irvine did not have an opportunity to say farewell to his players, and retrieved his belongings from the training ground the following evening, when the media pack had dispersed.

His is a familiar story of recurrent rejection and renewal, which underlines the breadth of his experience and the depth of his character. Barely 5ft tall at 15, he was deemed too small as a schoolboy winger. This led to unsuccessful trials at Leeds United, Manchester City, Rangers and Dundee United. He was even released, with goalkeeper Jim Leighton, from his boys' club team, Glasgow United.

He began training with Queen's Park, Glasgow's amateur club, while working as an insurance broker and studying for accountancy qualifications. He needed respite, the opportunity to grow intellectually and physically, since he would not mature and reach his current height, 5ft 10in, until after his 21st birthday.

'The great thing Queen's Park gave me was time. I had my setbacks because I was a baby, really. I'd been very quick and a good player when everybody had been much the same size, but the others suddenly shot away from me. My legs were still moving just as quickly but unfortunately their strides were covering a lot more ground than mine.

'My experience meant that, in later years as a coach, I never made a decision on a player at youth level because of size. I tell small boys and their parents to see it as an opportunity to develop technical skills, tactical understanding and game awareness. Become better at those things, when you cannot compete physically, and they will sustain you when your body catches up.

'I had good technique with both feet. I was aware of where I was on the pitch, because I had to be. The fact is I couldn't get into a battle with people. I played for the third team at Queen's Park. At that point, I was starting to stretch. I'd caught up physically, I was strong enough to cope, and I could run away from people. I also had these other attributes I'd been quietly developing.

'I missed out the reserves, made the first team, but still had to have a job. So I learned another important lesson, what it can be like in the real world. I worked from nine until five, jumped on the bus and went training, came home and studied for my qualifications, went to bed and did it all again the next day.

'The coach who took me under his wing at the time, Eddie Hunter, taught me the value of working hard. He was brutal with me. Honestly. A lot of Scottish coaching at the time was aggressive, screaming at players, pointing fingers, all that sort of stuff. But I knew Eddie liked me. That was the key for me.

'Funnily enough, many years later, I read that Damien Duff said I was the scariest coach he'd worked with. Whenever I see him he gives me a big hug, so that tells you something about a player's mentality. If they know you like them, you can do anything with them. You can be a real influence because when you need to be tough they'll have it, and when you take a softer approach they won't take advantage.'

Irvine's last game for Queen's Park was against Cowdenbeath at Central Park, on a pitch ringed by a stock car racing track. His first game for Everton, two months later in 1981, was against Inter Milan in Japan. His world had changed in more senses than one. He responded to the informality of Howard Kendall's management, without losing his sense of wonder.

'I could never get my head around anybody thinking, this is hard work. I've always appreciated the life football has given me. It was just incredible to get paid for what I had been doing for nothing in an amateur club. That feeling has never left me. People talk about the number of hours I do as a manager, as if it is some sort of hardship. What do I do when I go home? I watch football.'

Irvine began coaching when he moved to Crystal Palace at the age of 26. As a keen chess player, he related to tactical puzzles almost as an academic exercise. He loved the notion of being a student once again, even if his principal tutor, when he returned to Scotland to play for Dundee United, was a tortured soul with a tyrant's temper.

Jim McLean had his demons, but he was a figure of

some substance in Scottish management. He was ahead of his time as a coach, in terms of attention to detail and sophistication of planning. His training sessions flowed seamlessly, and his pupils were enraptured by the secrets they revealed. The only shame was they had to play matches, and confront the ogre.

'Jim was a massive influence, good and bad. I saw things and thought, I'm definitely going to do that. I saw other things and thought, I'm definitely not going to do that. He was a very, very good coach, but a terrible man manager, very aggressive. He just exploded. He couldn't control that, so it was a real problem for him. He did it so often.

'Everyone got it, and he got worse as he went round the team. You were sat there in the dressing room, hoping you were number two or three. If you were number twelve you were going to get the works. I remember watching his temper build for the first time, thinking, this is terrible. You could almost feel his anger as a physical force. He was so close to you.

'Ultimately it became ineffective. He'd be doing the same thing, weeks down the line. He'd still be close to you, being that aggressive, but you're now starting to separate yourself from the moment, not listening but looking at the sweat on his forehead or his pulse. You're just thinking, hurry up. Get this over with and move on to the next person.

'But Jim also created a real coaching culture. His

players were encouraged to think like coaches. A lot of us were a similar age; out of my group, Paul Sturrock, Paul Hegarty, Maurice Malpas, Billy Kirkwood, Dave Bowman, Billy Thompson and Billy McKinlay all went on to coach and manage. We used to go out for meals, and talk as coaches did.

'We saw how Jim controlled every detail that could be controlled in his training sessions. Everything was set up perfectly. The cones were completely straight, the goals weren't going off at a funny angle, there wasn't a big half and a small half. That taught me that clubs can create coaches, by making thinking players. As a manager, you have a chance to mould a person.'

The tradition endures. Sir Alex Ferguson's tough love nurtured thinking players at Aberdeen and Manchester United. Irvine worked for five and a half years with David Moyes at Everton, developing a similar group, including David Weir, Duncan Ferguson, Lee Carsley and Alan Stubbs, who were starting to make their mark in coaching and management.

Kenny Dalglish was not one for fusillades and florid speeches. There were few airs and graces in his finishing school, where wisdom was dispensed around a canteen table rather than delivered from a conference platform. He gave Irvine his first coaching role, running a satel-lite centre in the youth system at Blackburn Rovers, and eventually took him to Newcastle United as first-team coach.

'I did two years unpaid at that centre. Clarke Carlisle, Brett Ormerod and David Dunn came out of it. The fact is I didn't want to be paid, because they were giving me good players to work with, giving me the chance to make mistakes, to learn, to develop, to really go into my coaching in depth. I always tell young coaches to work with young players, because they will test you in terms of finding a way to help them.

'I would sit at lunchtime listening to Kenny and Ray Harford talking football. It was fantastic. Ray was very structured, very organised, a top coach of 4–4–2. He shared small details, simple messages to give players. He said things that seemed so blindingly obvious you'd think, why did I not think of that before?

'Kenny was just so different, so spontaneous. He couldn't really explain why he did what he did. He thought it was simple, but he was a genius. Kenny knew players. He knew the fine details about their habits. He was fascinating, because his knowledge was almost unstructured. I remember once asking his advice about James Beattie. We were trying to work with him on his movement.

'Kenny said, "I tell you what. You put the session on and I'll see what I see." He was as good as his word. He walked on to the pitch, got hold of James, and started pouring out all this information. I'm thinking, that's enough, because as a coach I was worried Kenny was scrambling his brains by giving him too much information in one go. But the stuff he was coming up with, without prior thought, was just fabulous.

'I'd played with top players, and when he took me to Newcastle I was working with the best, Shearer, Ferdinand, Asprilla, Ginola, Batty, Lee, and so on. I didn't get involved in picking the team. I wasn't involved in deciding what was going to happen on a match day. I was simply in charge of the training. From time to time Kenny would come in with a small piece of paper. There'd be four crosses on there. He'd say, "I want you to do that." That was my role, and you can't buy that experience.'

Coaches can be perfectionists; managers must be pragmatists. Irvine's work with Moyes at Everton bridged the divide, and gave him an insight into the cost of career advancement. Their relationship, forged on coaching courses, was honest, open and mutually supportive. They travelled across Europe together, as point guards in the recruitment process, and signed Marouane Fellaini despite his being sent off after 17 minutes when they watched him. Irvine was involved in every major decision, but shielded from the bitterest consequences.

'David made the final decision, but he always wanted my opinion. I could say anything to him and he would either dismiss it or take it. I wasn't looking to be a number one, but I was conscious that if I did go into management I had to be aware of the culture of impatience that has developed around it. That's really sad, because it holds the game back as far as I'm concerned.

'I've known Brendan [Rodgers] since he was a young coach who used to come to study my sessions. Look at the fantastic job he is doing at Liverpool, and there are still people who don't want to give him time to create. It is the same with Roberto [Martínez] at Everton. Give these people time.

'David would have done a fantastic job at Man United, given time. I have no doubt about that. People want results, right now. You have to have a certain mindset to put that to one side, because otherwise you'll get bogged down by it. You'll end up looking bad, feeling bad. That can't be good for you.

'Everybody knew David was stepping into an extremely difficult job, not just because of who he was following, but also because of what he was left with. When we were together at Everton we used to do an exercise, when we'd look at the team we were going to play and say, "Go on, then, how many of our players would get in their team?" Quite often it might be only two or three.

'I did that exercise when United played Everton in what turned out to be David's last game with them. There were only two of his players I would have put in the Everton team, Rooney and Van Persie, even though he wasn't playing that well at the time. That was me being completely objective.

'It was David who came to me when Preston wanted me to be their manager. He thought it was a great opportunity for me, and he talked me through what would happen, and what could happen. I don't know how I could have been better prepared, having been player, coach, academy director and assistant manager. I had my certificate in applied management and Pro Licence.

'I thought I knew what being a manager was, but I had no idea. Until you do the job you really don't know what it is like. The responsibility is huge, and you just have to cope. Suddenly, everybody wants you. Everybody looks at you whenever there's a problem to be solved. You can't actually tell people what you really think, whether that is players, fans, media or even club directors, because you're managing things delicately all the time.'

There was a revealing symmetry to Irvine's management career, before he joined Albion. He was sacked in strange circumstances at Preston in 2009 and at Sheffield Wednesday two years later. He took over each club when they were bottom of their respective leagues, and lost his job despite having a 40 per cent win ratio.

'I was absolutely gobsmacked when I got the sack at Preston. I'd got them into the play-offs the previous season, and we were three points off that pace, with a home game in hand. We'd played Sheffield United the night before and lost to a last-minute goal, one of those free kicks which misses everybody and goes in. I had the keys to the training ground and let myself in, as I often did.

'I'm watching the game when Derek Shaw, the chairman, called and asked where I was. He said, "I'll pop down." When he appeared, he said, "I don't know how to say this, and I can't give you any reasons, but we're going to move on." I said, "What do you mean?" He said, "We're going to replace you." That was the end of the conversation. It was bizarre.'

He called his wife, found a cardboard box for his personal effects, and delivered the bad news to his assistant, Rob Kelly. When he was succeeded by Darren Ferguson, conspiracy theorists began to speculate on the relationship between club owner Trevor Hemmings and Sir Alex Ferguson, who knew each other through horseracing, but it was ultimately irrelevant.

Wednesday approached him within three days. Irvine calculated he needed 11 wins from the 22 remaining matches to save them from relegation. Eventually, he failed on the final day. He took a two-week summer holiday, but since he oversaw the signing of seven players during that time he returned home with hotel room pallor.

Wednesday started the season well, and were top of the table, with five wins and a draw in their previous six games, when Milan Mandarić, the former Portsmouth and Leicester City owner, bought the club for £1, and promised to clear the debts. Irvine knew he was on borrowed time, the players sensed his vulnerability, and his departure, within three months, became a self-fulfilling prophecy.

The callousness of regime change hit him hard. He felt mentally drained, physically depleted. His friends worried that he had lost his natural optimism and eloquence. He was 'wiped out', so alienated by football, the game which had given him a life, that he could not bear even to watch it on television. He regained trust in his trade slowly, working with the England Under 17 squad before returning to his roots, as Everton's academy director.

'I had a job for life. A very good job, a very well-paid job, a job where the support I received was phenomenal. But it was bland. Don't get me wrong, I knew I was extremely fortunate, but there was a telling moment when I went to Goodison Park for David's send-off, before he went to United. It was a Sunday; I'd taken the under elevens that morning, because their coach wasn't there.

'I enjoyed the involvement, but when I sat in the stand watching David, it made me think, what am I doing here? All my contemporaries work at first-team level. It was a really strange situation. I realised how much I missed the excitement. It was crazy, because I missed waking up at three in the morning, thinking, have I picked the right team? Have we done the right work? What will the subs be? What will I say to the press if this happens?

'I missed the game still being in my head. I've never applied for a job in my life, and I had immense respect for Everton, so at no time did I put my name in for any jobs, even though I had agents phoning at different times saying, "Do you want us to try for something for you?" I reasoned that if a club wanted me they would know where I was.'

Albion's initial approach was made by Terry Burton, and Irvine was comfortable with the parameters of the role. 'I know how the club is run, in a very prudent and sensible way. The fact is that the club will never overstretch itself, and why should they? They've been extremely successful working with the model that they've got.'

I studied his methods and doctrines concurrently with those of Ronald Koeman at Southampton. Both clubs were run on similar principles, which Albion quickly modified to facilitate the arrival of Tony Pulis, whose appointment as their fourth head coach in a year was confirmed on January 1. Unlike Irvine, he had autonomy on all first-team matters, including the buying and selling of players.

Southampton had greater resources, but operated with greater efficiency. Their recruitment was insightful and strategic. Their philosophy, of long-term growth underpinned by enlightened player development, was ingrained into the fabric of the club. There was a continuity of purpose and principle, from the Under 9s to the first team.

Koeman, a deeply impressive coach, lacked Irvine's natural warmth. There was a scholastic air to his sessions, which were timed to the second and smoothly sequential. Players maintained eye contact as they shook the hand of strangers; they had respect for their talent and surroundings. They trained in virtual silence, a contrast to the bovine atmosphere at most British clubs.

A squad ravaged and rebuilt during a turbulent off-season were the season's great surprise. Their respect for Koeman was tangible; they knew him as a player, winning the European Cup for Barcelona at Wembley in 1992, and effectively eliminating England from the 1994 World Cup in Graham Taylor's 'do I not like that' moment in Rotterdam.

They relished Koeman's interpretation of the fusion of beauty and passion which created Johan Cruyff's kaleidoscopic Dream Team. Once his ego had been parked, a feat of modern engineering given that he exuded the trademark arrogance of leading Dutch coaches, he shared the lessons of Louis Van Gaal's flair for organisation.

The business rationale for his appointment was undeniable. He had proved, in Portugal, Spain, Belgium and Holland, that he was comfortable regenerating teams splintered through financial expedience or necessity. Les Reed, Southampton's executive director, had been monitoring his progress at Feyenoord for three years.

The Rotterdam-based club were not out of the top

three in the Eredivisie in that time, despite the burden of debt, which necessitated the annual sale of their best assets. Koeman merged academy graduates with unheralded bargains, loan signings and veterans of appropriate character. He made a profit, prepared new products for the market. He had an MSc in human chemistry.

Reed saw the relevance of such experience and acumen. He moved quickly when the Premier League's pecking order reasserted itself. Southampton conformed to the pattern of a selling club by reluctantly allowing Mauricio Pochettino to join Tottenham, yet they yearned for the sort of solidity provided by cohesive coaching.

Koeman offered reassurance, in a distinctive form of English: 'We had our problems, because there were a lot of changes in the summer, but we still have our philosophy, our ambition, our spirit. I am not always in the dressing room, so I need players who understand how we train, and how we live. We train to improve ourselves, and have better organisation of the team.

'I don't take them running in the wood for an hour. OK, that can be mental training, conditioning, but it isn't football. Running with the ball is much nicer than running without the ball. I hate to see sessions when players are told "just go and play". They need to be concentrated, and when you give them different exercises, they love it.

'Southampton is a club which is growing up, and here I can give young players possibilities. I learned in Holland, you have to work with young players thoughtfully. If not, they go left when the rest of the group goes right. I am a guide, and a father of them. I teach them how I like to play, and how to behave, as public people.

'I give them chances to make faults. Everybody can make mistakes, because they are human persons. Sometimes people need five or six years to improve themselves, to understand what they did wrong. It is not only the qualities in your feet which matter in professional football. What is in your head is more important. How many players get to thirty and wish they had done things differently at eighteen?

'I had [Zlatan] Ibrahimović at Ajax. I saw his great qualities from the beginning, but he had come from Malmö, where he played with two strikers in front. He had to be our target man, and Ajax is not an easy crowd. It was a difficult change for him but we gave him time and confidence. There were little problems with him, because of his character, but you have to be patient with that kind of person.

'I wanted to manage in the Premier League because it stretches me. It is at a very high level. I like the way clubs are working. I like the ambition and a lot of money in the football. I like the atmosphere in the stadiums, how you watch the games. I play for win. I am a very bad loser. We will get new players in, good ones, and we will reach what we did last season.'

Koeman, bold and barrel-chested, had the calculating air of a mercenary. Irvine, sharp-featured yet understated, had the earnest demeanour of a missionary. He loved what he was doing, despite the 18-hour days and the seemingly endless self-justification, because of the release he found on the training ground.

Pulis is renowned for turning his training ground into a drill square that would do justice to those preparing for the Trooping the Colour; his teams become resilient through repetition. Albion's results improved, though Irvine did not deserve to be dismissed as an irredeemable failure; it was a convenient fallacy for those who had justified his prediction that 'they'll make their mind up about me after three or four games'.

I had watched him take an early-season session which concentrated on the relationship between his first-choice back four and two holding midfield players. The group were engaged by the intelligence of his interventions and spirits were high. He did not attempt to impose his personality on them; he was a facilitator rather than a dictator.

Albion were operating at a disadvantage from day one, because, due to injuries and late recruitment, eight out of 19 outfield players lacked sufficient match fitness to make the anticipated impact. Yet Irvine exuded enthusiasm; his desk was littered with Post-it notes from assorted hotels containing reminders of calls to be made and fixtures to attend. As I rose to leave that day, he looked up: 'I hope you're coming back to see me around February.'

We laughed in unison, uncomfortably aware that the odds stacked against true believers like him are not remotely funny.

14

No Blacks, No Irish

Willie Hughton is a former medical student from Ghana who settled for the security of a job in the Post Office. His wife, Christine, is from Ireland, a homemaker and fiercely proud mother of three. They still live in the terraced house in which they brought their children up to do the right thing, in the right manner, for the right reasons.

Before they found that refuge in the east London borough of Newham, ten minutes' walk from West Ham United and the Boleyn Ground, they were obliged to endure the endemic racism of 1960s landlords. They became inured to insults, signs in front windows which spat out the message: 'No Blacks. No Dogs. No Irish.'

Their world changed, superficially at least, but their principles passed down the generations. Their eldest son, christened Christopher William Gerard in deference to family tradition, has given them four grandchildren.

He is 56 now, a quietly spoken, dignified man with a wider sense of purpose. Tight grey curls are beginning to colonise his dark, neatly trimmed hair, but he looks younger.

His lean body hints at athletic achievement. His measured personality, which prompted him to qualify as a lift engineer as insurance against football's inherent insecurity, lends him a certain serenity. The strength of his social conscience, expressed through support for the anti-apartheid movement long before the release of Nelson Mandela, is another indication of the enduring influence of his parents.

Chris Hughton's return to management with Brighton & Hove Albion on December 31, 2014, seven months after being sacked by Norwich City, was widely welcomed. For five of those months, there had been no black, Asian or minority ethnic managers (BAME) in the 92-club pyramid. Hughton's appointment ensured there were five who entered the New Year with differing priorities.

Jimmy Floyd Hasselbaink was flying at Burton Albion in League Two, where Keith Curle was preoccupied with keeping Carlisle United out of the relegation places. Fabio Liverani, a former Italy international of Somali descent, had become Leyton Orient's fourth manager of a chaotic season on December 8. Chris Powell, sacked by Charlton in March, was successfully rebuilding his career at Huddersfield Town.

Evidence of enduring inequality had been collated in

an LMA report. Seventeen aspiring BAME managers held a UEFA Pro Licence. Eighteen per cent of candidates in coaching courses were from BAME backgrounds. Four of the 18 students taking the LMA's newly launched Diploma in Football Management were minority representatives. A significant proportion of the 46 BAME managers employed over the past 55 years, 60.9 per cent, have managed only one club.

As Hughton became 53rd and last management change in the calendar year 2014, the game's recruitment processes had rarely been more obtuse and illogical. Political pressure was growing for positive intervention, but establishing a consensus for change was as frustrating as attempting to eat jelly with chopsticks.

When the mandarins at Radio Two, that Valhalla of easy listening, insist on additional representation of minorities, such a sensitive issue has social momentum. Yet, in football, it was cheapened by politically correct opportunists who admired the window dressing of policy launches in the House of Commons while averting their eyes from the old boys' club, convening in a dingy back room.

Despite it all, leaders of genuine substance were starting to emerge in isolation. Kick it Out, the revealingly underfunded campaign body, featured two of football's most socially important figures, Lord Herman Ouseley and Troy Townsend. Jason Roberts retired as a professional footballer with Reading and reinvented himself as a professional irritant, through pungent commentary and an equality-driven charitable foundation.

Hughton's status within a fractured fraternity was keenly felt and increasingly relevant. We discovered we had a mutual friend, Sam Ramsamy. At 77, the former primary school teacher is one of the most respected IOC members. Hughton and I first met him independently in London in the 1980s, when he led opposition to South African involvement in world sport through SANROC (South African Non-Racial Olympic Committee), a focal point of anti-apartheid activism and advocacy.

Though he is too discreet to admit it, Sam was my unseen guardian angel on the rebel cricket tour of South Africa in 1990, which collapsed in the build-up to Mandela's return to society, as the founding father of a rainbow nation. It was a fraught, surreal experience, involving clandestine contact with the then-banned African National Congress.

British sportswriters were shadowed by agents of BOSS, South Africa's security service, and spat upon by spectators, who were encouraged to regard us as the enemy within by the Afrikaner media. The tensions led to play in one match being temporarily suspended, while we settled our differences in a full-scale brawl in the press box.

Such self-indulgent reminiscence, as we sit on a blustery afternoon in the manicured gardens of the north London hotel which used to host England teams managed by Don Revie, Ron Greenwood and Bobby Robson, coaxes a typically thin smile of recognition to Hughton's face.

'I've had many conversations with Sam over the years. I have a real affinity with individuals I believe are absolutely genuine in what they feel and what they show. I wouldn't say I am particularly active politically, though I've been a member of the Labour Party for a long time, but I get a feel for those who believe in a cause. Sam believed one hundred per cent in the cause.

'Mandela, obviously, is a great hero of mine. I'm guided by my background. My parents are incredibly down-to-earth people. I had a grounded childhood and I've always found importance in social issues, education and health especially. I am conscious of references to myself being a good role model for young coaches and it's something I'm very proud of.

'Another person I've always looked up to, and he's one of my best friends, is Garth Crooks. He's always been socially aware, and very articulate. He's one of those people you need as a manager, dealing with a lot of difficult situations. You can lean on him, and he will tell you the truth, rather than what you want to hear. He has always been good that way, he's very close.

'In a day and age when we are still asking why there

are not more black and minority managers, why there are not more ethnic personalities involved in all aspects of the game, we need more people like him. I am seeing more black coaches at academy and grass-roots level, but there is a massive gap between that and management roles in what we regard as senior football.

'There is no doubt there was a time when we were regarded as good players, athletic, but not looked upon as good management material. It's about changing that mentality, changing how people see you. Talking to Sam about how quickly things changed in South Africa gives me hope.

'Garth and I played in the era of monkey chants and banana throwing. I said something to him recently which I later realised sums up that era: you could feel racism in the room. Something would be said, a racial comment, and everyone would realise there was a black person there. This was a time when a week wouldn't go past without us getting abuse from an opposition crowd.'

Football favours neatly packaged solutions to multi-faceted problems, so it was unsurprising there were increasingly strident calls for the introduction of a form of the NFL's Rooney Rule, which requires teams to interview at least one minority candidate for any vacant coaching or senior management role.

Despite suspicions some franchises staged so-called 'courtesy' interviews, it had a measure of success. When, on January 15, 2015, Todd Bowles was appointed as head coach of the New York Jets, he became the fifth black man in such an exalted role in the 32-club NFL. The others were Cincinnati's Marvin Lewis, Detroit's Jim Caldwell, Pittsburgh's Mike Tomlin and Tampa Bay's Lovie Smith.

Hughton understands the danger of tokenism. 'The American experience is very different to ours, but the more I think about it, there are aspects of the Rooney Rule which make sense. When I speak to the prime people at the FA, I sense a real enthusiasm for change. They have a very big responsibility, and a very big opportunity.

'If there is that enthusiasm, they have to demonstrate it. For me, that can only be through peer pressure, communication with the clubs. Say there is a vacant role for an under twenty-one coach. The FA should contact them, and ask how many black and ethnic coaches have been interviewed. They have the opportunity to speak to each and every club about what they intend to do about these issues.

'There is always going to be this feeling that the best person for the job is the best person for the job. And I think that is right, as a principle. But we are still in an age where there can be racial influence and racial prejudice. I don't think we can totally ignore that. The FA are our governing body. If they feel the balance is unfair they should act.'

Someone with the solidity of Hughton's background is increasingly rare. He accepts the nature of the modern footballer has changed with society, and argues that management will, by necessity, become a much more delicate balancing act. The new breed of owner demands success whatever the human consequences, and the modern player yearns for emotional succour.

'Management is becoming much more about developing the person and the player. The senior pro you bring into your first team is generally going to have a good support system. He will be on good money and have the security of a contract. That enables him to work around some of the issues, like affordability of housing, for instance.

'The younger player needs more emotional support. There are some very stable individuals in the youth system; their parents tend to watch them play in every game. But as a manager you have to have a feel for those with problems. A big example of that is probably Nile Ranger, whom I had at Newcastle.

'We knew his background was difficult. He was different as an individual. I had to work harder with him than I did with others, simply because he needed it. You have to relate to the human being, because ultimately what's going to determine that young man's progress in life is what he does on the football pitch. Success there will bring him some stability as regards contracts and finance.

'I try to develop players as grounded people who are able to cope with money or hardship, success or rejection. I've always told players they are going to be released, whether that's from the academy or as young professionals. That gets no easier the longer you are in the game, but I become personally involved because I hope I will, in some way, be a positive influence at a difficult time.

'I'm lucky I had a very humble upbringing. I did a four-year apprenticeship as a lift engineer before going into the game at twenty. I was at Tottenham from the age of thirteen and at sixteen they asked me to stay on as an amateur. I did well enough for them to want me to sign professional forms at eighteen, but I chose to complete my engineering apprenticeship so I had something to fall back on.

'My parents agreed, but they made sure it was my decision. I was encouraged to be independent from a young age. I was brought up in an era where you played out on the streets, where you were allowed to jump on a bus, or get the train by yourself. I didn't have parents who mollycoddled me.

'They valued work, but they let me choose my own path. It is so different today, where parents jump at the opportunity of a young lad going to a big club like Tottenham. My parents didn't see me play every week. They worked and spent time with my younger brother and older sister.

'Today, little Johnny is nine years old, and training at a professional club two nights a week. He's taken there and back, sometimes by the mum, sometimes by the dad. That takes up four hours each night. He plays on a Saturday or a Sunday. He gets to twelve and trains three nights a week. He gets to sixteen, and doesn't get academy forms.

'His parents have been with him at the football club for at least seven years, so that becomes a family issue. It's like a bereavement, because it has taken such a big chunk of that family's life. My parents wanted me to do well. My brother Henry, who was self-sufficient like me, also played professionally, in a very good side at Leyton Orient. But football wasn't the be all and end all.'

There is a theory in football that Hughton is too nice for his own good. It is based on his casual maltreatment by Mike Ashley's regime at Newcastle, but overlooks his quiet ruthlessness in isolating the financial and administrative chaos he inherited at Birmingham, where owner Carson Yeung was imprisoned in Hong Kong on money-laundering charges.

Unemployment, for a football manager, is a place of light and shade. Hughton found the summer of 2014 debilitating, because it was the first time he had been out of the game in pre-season for 35 years. He maintained a high profile through media work, but his most significant venture was to undertake a course in corporate management.

Owners and directors can no longer be fobbed off with a few war stories in the manager's office, where the post-match testosterone high was once traditionally shared with club tsars in suits. Hughton was smart enough to realise he needed to relate to modern business principles, so he could be more effective in the boardroom.

'I'm not the most confrontational person, but I can also look after myself when I need to. I am not the type of individual to back down in a fight. Managers need to react to circumstances these days. The new type of owner, chairman and CEO has a target mentality, taken from other walks of life. They have no fear of continual change if those targets are not met.

'The decision to dismiss a manager was once a big club issue, a board decision. You felt it was almost done reluctantly. Now individuals are used to getting rid of people, again and again if necessary. It is part of working life for them. That means, inevitably, you will begin to see a different type of manager.

'I've always believed the right way to do the job is to totally immerse yourself in the club, and what it stands for. The new type of manager, a coach really, has a different outlook. He thinks, there's no point looking over my shoulder, because I know what's going to happen. He doesn't concern himself with the development of young players because he thinks, I might not be here next year. I have to win today.

'That won't take anything away from how much I put into the job emotionally. There might be a perfect manager or head coach out there who finds time for himself and his family, and has a rounded lifestyle which prioritises things which really matter, but I've never met him.

'There is a feeling now you have to be seen to put even more into it. Results and expectations are generally decisive in you losing your job, but the one thing you really don't want is your bosses saying, "He never put enough into it."'

That could never be said of Brian McDermott, whose return to football, in a senior scouting position at Arsenal, was welcomed by the brotherhood. Admired as a man of unchallenged integrity and deceptive sensitivity, he was respected professionally for the manner in which he survived a brutalising experience at Leeds United.

We first met there, for the purposes of this book, in August 2013, when the paucity of his inheritance from Neil Warnock was immediately apparent. McDermott had a supposedly strategic brief to rebuild the club, from the bottom up, over three years. Elland Road, as evocative a relic as the sock tags of the Revie era, seemed trapped in a time warp.

The club had no scouting system and lacked basic analytic tools. When I watched them later that season, at home to Bournemouth, McDermott's staff had been forced to borrow performance statistics on their own players from Leicester City. Leeds' recruitment policy was informed by a personalised database of more than 1,000 players, maintained by the manager on his BlackBerry.

The main training pitch was undersized, poorly drained and rarely usable. A previous regime had felled surrounding trees to enable the manager to watch from his second-floor office without the inconvenience of leaving his leather chair.

Now there was a long-suppressed spark of humanity about the place. The sound of children playing filtered through the long dark doors of McDermott's office. He had been struck on arrival how staff seemed 'almost in shock, downtrodden.' He had given permission for them to bring young families into work during the school holidays. There were toys on the floor, smiles on the faces.

His assistant Nigel Gibbs, whose subsequent treatment by the Cellino regime would lead to a legal claim for constructive dismissal against the club, reflected: 'Brian is very much a people person. His man management is one of his great strengths. He trusts his staff, and is inclusive with the players. People want to do well for him.'

McDermott picked up on the theme during training, which was taken by Gibbs. 'I'm scanning, looking around,' he said as we walked diagonally, past a pair of drainage workers drilling a borehole to a pitch staging a small-sided game. 'I'm very aware of how I speak to people, what words I use. It's really important that you think about what you say.

'Does that mean that you're not relaxed around someone? I don't think so. I think it's important you speak to people in the right way and pick up the nuances of a conversation. Most make statements but don't ask questions. As a manager you ask questions. If you don't you might miss things.

'Somebody might not be in a good place. You don't know what's going on in that fella's life, so you have to find out. And if you don't, then you're in the wrong, because you've failed in your responsibility to him. I can't speak for other people in football, but I know how I want to be treated and how I want people to talk to me.

'It's funny. I know I'm going off on a tangent here but when I was at Reading I thought, well, when I walk out of here, this place is going to fall apart. It didn't. It was a case of, here today, gone tomorrow. I learned from that. I didn't resent it. I thought, you know what? Enjoy the time you've got, do the best you possibly can.'

He spent 12 years at Reading, after being recruited as chief scout by Alan Pardew, 'when I was wet, cold and out of work', following spells as manager at Slough Town and Woking. His playing career had meandered to a close in Hong Kong before he returned to England

at the age of 32 'to find out what I didn't want to do'
by spending a year working in insurance.

His demeanour was equally wistful when he invited
me into his office at Elland Road in the hour before
kick-off against Bournemouth. It was an unprepos-
sessing room, narrow and flanked by blue-cushioned
chairs. A tray of chips simmered im fat uninvitingly
under a heat lamp on a plastic catering trolley.
Immediately before a 2–1 win, his stream-of-conscious-
ness reflections were ethereal, fascinating.

'Is this a normal job? I'm just going to go out and
do it in front of twenty-five thousand people. That's
not normal, however you define normal. There is no
past, no future, only the now. This is a big club to play
for. You have to have big people. Can I create confidence
and arrogance? I can tell them to wave at the crowd in
the manner of the old teams, but do they believe it?

'There is no point going mad with them. I learned
my lesson as a young manager at Slough Town. At that
time I was everything I hated in a manager when I was
a player. I once went into one at half-time, and my false
tooth fell out. How silly did I look? The lads just started
laughing. I had to laugh with them.

'I've still got that side to me. I don't mind confrontation, believe it or not. I avoid it, but I don't mind it. I
don't encourage it, but I don't have a problem with it.
Genuinely. If someone fronts me up, in a bad way, I am
very comfortable with that.

'This job examines you. When I was at Wembley with Reading in the play-off final, there were eighty-six thousand there. It was impossible to believe how lonely I was. It's bizarre. You retreat inside yourself. I talked to Sean Dyche about it. "We all want the same things," he said. But what makes us different?'

Like Hughton, McDermott was a child of circumstance. His father, Jack, who hailed from Sligo, was a decent footballer and part-time boxer who provided for his four children through a variety of jobs. He was a disciplinarian who instinctively hid his tender side, and died from a heart attack in 1985, aged 60, when Brian was 24. The pride he showed in his son, despite the conventions of his generation, is his legacy.

McDermott's mother, Bridget, was from County Clare. She was a caring woman, an emotional rock. She sensed his vulnerability, which was exacerbated by a particularly insidious form of snobbery, almost designed to highlight natural childhood assumptions of inferiority.

'I was a Catholic council house kid who was always being told he wouldn't amount to much. I had a talent, I was a good footballer, but those attitudes held me back. I nipped through my eleven plus by the skin of my teeth, and went to a technical school, Herschel, in Slough. I was never ready to go to a school like that. It was just too much for me.

'Every Christmas and Easter they used to read out

the names of the twenty people who were bottom of the class. It was humiliating, completely humiliating. My major driving force was football. I knew I was destined to be a pro. I just wish I'd known then what I know now, because my career would have been different.

'I did get three promotions, but I never played for Ireland, which I should have done. Don Howe suggested I play for England under seventeens. I wasn't English, though I was born in Slough; I was Irish. Don was the big man at Arsenal at the time. I had no confidence, and just went along with it, almost to protect myself. Dad was worried about upsetting anyone.

'That's a real driver for me, now. My life goal is to manage Ireland. I don't blame Don for anything, because when you play at a big club like Arsenal, you have to have real belief in yourself. I played more than sixty first-team games, but I felt like a nobody. I was never made to feel special. I never felt good enough, however hard I tried. That's probably down to my background.

'I went to Oxford from there and really struggled. I only played twenty-odd games under Jim Smith. I found him very hard. He was a successful manager, but very, very confrontational, especially with wingers like me. He drained me of confidence, quite frankly, though he tried to sign me for QPR afterwards.

'I worked for Frank Burrows at Cardiff. He was very good for me, very strong but very good. I loved playing for Terry Cooper at Exeter. But I always had my teachers in my head, telling me that I wasn't going to do much. They never encouraged me. It was always "You have to be careful, you have to watch yourself, it might not work for you."

'It was, "You won't, you can't, you ain't," words I try not to use any more. The word "but" is the worst in the dictionary. If I use that word to you, you'll stop listening. You'll only hear the "but", and be waiting for a knockback. You know, "You're a great guy, but your gear's shocking." I'm always waiting for that word, and when I hear it I just want to walk away.

'I have a theory there are a lot of depressed people in football, but they probably don't even know it because they are conditioned by the game. They are expected to overcome brutal things they regard as normal practice. People like me tell them they're not going to get a new contract, they're not in the team, they're thirty-five and they can't play any more. Where do they go from there?'

Most never go beyond ill-focused attempts to remain in the game. The tiny minority who graduate into management are obliged to develop a second skin, with characteristics similar to those of the heat-resistant tiles which protect space modules on re-entry into the Earth's atmosphere. Nothing, however, could prepare anyone for the mad cabaret which began on 'Mad Friday', January 31, 2014.

McDermott took a call that evening from Chris Farnell, a Manchester-based lawyer who was representing Massimo Cellino, the Italian entrepreneur who had previous convictions for deception and false accounting. Cellino was in the process of becoming the new owner of Leeds United, and he evidently intended to live up to his nickname of '*ll mangia-allenatori*', the manager eater.

'I didn't know the number. I didn't know the person speaking to me. He said he was a lawyer, calling out of courtesy. They were terminating my contract, and I was to expect a letter. I said, "OK." I didn't need to say any more. The next thing I know it is on TV that I've been sacked. At the time Massimo didn't officially own the club.'

Even for someone with McDermott's grasp of the absurd the next 48 hours were unique. The legal letter never arrived, amidst rumours Cellino's staff were under orders to shred any copies should they be unearthed. McDermott was advised not to attend the following day's game against Huddersfield, a 5–1 win overseen by Gibbs after much heart-searching, before being reinstated by the group who were selling majority ownership of the club, Gulf Finance House.

His experience shocked the unshockable. He was inundated by messages of support from fellow managers, who sensed a line had been crossed. McDermott did what he was trained to do, and concentrated on the next match, on the Tuesday night, against Yeovil. They won 2–1.

'You feel a lot of empathy in those circumstances. I appreciated so many people in the game taking the time to write, text or call. But, strange as it sounds, my fundamental aim was to get a result against Yeovil. It was surreal.

'Everything was played out in the public domain. When I went in on the Monday I did a press conference which was live on Sky for forty-five minutes. I didn't know Massimo. He didn't know me. We got off on the wrong foot. I get on with him fine now, believe it or not. He rings me, wanting to know about players.'

Cellino, who still faces unresolved charges of attempted embezzlement and fraudulent misrepresentation, purchased a 75 per cent stake in the club through his company Eleonora Sport in April 2014. He was disqualified by the Football League that December, after they obtained Italian court documents relating to his alleged role in a tax evasion case, and asked him to resign from the club until April 2015. He did so, while pursuing an appeal in the Italian justice system.

McDermott has maintained his equilibrium. He faced a far-reaching decision in the summer of 2015, when his initial agreement with Arsenal to operate as a senior scout until the end of the season expired. He was trusted and respected at the club which once stimulated his worst fears. He travelled extensively and worked well with Steve Rowley, Arsène Wenger's chief scout.

'Arsenal have been fantastic for me. I've known Steve since I was sixteen. They do things right. They do their due diligence. They know everyone. I needed to get out there and watch games, re-educate myself. I won't go back into management unless the club is right, and the owner is right.

'Leeds hasn't put me off, but it is real unfinished business for me. I know people will smile at this, but it was a real honour to be their manager. One day they're going to get back into the Premier League. That's going to be some day, some night, some week, some month. Whoever does it, good luck to them.'

Inevitably, he was not allowed to leave with greater grace. He was sacked by Cellino in late May 2014, but not before one final insult, a tirade inspired by his perception that McDermott had taken 'a holiday' after the last game of the season. It was the sort of rant that, by then, had become familiar:

'Who's managing this club? Brian. Where's Brian? I send a letter to Brian. Help us. He's on holiday to get some rest. He was tired, I can understand. But just let me know what he's planning for pre-season. What he's thinking for the future. What's his plan? What are his ideas? Where are the people that we pay wages to every month gone? Who gave them the permission? Who organised that? He's the manager.'

McDermott was, instead, fulfilling a sombre, sacred duty. 'I left at the start of May. I had to because my mum was dying. I had to be there for my mum when she died. I did the right thing by my family. I don't have regrets about that, because I was three hundred miles away from her when she was struggling. It was important that I spent that last precious bit of time with her.'

Cellino sent a letter of apology, when he learned of the death of his former manager's mother, but hearing the sadness in McDermott's voice made me recall an earlier snippet of conversation.

'Do you forgive easily?' I asked him.

'Yes. Yes.'

'Do you forget?'

'That's a tough one. Subconsciously, probably not, is the honest answer. Consciously, I try to. But I need to work on that . . .'

15

Daddy Day Care

The session was winding down with a standard set-piece drill, practising movement at near-post corners. Dele Alli made a steeply angled run across the area to the right-hand edge of the six-yard box, rose high, and cushioned a deliberate back-heeled flick over the covering defender at the far post. The net shivered as the ball found the only unprotected target, a small area at the top of its inside panel.

'Whaaaat?' exclaimed Karl Robinson, his manager, as he dissolved into a fit of giggles. Alli was abused and bundled to the ground by his teammates in the manner which signals professional respect. He emerged, grinning, and sauntered over to where we were standing behind the goal.

'Did they get it?' he asked, motioning towards a film crew who were, instead, concentrating on the atmospheric image of a low sun, shot through the skeletal frame of an abandoned cricket net on the far side of MK Dons' training ground. He grimaced theatrically when informed he had suffered for their art. Then he produced his next party trick.

Alli spat a wad of chewing gum into the air, controlled it on his knee, and let it fall on to his right boot. He flicked it casually on to his left foot, and in a single fluid movement volleyed it upwards, back into his mouth. The dental hygienist might have had a problem with such audacity, but the man-child, only 18, was inordinately pleased with himself.

'Behave, you,' said Robinson with a smile, before lowering his voice to a church warden's whisper. 'Best young player I've worked with. He does things in training I've never seen before. He scores goals, wins penalties, beats people with back-heels, nutmegs them. He's got pace, strength. He drives inside, wins headers and tackles.

'Sure, he's got an air of arrogance and confidence about him, but he's a good kid. He's given only a percentage of his wages, so he understands what it means to save. He doesn't mind a row on the pitch, but we've a special signal. If it is getting a bit tasty – and teams do try to kick him out of the game – he winks at me to tell me he is still in control. He can be anything he wants to be.'

This was not a manager acting as market trader, shouting up the price. This was a father figure, radiating pride and mentally preparing a safety net. I had seen

Alli intermittently over the previous year or so; Robinson asked me, as an objective observer, to talk him through the complexities of fame and, in particular, the instant adjustment Gareth Bale had made to sudden and startling celebrity.

He was subconsciously channelling his mentor, Steve Heighway, who cites Bob Paisley as the best exponent of one of the most subtle arts of management, creating a supportive environment without compromising the enforcement of discipline. The endgame approached on January 29, four days before the closure of the winter transfer window.

Liverpool, long-term suitors, were strangely reluctant to commit. Newcastle were ready to pay £5 million. Aston Villa and Tottenham Hotspur had confirmed their interest. The following day, a Friday, Robinson called Alli into his office. He directed him towards the long, low black-leather seat along the wall in front of his desk, on which drinks coasters, inscribed with the wit and wisdom of Bill Shankly, were placed.

This was the most important conversation of Alli's young life, the natural conclusion to a story which began when he joined MK Dons as an 11-year-old. He had the athlete's sheen of self-belief, but a complicated family life, offset by strongly supportive grandparents. He was living with the parents of teammate Harry Hickford, a defender who had just returned on loan to Chelmsford City, in the Conference South.

'Seeing him sitting there, I had a tear in my eye. I had known for a long time, across at least three transfer windows, he was going to go. We turned down a million, two million, two point five. Now it was five. This was it. I asked him, "Do you want the deal to be done now, mate?' The way he said, "Gaffer, please," convinced me. 'There had been enough talk, enough "what if" scenarios. This was the first time I knew he knew what he wanted. Funnily enough, he looked his age for the first time in a long while. I saw fear in his eyes, good fear. He was worried about getting injured and losing the chance. He kept saying, "'I back myself, gaffer.'"

'We had sworn we'd tell each other everything, whether either of us liked it or not. I said, "Del, the deal is done." His eyes lit up. I saw a weight lift off him. "You've got two clubs to see on Sunday. You make a decision, mate." I knew this kid's story. I knew he'd had that dream for a long, long time. They all have it, these kids. Having the dream is one thing; fulfilling it is completely different.

'All the talking in the world is irrelevant unless you see substance in the individual. Dele has backed my words. All I have tried to do is care for him. I wanted to groom him as the whole package, on and off the field. It is not for us to judge his background. All I know is he has good people around him. He has a caring way about him, and a cheeky smile, which helps in this industry.'

Alli played in a 5–0 win at Crewe Alexandra on the Saturday, and visited Aston Villa's Bodymoor Heath training ground the following lunchtime. Perhaps portentously, the monitors were showing live coverage of Villa's 5–0 defeat at Arsenal. He travelled on to Tottenham's complex near Enfield. At 5.30 p.m. he called Robinson with a question to which he had already prepared an answer: 'Gaffer, what would you do if you were me?'

He had been excited by Mauricio Pochettino's vision of a young, urgent and smart team, ushering a storied club into a new era in a new stadium. He was excited by the modernity of the surroundings, the 15 pitches in the shadow of a gleaming building which contained pools, hydrotherapy facilities, an altitude room and a world-class gymnasium. He felt he belonged.

The deal involved being loaned back from Tottenham to the Dons for the rest of the season. Robinson's reputation as a development coach ensured he would be able to augment his team during their promotion push from League One with two more prospects of the highest quality, Chelsea midfield player Lewis Baker and Manchester City striker Devante Cole, the son of Andy.

His empathetic approach is another example of the legacy created by adversity. Robinson's playing career, undermined at the age of 16 by a serious back injury, reads like a railway timetable from the days before Dr Beeching laid waste to the network. It began at

Caernarfon Town and ended at Warrington Town, with stops at Bamber Bridge, Marine, Oswestry Town, Rhyl, Kidsgrove Athletic, Prescot Cables, St Helens Town and Alsager Town.

He was one of six young coaches taken under Heighway's wing at the Liverpool academy. The former Republic of Ireland winger, a singular character signed from Skelmersdale after he had completed an economics degree, urged them to push personal boundaries. He quietly inculcated the values he had absorbed under Shankly and Paisley in the 1970s.

'He once asked me what my dad did for a living. He was an electrician, and Steve directly related that to my coaching. "He'll have all the right tools in his van, Karl," he said. "Your job is to fill your van with the sort of tools which will help your players." Steve had a vision for us. He taught me to love the purity of football. He trusted me to work with some of the best kids in the country.'

Robinson is a noisy, engaging figure on the training ground. His sessions, a tribute to the intelligence and insight of his mentor, are sharp, full of movement and designed to make his players think. The squad is broken down into individual units after intense small-sided possession drills. Robinson circulates easily, cajoling and challenging without wasting a word. He can be waspish, but he has a teacher's patience.

On this particular day defenders worked on switching play and the discipline of monitoring and maintaining a high line. Midfield players, pressurised in possession at all times by two squad members in yellow bibs, were expected to rotate seamlessly and pass quickly and accurately. Strikers were being asked to split and make runs, at different times and angles, through four mannequins, lined up on the edge of the penalty area. Following a difficult sequence of results, Robinson had written three words on the dressing-room wall: 'Basics. Responsibility. Fear.'

'Football is the same as any other walk of life. If you are having a bad time, you go back to basics. You take responsibility for that process, and that eradicates fear. But if you are anxious, fearful of responsibility, you forget the basics. That's when you find yourself in a constant downward spiral. My players have to police themselves, to a degree. I am here as a support mechanism.

'Each player will respond differently to a particular management skill. Football is a creative industry. I have to be honest, caring, loving, strict. I've seen so much in this game. I've seen amazing parents and those who don't care for their sons. I've seen good agents, bad agents. I've seen kids in tears, frozen by fear. They've never experienced the struggle and they don't know what to do.

'Fear of rejection is part and parcel of being a human being, and, as a manager, I hope my values determine that my players will respond positively to me. The training ground is my home. It is where I think, where I breathe. I'd describe myself as being a very strong-minded coach, opinionated and forward-thinking. I am not trying to create the wheel; I'm just trying to make it turn a little easier.'

His subsequent team talk was measured in tone, but passionate in nature. It rose in pitch and intensity: 'You have to be braver. I don't care who you are, you need a work ethic. Don't talk to me about a lack of confidence. That is the biggest excuse in this world. It's a shithouse's way out, a failure's way out, an amateur's way out.

'I won't shout, because shouting only creates anxiety. This is about quality, intensity, hunger and desire. Who is going to be the man? Which one of you is going to stand up and say, "I'm there. I'll suffer. I'll take the ball in the face. I'll give everything"? Challenge yourself.'

The callowness of the group was startling. Training had been completed by a nine-a-side match between the Oldies and the Young 'Uns. Three 21-year-olds were in the veterans' team. MK Dons may be branded by the brutality of their birth, but, as a new city grew up around them, the club embodied the hope and vivacity of youth. A slogan emblazoned on a wall adjacent to the dressing room captured a state of mind: 'It's us against the world and the world doesn't stand a chance.'

Robinson initially joined the club in 2007 as Paul Ince's first-team coach. He followed him to Blackburn

Rovers, where he also flourished under Ince's successor, Sam Allardyce. He returned to Milton Keynes, again under Ince, and became the league's youngest manager, at the age of 29, when Ince resigned in May 2010.

'People saw something in me, but I could easily have crashed and burned. I was lost for a while, big time. I was living on my three a day – coffee, Nurofen and red wine. Was the job too big for me? Possibly, possibly. I had a hard time for six months. No one knew me. Some didn't want me. But, arguably, that made me, because I had to pull myself around, with help from my loved ones.

'Fans don't see that. They rarely look beyond win, win, win. It is a balancing act. You can go either way. It is wonderful when you are deemed to be successful and allowed to enjoy achievements. When things go badly there is only one way to recover, and that is not to be in the game. Public demand doesn't allow you to stay in it and recover.

'I am one of the few who has gone against the grain, and worked my way up from the under nines to the first team. Brendan Rodgers has done it. I watched him from afar, long before he went to Liverpool, the club I love. Everyone spoke very highly of him as a coach at Chelsea, and he did well at Watford.

'Yet at Reading he got the sack. A lot of people said that was that, but here he is, managing one of the great clubs in world football. It is such a precarious job. It is not like being a surgeon, who knows that if he sticks to procedure, the job gets done. We can stick to procedure and principle, but our team can lose a silly goal, lose confidence, and we end up losing our job.

'Man management was probably my strength at the beginning. I had icebreakers: music, trends, buzzwords. A few of the squad were the same age as me. I've always been quite good at relating to people, dealing with them. I let them in, and sometimes that is mistaken as weakness.

'I am very straight when I want a player out. If I don't think he is good enough I will tell him to his face. I know I am affecting them. They have families and kids; I am ruining their lives as well. But as a player, you live by my rules. I will give you a chance; stitch me up and you are out. It is that black and white. If it is not working I will tell you why.

'The best side of the game is working with young players. I watch kids like Dele, Lewis, Devante, George Williams, playing the game with such joy. They ask me, "What makes you happy, gaffer?" They tell me I am never happy. It sounds a bit lame, but I tell them I can't show them what I truly feel, the pride I will have in them when they maximise their ability in the Premier League.'

His denial that promotion was essential, after four seasons of relative overachievement punctuated by appearances in two play-off semi-finals, was not entirely convincing. The logic of his argument, that progression would continue to be underpinned by harvesting the assets of a strategic approach to youth development, was sound, yet there was a sense all was not as it seemed.

Robinson is a deceptively deep character, ill-served by Scouse stereotypes. It took time to peel away the layers of his personality, to answer those who saw him as an inveterate self-publicist, constantly linked to jobs for which he was not being considered. At 34, and established as the third-longest-serving manager behind Arsène Wenger and Paul Tisdale, he was growing into his own skin.

'I've changed massively over the past eighteen months,' he admitted. 'I felt I had to prove things to people who had no influence on me. I felt I was living a bit of a lie. I know I am a good coach. I have got this far on that talent. I got carried away with myself. If it wasn't for my wife – she said, "You are going to have to go back to being who you were, the person who got you to where you are" – I'd have been lost.

'I started reading some of the things I said. I realised what I thought was passion and intelligence could be perceived as arrogance. A lot of people had a pre-conceived, subjective view of me. I thought, oh my God. That is the complete polar opposite to who I am. I needed to address the image.

'That is the problem with this job. People are conditioned to thinking that they know us, when they have never met us. They prejudge us, as strangers. It is idiotic. We are the pantomime baddies, who are always judged after the event. If Billy Hindsight was a manager, he'd be top of the league.

'There are sides to us we can't ever let other people see. They don't realise the strength of our feelings, the extent of the worry and anger. You don't go through life without having some valve to release that sort of emotion, but we cannot allow them to see what the valve is, and how we let it all go, because we would be perceived as being weak.

'I've heard it all. You know what I'm on about, comments like, "If you come from Liverpool you'll either end up as a footballer or a robber." Mum and Dad brought me up on strong principles. They taught me to treat people correctly. I would like to think my players would say, "He cares for me. Whatever time of day, whatever I have done, the gaffer will be there for me."

'But I knew something had to change. I needed to strip things back a bit, be a little less raw, stop chasing and settle down. I have become a lot more open, a lot softer. I am not scared to be me. Before I didn't think being me was good enough. I've learned you can't always rely on yourself.'

He had been working for a year with Simon Edwards, a so-called 'behaviour strategist', based in Harley Street. His website speaks of 'developing effective, dynamic and measurable techniques for discerning clients'. His trademarked approach, 'Mind Measuring', is designed to 'overcome the restrictions of fears, phobias and common psychosomatic conditions to release talent, skill and confidence'.

In essence, he counselled Robinson on the harshness of language and the complexity of his fundamental professional relationship with his players. This inevitably spilled over into his personal life, and reinforced his parental responsibilities to his eight-year-old daughter, Jasmine.

'Simon talked me through various behavioural examples. I was once having a go at a player, and lost the plot because he wasn't looking at me. My opening line was "ignorant prick". Simon argued that he didn't have to look at me to listen. I replied that it was a matter of manners. He then made me think, maybe he is shy. He is scared, because he knows you're going to shout at him. You don't know about his background.

'If you get told "no" every day of your life as a kid it becomes an automatic cog in your head. "Don't do this. Don't do that." As a parent I've become aware of negative words. At home I tell Jasmine I love her a hundred times a day. I tell her she is perfect, she is clever. She can do it. I tell her she can be what she wants to be. I want to be someone she is proud of as she grows up.'

We were speaking in his office on a Thursday evening, prior to the season's final loan deadline. He was, to use his phrase, playing the role of 'Daddy Day Care' since his wife, Ann Marie, a former *Brookside* actress, was appearing on stage in the Theatre Royal, St Helens, in the comedy 'Rita, Sue and Bob too'. He had picked Jasmine up from school and was helping with her homework, in between concluding negotiations with Wales Under 21 defender Joe Walsh and attending a supporters' club function.

His daughter knocked on the door, opened it and blew a referee's whistle, which hung around her neck. Her mobile phone, operating in face-time mode, was held at arm's length. It took several seconds for us to realise this was a preordained signal to her cousin, who was watching in Liverpool, to cartwheel down the landing of her home. 'Can you believe that?' Robinson exclaimed, once his laughter had subsided. 'What is she like?' When Jasmine left, his mood became confessional.

'I picked her up the other day and shouted at her in the car, because she had left her coat at school. Something had happened at work, and it had spilled over. When we got to the house I went upstairs and sat on the bed with my head in my hands. I said to myself, that's not her fault, Karl. I went downstairs and said, "Oi, come here you. I'm sorry." She said, "What for? You're always shouting." Makes you think, eh?

'Coincidentally, I was on the phone that night to Robbie Fowler. He's a mate, and was going to London to do a show called *Big Star, Little Star*. That's when a kid goes on TV and answers questions about his dad. He said his son was going to cane him. I told him to bribe him on the way down. When I told Jasmine she said, "Can we do that, Dad?"

'It was a typical night. We were lying on the couch. I'm watching football on TV, and she's watching a film on her laptop. "Right," I said. "Give me three bad things about your dad." She thought for a moment and said, "Well. You never answer me because you are always on the phone. You're rubbish at cooking. You swear when I am in the back of the car."

'Guilty. I try to hang football up on the peg when I get home, but it is not that easy. I take my daughter swimming, early on Sunday mornings. We also go out for a coffee, and walk around the local lake. She's lovely, so innocent. One day we were laughing, messing about. Someone came up to us and said, "You find losing funny, do you?"

'It was incredible. What a stupid thing to say. This was someone I didn't know, intruding on my time, my family time, but I had to close my ears so as not to cause a scene. That's why so many managers become almost a recluse the day after a game. People are all too willing to tell you what you should have done, what they would have done.'

A child's logic is both poignant and powerful. It came to the fore when Peterborough United sacked Darren Ferguson, following a 3–0 loss at MK Dons on February

23. He had been in philosophical mood in Robinson's office after the match; the pair are not particularly close, yet their affinity did not require restatement.

'Darren is such a good manager. We have a healthy rivalry. I love beating him and he really enjoys beating me. We were playing their reserves on the Monday, and Bradford were playing at Swindon on the Tuesday. We agreed to meet there, to have a coffee and a chat. The next thing I know I get a text off my kit man, who is at the ressie game. "Darren's gone," it read. I went, "Darren who?" I didn't put two and two together.

'It felt really weird. I mentioned it when I got home that night. Jasmine asked me, "Does that mean we will be sleeping on the street one day?" I realised immediately what she meant. We had been watching a documentary on homelessness together. She wanted to know how people end up on the street. I spoke about personal problems, illness and unemployment. That's where the idea came from.

'You are never safe in this job. The fear of being sacked drives me on. There's not a day goes by when I don't get into my car and think this could be my last. I walk around the place with my biggest smile on, saying hello to everybody, but what happened to Darren shook me. I thought to myself, this game is not right. It is not right.'

He prided himself on the inclusive nature of his management. He had replaced Gary Waddock as first-team coach with Richie Barker, who needed time to breathe after punishing spells as manager at Crawley Town and Portsmouth. Former Republic of Ireland midfield player Keith Andrews, a friend re-signed on loan from Bolton Wanderers, was taking his coaching badges and working informally with the Dons' development squad.

Robinson's remit has rare breadth, since he sets and sustains the club's philosophy from the academy to first team. He was looking to strengthen the youth system with a similarly far-sighted coach, and was advised to consider Joe Dunne, who remained out of work, six months after leaving Colchester United.

'Joe is one of the best coaches and tacticians out there. I know this sounds harsh, but he got himself sacked. He's an amazing motivator, but took too much on his shoulders. It made the job unbearable for him. I saw him change, look more tired. He wasn't himself. He came out after a game here and said, "I should be sacked for that." That's something you should never do.

'What defines a good manager? Spending millions in the Premier League or surviving with no money? Success to a Burnley is not success to a Chelsea. In our league success to Colchester won't be success to Bristol City. A chairman and manager must understand what winning means for them. Joe is a good man, and you never know what was said behind his back. Everyone thinks they can do this job better than others, and there's only one way of finding out.'

Dunne remained positive, despite lingering, lacerating frustration. He had fulfilled a long-held promise by moving to Suffolk, but, having turned down an early chance to manage in the League of Ireland, he was willing to move abroad to renew his career. He had been narrowly beaten to the assistant manager's job at Portsmouth by Waddock.

'Karl's got my CV,' he chuckled. 'It has gone to the four corners of the globe. Doors get closed on you all the time, but you become a stronger person for it. You have to persevere, stay positive, and hopefully one day you will be the one who gets a call. I know when I get back in the game I will be better at my job.

'I was put in for the job in Ireland by Steve Cotterill, who has been a good friend. They wanted to speak to me on Skype, but reception in my new village is very poor, so I had to drive to a lay-by after dropping the children off at school. I talked to them for forty minutes and things went well. They invited me over to complete the formalities, but I just sat in my car afterwards, weighing up the decision.

'I liked the sound of it. They wanted me to remould the club, rebuild from the bottom upwards. For the previous two years, at Colchester, I had given it my all. I had sacrificed everything. I put so many things at risk. I have been in football for twenty-six years, and have been married to Natalie for twenty-five of those years. It was time to put my family first.

'I called the club back, thanked them for their interest, and told them to go with someone else. People said, "What are you fucking doing?" but I don't regret what I did. There's no point in regret and bitterness. I feel good, focused. I'm still ahead in my career pathway. I originally wanted to be a manager by the time I was forty-five. I made it at thirty-nine. I'm now forty-one. The longer this goes on, the more I'll need a break.'

Sean Dyche was two years older. He was exactly where he needed to be.

16

Seeing Through the Noise

It was the sound of the first cuckoo of spring, shrill and self-regarding. José Mourinho condemned 'criminal' challenges, citing four incidents in a home draw with Burnley to support his latest conspiracy theory. In so doing, he traduced a team he evidently considered to be at the knuckle-dragging end of football's evolutionary scale.

Sean Dyche did not get mad. He got more than even, in a 10-minute 47-second monologue into the lens of a single camera. It was a masterly point by point rebuttal of the Chelsea manager, in which repeated assertions of respect were as acidic as his rationality, professional insight and forensic analysis. He protected his players and, for good measure, concluded his case with a video clip which exposed the champions-elect as cheap and faintly nasty.

Anyone with Dyche's shaven head, sculpted goatee

beard, piercing eyes, furrowed brow and pebble-dashed voice gets used to lazy stereotyping. He is routinely compared to a nightclub doorman or the sort of 70s detective who imposed order by fitting up the manor's more troublesome villains. This showed him in a new, authentic light; he demonstrated a QC's ruthless articulacy and sensitivity to the human condition.

It added to his lustre as an emerging manager of the highest quality. It was one thing to get Burnley promoted into the Premier League on one of the lowest budgets in the Championship, entirely another to keep them there while spending the equivalent of a string of shiny beads. His group were mainly English, prodigiously hard-working, impeccably organised and imbued with a Churchillian spirit of defiance.

This was his idea of a day off. He had arrived home in Northampton at 2.15 a.m., after a game at Turf Moor. He was up for the school run five hours later, and, apart from a brief diversion to sort out the builders as they installed new windows, spoke engagingly and knowingly until it was time for a return trip across town to pick up his son, Max, at 3.30 p.m. They then went to watch his daughter, Alicia, ice-skate.

His intensity was leavened by moments of self-deprecation. He was no glib propagandist; he thought deeply about what he was saying, and was unafraid of screaming silence. He combined the components of a journeyman's playing career with experiences as coach and manager at Watford, who sacked him in adopting the business model developed by their new owners, the Pozzo family.

That was not the sort of dismissal to deface a CV. He was the first of 12 candidates to be interviewed for the Burnley job, when Eddie Howe returned to Bournemouth in October 2012. He impressed with his respect for the club's ethos, and was called back for confirmation that the caricature of a Rottweiler centre half could not be further from the truth.

He understood: 'You look like me. You've had a career like me. Everybody thinks I was this mentalist as a footballer. I was only sent off twice, only once for a straight red, when I was thirty-six. I was never suspended for bookings; the most I got in a season was three. Now, either I was the cleverest hard man in the world, or I actually played quite fair, quite tough, and gave out body language that I meant business.

'I was a tricky centre midfield player as a kid at Nottingham Forest, a passer. The lower leagues moulded me into what I became, because you have to learn to fight. They were more brutal then than they are now, I can assure you. Here's the other thing about perception against fact. When I left Watford, I started doing Sky. I was on the panel there. Very quickly, things started turning.

'I'm not up my own arse about it, but people started going, "Hang on, there's more to this ginger skinhead.

He's got some good thoughts on the game. He's actually thinking." We do question the media at times, but the power of the visual media was invaluable to me. People see how you say things. They see your authenticity, see you care.

'The term I use is "seeing through the noise". That may not make sense to some, but imagine this scenario. You walk into a bar and your mate's on the other side of the room. It's hectic, mental. You can't hear yourself think, but you still catch eyes and know what's going on. That kind of analogy works in football management.

'There's all this stuff on the outside, media talk, internet sites, perception against misperception, fact against fiction. Your job is to see through all that, and even see through results at times. We are arguably the biggest underdogs the Premier League has ever seen. Maybe Blackpool were similar, but I don't say that for effect. We have nowhere near anyone else's resource base.

'We didn't win for the first ten games, so one reporter asks, "Will you ever win a game?" I said, "What, ever? Ever again?" You know, just scoffing at him really. Having fun with him, not trying to be offensive. Then someone else said, "They'll only ever win a game when they get relegated," and everyone gets involved.

'You have to look through that noise. I'm looking at the players' performances. I'm looking at the analytics. I'm looking at the facts. It's about being a motivator, an organiser, being empathetic, sympathetic, psychologically strong. It's about being a developer, an innovator, though I'm not keen on that word to be honest, because it implies you're reinventing the wheel, which I'm certainly not. This game has been going for a hundred and fifty years, so you pretty much find that every tactic, every organisational trend, has been used before.

'People rebrand it, repackage it, sell it again, but that's not really my bag. I'm currently trying to get everything to work at once, because we can't touch what we really need. Experienced or recognised Premier League players are out of our world financially, not just with the fees but the wages.

'Seven of the clubs in the Championship have got a bigger wage bill than we've got in the Premier League. You'd be amazed at some of their numbers, amazed. They have players on thirty-five grand a week, and then some. I've got to try and build a club for the future. I believe in what we do because I'd describe myself as a custodian. My job is to look after the club.

'Other managers have been saying, "Why don't you go out and get all the money you can and spend it?" but I was brought up a certain way by my parents. My dad was in business. You don't risk what you've built, unless it has to be done. People forget Charlie Austin was sold a year ago to allow the club to move forward financially.

'Are you really going to throw all that Premier League money on to the pitch and keep your fingers crossed, knowing that in two years' time you're going to have to sell someone to pay the electric bill? Because, believe me, there aren't any sugar daddies at Burnley. They're wealthy, but not football club wealthy, where you can throw away twenty million a year. That's what it takes now.

'The board, the club and myself have a realistic way of working. If that alignment goes, that's when you see trouble. When the manager starts saying, "Why are they doing this?" the board start saying, "He should be doing that." The players will say, "Well, where do we fit into all this?" It's not helpful to anyone. I can't see how that is healthy.

'My parents had good moral fibre. I put a lot of my way of working down to that. I was brought up in an era where if your job was to clean the floor, you'd make sure it was the cleanest it had ever been. If your job was to paint the fence, it was painted properly. If your job was to do your schoolwork, you didn't just do the basics. I still insist on those standards, even now.

'My team is built on respect, honesty, desire, will, demand, self-demand, pride, passion, all the things that are seemingly unfashionable in this country. I feel quite strongly about it, because I see some ridiculous things going on with our youth footballers, and nobody wants to stop it. I've never seen anything like it.

'Parents need to be educated. I'm not getting on my high horse about how they bring their kids up, but I'm referring to football education. Some old-fashioned beliefs are absolutely relevant to the modern game. We've got so drunk on technical detail that people have forgotten about moral fibre, about what it takes to walk out in front of seventy-eight thousand and deal with it.

'There are thousands of young, lovely-looking foot-ballers who can receive on the back foot. They can pass, but when the ball's coming into the box, I'm not seeing so many centre halves who want to head it. They want to block it, kick it. I don't see many wide players who want to take the risk of dribbling past someone and beating them.

'I don't see many centre forwards who want to head it like their life depends on it. I see lots who want to score a trendy goal. That seems to be the in-vogue thing. I just like people who score goals. They can score them however they want. I'm not trying to be a dinosaur here, but in the old days you had to earn the right.

'I left Forest, to go backwards to go forwards. I played two hundred senior games before I earned a contract that you would recognise as being decent. Now, there are players in youth systems earning more than I ever earned as a player, and they're probably never going to kick a ball in the first team. I find that astonishing.

'There are a lot of players whose desire has gone by

the time they're twenty-one. Basically, they're confused. They've been paid a hell of a lot of money almost to the point of it being life-changing, but they've never played in the first team at their own club. There are some really conflicting messages out there.'

Don't run away with the notion that here is one of life's regimental sergeant majors, pining for the return of National Service and the brain-numbing conformity of square-bashing. Dyche is inclusive by nature, but uses freedom of expression in a subtle, educational manner. His first act as Burnley manager was to give his players a questionnaire, to gauge individual and collective character.

'It was very simple. They had complete anonymity. I wasn't interested in who said what. I wanted them to be respectful of the process, but if they wanted to be flippant, they had the right. I just told them, "Fill it in, bring it back. I'm just interested in knowing what your thoughts are." You can quickly tell the ones who take it seriously even by watching them disperse around the room.

'You immediately see the ones looking at someone else's answer, like when they were at school. You see the one who has his arm covering his sheet, because he might be saying something he doesn't want the others to see. You see the one who has his shoulders back, telling you, "I'm prepared to say it all."

'You watch out for those tiny nuances, those little

idiosyncrasies. You get them in and feed it back. You say, "Right, this is where you've told me we're at. These are the things you want changing. These are the reasons why." You then go through the negotiables and the non-negotiables. My non-negotiables are really basic things.

'We work hard at all times. We show respect. Honesty and endeavour are a given. Show enthusiasm or say goodbye. We won't have people wandering around with headphones on. That might change in the future, because it's fair to say there are certain cultures where that is important. As Brian Kidd once said, you can have a fight every day; it's which fight you want to win.

'Don't get me wrong. This is not set in stone, because if I went into a different group with a different culture, I might have to be flexible. I try to debate, to nurture. I try to get them to open up in small groups. Then we'll put ideas and views to a bigger group, and build it into a collective voice.

'There are different kinds of leadership. I was deemed a leader as a player, because I've got a big mouth and I can shout instructions. David Beckham wasn't a big voice, but he delivered by example. His stats were phenomenal. His message was: "I will do it for you. I'm willing to run for you. All I expect is for you to do everything that you can to deliver." It's almost subliminal.

'I've learned over the past six months how quickly

people become affected by success, and change. I don't think I have. I've learned there's no magic answer, and that people can't wait to drag you down. It is almost a jealousy thing, within football managers and coaches. It creeps in from the outside, which is strange. I enjoy people's success, and I tell them so.

'I don't do envy. I've known John Still a while, from when I was at Watford. He'd bring his team over and we'd play. I send him texts now: "Hi, mate, brilliant what you're doing." I do that a lot to people because I know how hard it is. It's my personal choice, but I don't do debranding of managers. I don't do slagging off of other teams.

'What do I mean, debranding? The favourite way to debrand another manager is to comment on how they play. It's like a vicious sting; if you kick the ball more than thirty yards, they tell you that you play direct. We had that all last year, so I don't even bother with it. I can show you the pass notes. I can show you the stats. But what's the point? We got promoted. I choose not to get involved.'

It was tempting to close my eyes, to kill the image of this physically imposing man, edging forward to make his points. A cold page can strip words of their warmth, their life force. This was a process of greater sophistication than a settlement of scores; it was someone searching within himself to share the truth of who he was, and how he worked.

He was ahead of me: 'Psychology says that within four seconds of meeting someone you've formed an opinion, without even speaking. So it's fair to say, if you walk into a group of footballers you are immediately scanning the room. There's no definitive answer to this but I'll give you a feel of it. If I walked into a dressing room, I reckon within a morning I could go back to the manager and say, "Right, he's that, he's that, he's that." I reckon my strike rate would be pretty good.

'Loads of managers and coaches could do the same. You can sense it, smell it. Just by a very few conversations, watching and listening to the group, you'd know the leaders, the followers, the alpha males. You'd know the fraud, because you always get the fraud, the one who thinks he's the alpha male but if you scratch the surface he's got nothing. It's amazing.

'One of the biggest achievements in management, because it has changed massively, is softening egos, getting rid of agendas, getting them to understand that the group will sort out everything. I sell that to players all the time. When the group achieves, even if you're out of the team, you'll be looked upon differently.

'I'll give you an example. We were top of the league last season, doing great. Some of our subs moved on. The reason they got another club is because people thought, oh, they were part of a really good team. Think of what happens when the group underachieves. You're at the wrong end of the table, you're not in the team, and you've got your agenda. You're giving it big ones and you're mouthing off. Trust me, no manager is going to be looking at you when you are let go.

'It's rare that you get a group that aren't giving their all, but you do get it. I've been in a couple where, to use that favourite expression, people have downed tools. It comes and goes, it's strange. Clive Woodward talked about "sappers" and "energisers". Paul Sturrock called them "crows" and "pigeons". Others speak about "terrorists" and "mavericks", or "assassins" and "mavericks".

'It's bizarre. You can remove three individuals from a dressing room and the whole feel changes. Sometimes you only need to remove one. I was talking to another manager about this the other day. Every one of us would take the maverick, touched with a little bit of genius, but nobody wants the terrorist, however talented, because he will quickly change the dynamic of the group.

'You know when you're in a good group. I went through the divisions, played at a few clubs, and you can sense it very, very quickly. There are a few in the middle, where it's good, but not going to get you where you need to go. I've had four promotions as a player and one as a manager. Every group has been right, for that season. And I've seen it quickly turn.'

Some questions accelerate time; others make it stand still. When I asked him to consider what Sean Dyche the manager would think of Sean Dyche the player he paused for what seemed an eternity. He puffed his cheeks out, gazed into the middle distance, and allowed a small smile to play on his thin lips.

'Full-on. Opinionated. Not tough to deal with, but I'm going to have to deal with him at some point. I'd very quickly say, he's going to stand up and do it for me. If he moans, I'll take that because he'll still get it done, whether he thinks it's right or wrong. If he has a fallout he's going to sort it. The dressing room's going to be good because he'll make sure it's good. Underneath any edges he's got, he knows the fundamentals of how the group should operate.

'I've worked this out about myself. When John Duncan and Kevin Randall came in at Chesterfield it was a big turning point in my career. I was a young player, and didn't understand what they wanted. They didn't understand what I didn't get about what they wanted. I had a season of that weirdness, and nearly left.

'I went to Crystal Palace for a trial, as part of a swap deal. I was on a real low when I went there, but they wanted to sign me. That was a great boost, because they were at a higher level, but the money didn't work, so I had to go back. I delivered really good performances, and do you know why? One day John had me in and actually asked my opinion. It was about defensive positioning.

'That's all I really wanted, that little moment to be heard and rationalised. I didn't even need to be agreed with. I just felt, I can't get through to these people. They see me as this cocky Herbert who's got a lot to say for himself. He's a young player and should do what he's told. To be fair to John, he thought, he's got something to offer here. It was almost like a flick of a switch.'

Tellingly, Dyche still regards Duncan as a mentor. A pivotal personality in Chesterfield's run to the FA Cup semi-finals as a third-tier team in 1997, he earned what seemed to be an ideal move to Bristol City. He made only 17 appearances in two years, and underwent another unseen rite of passage.

'There was a hard core of about five or six players who were the daddies of the dressing room. They were getting a bit older, a bit cliquey. I was twenty-six, had a great season with Chesterfield the season before, and it is fair to say I was not backward in coming forward, without being disrespectful. I was a strong character and they immediately thought, hey, he's a threat.

'Off the pitch it was difficult, and on it I kept getting injured. The mix wasn't right. I had started thinking about coaching, management, team modelling, team thinking. It formed me as a manager, without a shadow of a doubt, because it gave me an understanding of the realities of the ugly side of football.

'I went there as quite a big signing. The fans didn't take to me. I learned about the human element, how you should and shouldn't treat people. I learned about dealing with media spin, because Bristol City is quite a big club in that neck of the woods. They saw themselves as massive, which was interesting in itself, because they were in the third tier of football at the time.

'It was intriguing, because I had an insight into support systems for injured players. I thought it was going to be hand in glove, but they were not getting me and I was not getting them. It was a big shock, really odd to have this feeling of "me and them". That's why, as a manager, I've tried to keep a handle on the balance of my dressing room.

'Players speak to the staff, rather than the gaffer. I value my staff and make it clear to them I don't want tit-for-tat stuff. They know they only tell me something that really needs influencing because it could hurt the group. Footballers moan a lot. There's moaning for moaning's sake, when we all know it's flippant, and a damaging moan. It sounds ridiculous but you fathom the difference very quickly.

'It's the difference between a maverick and an assassin. Mavericks moan but you know they're going to do it. I was a bit like that, I suppose. Not in my skill level, but I would have a moan at the manager, which he accepted because I dealt with things in the dressing room. I could work players out, even the cute, clever ones who say all the right things and do all the wrong things.'

His growing stature led to an invitation to address candidates on the FA's Pro Licence course in March. They included fellow managers Mark Warburton, Jimmy Floyd Hasselbaink, Dave Flitcroft and Andy Awford, in addition to his assistant at Burnley, Ian Woan. His treatise on leadership – "I'm not here as a guru, I'm not here as the font of all knowledge, and I'm not here to pontificate" – contained insights from the original maverick, Brian Clough.

He knew Dyche as 'young ginger', an apprentice whose year-long growth spurt made him five inches taller and two stones heavier. Clough expected his garden to be tended, but would invite him into the first-team dressing room, where his unorthodox approach intensified the clarity of the message.

'There's an art to delivering information in a dressing room. It has to be done in a manner that, even if it's theatrical, it's believable. Brian Clough was the best, because he could do it in very short blasts, in the most surprising ways. It wasn't always about tactics. It was the mood, the feel, the timing, the love, the hate, the power, the anger, all at the right time.

'I remember distinctly seeing Forest come in three–nil up at half-time and he absolutely ripped them to bits. I've seen him at three–nil down saying, "Well done. You're doing terrific, lads. That's how we play at Nottingham Forest, we keep playing like that." They then go out and get a three–three, or something. He used to say, "Hey, young ginger. Go and sit next to someone who plays in your position."

'One day me and Steve Stone, who's a big mate of mine, were in there with another lad, Craig Ball, to get a feel of things. I'm not kidding. Cloughie got on his hands and knees with a towel, and crawled over to the middle of the dressing room. He curled the towel up, put a ball on top of it, and went on his hands and knees back to the benches.

'It was quiet. They didn't have ghetto blasters in those days. He simply started pointing at the ball. When the referee's bell goes, he keeps pointing and says, "There she is, look after her. All the best, captain." That was his team talk, done. The players get up, line up, get out there and win two–nil. Now imagine me going home and telling my dad that story about the legendary mystical tactician, the brilliant manager.

'My dad's going, "you're kidding me." And I'm going, "No, Dad, I swear, Dad." The simplicity of it was genius. The hardest thing as a manager is to say a lot in not many words. At half-time, for example, when there are a million things going through a player's brain, you can lose them with too much information. Psychologists say go for three points they will remember, particularly three buzz words. But you can imagine what I'm thinking as a youngster: wow, what is going on here?'

His influences are eclectic. Lennie Lawrence reignited his playing career on loan at Luton. Mark McGhee and the late Ray Harford made him think at Millwall. Aidy Boothroyd's acerbic honesty, in releasing him as a player at Watford and re-employing him as a coach two years later, was cleansing, for both. Brendan Rodgers, Boothroyd's successor at Vicarage Road, remains a friend.

When we piece together the jigsaw of what makes a successful manager, it contains shards of bone, scraps of sinew and slithers of grey matter. Dyche's sensitivity may not fit the stereotype. His assertiveness does not translate easily. Yet he appreciates the mechanics of getting the best out of himself. He has developed the confidence to change.

'If you want me to be brutal, if you're going to bullshit people, you'd better remember your bullshit. But if you're going to be honest, you don't have to remember anything because you've just told it how you see it. That's why I won't project to my players about honesty or authenticity without delivering it. I don't spin. I'm not trying to work an angle.

'Five years ago I was typical. I came out of the game with a bee in my bonnet. I'm now not afraid of money being someone's key driver. It's not mine, but if it is someone else's, fine. Last season we were saying to the players they had every possible means of fulfilment within their grasp.

'We told them, "If you want money, go for it, and you'll get money. If you want kudos, you'll get kudos, if you get this job done. If you want local fame, you're going to get it. If you want national fame, you're going to get it. If you want to nick a bird, you'll get a bird on the back of what you're doing now. If you want the car, you'll get the car. And if you just want plain old-fashioned winning and success, you're going to get that as well."

'So I've got no problem, as long as a player is stimulated to drive forward and get what he wants. Like most, I used to go, it's disgraceful, all they want is money. Well, so what? As long as you're giving everything to me, the team and the cause, you go for your life. My personal thing is winning. That's what I do it for, that's my buzz. Get that right and everything else will come anyway.'

He is not keen to amplify recent praise from Sir Alex Ferguson, since 'your peer group go, "oh, do me a favour. What are you doing? You egg." He is, though, quite happy to rationalise his habit of cold-calling fellow managers, if he hears they have been at a Burnley match.

'Friends will tell you what they think you want to hear. Family will tell you roughly what they think you want to hear, but managers will tell it as it is. You can usually get a number for them in our business, so I ring them: "Hi, Sean Dyche. What did you think? Tell me the brutal truth." It is important to get that outside view. It can help if you are emotionally or physically stretched. Sometimes you've been working so hard you can't see the wood for the trees.

'I'm lucky because I have a hard core of mates. We've known each other since we were five. Quite frankly, they don't particularly give a toss about me and football, they never did. They like football but they're not of football. They are my go-tos, for my ups and downs, ins and outs. Hopefully they are always going to be there for me.

'We have a curry night now and again. All the stories come out. The fish gets bigger, the bird gets uglier, we drank more; we tell the same stories a thousand times over, and wet ourselves laughing to the point where our wives do that face that women do, like, what are they on about? Idiots. I don't think my mates realise just how important that is to me.

'This job is intoxicating. You can morph into something different. I'm forty-three, pretty young to be doing what I'm doing. Imagine if my future keeps going on an upward curve, and I end up at what you'd regard as a really big club, with no disrespect to Burnley. You might meet me in four years and think, where's the geezer who was popping home to see the builders and get his hands dirty and then coming out for a coffee?

'I'd like to think I won't change but I can't guarantee it. This isn't about management but about life. I really like music, and saw Kasabian after a show the other day. We were in a small room, maybe thirty feet square. There were friends, family, people they've known for years. There's drink, and the stereo goes on. No lights, just a big speaker with a phone.

'For three hours it was mayhem, laughter, dancing, joking. These guys are going to be regarded as rock legends, yet they know the world they live in is false. I'm the same. I take great pride and enjoyment in some of the doors that open because of football, but I know where I live, that's my point. I go off home to my kids, my family, that's my number one priority. Bar none.'

17

Back for Good

A solitary car, a black Range Rover, is parked outside the main entrance at Dean Court. Dawn is beginning to break, a grey watercolour wash giving texture to the poplars and silver birch trees which line the pathways on adjoining parkland. It is 6.35 a.m., and a light from the stadium's first floor signals that football's most coveted young manager is already at work.

Eddie Howe is on his laptop in his office, methodically analysing another victory. He clips small sequences of play, both good and bad, and transfers them into the electronic folders of individual players. He seeks to praise whenever possible, and caution privately, in one-on-one review sessions designed to remove ego and insecurity from the learning process.

Outside, joggers in high-visibility cagoules are purging their souls, while defying their body clocks. Office workers are starting to fill the other 399 spaces in the car park. A security guard goes on his final patrol of the night shift, past the East Stand and beneath the Bubbles Champagne Bar.

Assistant manager Jason Tindall and first-team coach Simon Weatherstone arrive, primed to add depth to the debrief. Training plans, colour-coded, position-specific and designed to address individual strengths and weaknesses, must also be confirmed if they are to stay ahead of the game.

The players have been given the day off, but the majority report for a warm-down. Rituals reassure as a long season reaches its pinch-point; they log on to computers each morning to reflect on their mood and give a sense of their physical well-being. Any potentially stressful incidents, including domestic issues and family illnesses, are also recorded.

Circular tables in the players' lounge are designed to encourage interaction between teammates. The PlayStation console and ubiquitous table tennis table must not be used until after lunch. Howe decrees that if players are there to work, they require no distractions. The atmosphere is aspirational, with honours boards in club colours – black, white and cherry red – lining the wall.

The prize is glinting in the near distance. AFC Bournemouth are setting the pace at the top of the Championship, which is as crowded as a nightclub dance floor in the pheromone frenzy of the last lunge just before 2 a.m. Doubters who dismissed them as insubstantial adornments have dissolved into the background. A place in the Premier League is within reach of a club which six years earlier was 92nd in the 92-club pyramid.

Howe entered local legend by managing Bournemouth through administration and a 17-point deduction. The club's future was secured in the last home game of the 2008–09 season, when they came from behind to beat Grimsby 2–1. One of the items on his 'to do' list is to find a suitably inspiring image of Steve Fletcher scoring the decisive goal with ten minutes remaining. He intends to have it magnified and installed in the stands.

'That was a spine-tingling moment. I'll never, ever forget it. It was one goal, but it was the goal that kept us in the League. It was scored by the guy I'd re-signed on a free transfer. Steve was such a key figure in the club's history. He was thirty-six, our appearance record holder. That was his one hundredth League goal. I was nearly in tears on the touchline, because of the incredible way in which events unfolded. The football club was safe. That was the biggest thing.

'I don't want to over-egg it, but you couldn't really write the story of how and why we took over. I was so young, thirty-one. I'd no previous managerial experience. Several board members told me, "If we go down into the Conference this club is finished." It might have been all over anyway, because the bailiffs were in literally every day. It was, "We want kit, we want money, we want this, we want that."

'The players weren't paid for two, two and a half months. We couldn't pay for the training ground, a local school, so they were threatening to kick us out. I don't think the scenario could have been more grim. I would be negotiating about the electricity bill, having conversations with the water company about not cutting us off. It was surreal, because I look back with such fondness at those times. I absolutely loved it and learned so much.

'We had nothing. I knew we had to build a really good team spirit. We had to use adversity to our advantage by creating a siege mentality and almost turning players against everybody else, including our own board. I don't think we realised how serious it was for them, having to explain things to their wives and families.

'I've experienced instances of results having an effect on people's jobs. It's not necessarily the players who are affected. It's those in supposedly smaller roles at the club. It doesn't sit easily with me, it really doesn't. That burden of responsibility is one of the things which motivate me to get up in the morning when it's still dark, to come in and try to make the team better.

'When you take the job you know you're going to have to accept the consequences. I'm always here by six thirty and I still don't have enough time, because things run away with you. The morning is the key time, where you plan and organise. That's when you earn your money because your training session is going to dictate what's going to happen on a Saturday.

'I know it's a bit of a cliché, but the thing I enjoy the most is the planning of the sessions. You've got a blank page. That's not to say we don't repeat sessions, because there are key things which confirm what we're about, but in the main, I'll always say to the guys I want something new and fresh. The aim is to come up with something which stimulates and tests the players.

'Jason, Simon and I bounce off each other really well. We work things through together, and throw ideas around until we develop a plan. We're pretty hands-on here, and when we meet up with the players the first thing we look for is body language. That's huge; you can tell straight away whether someone is happy, sad, upset. You can sense good moods and bad.

'I'll try to speak to everyone before we train. They're not long conversations, more like, "How are you? Is everything OK?" but those little gestures are so import-ant, you can't underestimate them. I can only speak from experience, but the emotional side of the game affected my performances probably more than even I realised at the time.

'When I was playing it was, "Get on with it. You're here to do a job, train and play, so it doesn't matter if your kid is sick." I try to be a shoulder to lean on, to help in any way I can in those circumstances, because it can only help you, as a manager, and the player himself in the long run.

'Attitudes do change. We all move on. Some players can take personalised reviews of their performance, but you do get "Why are you telling me this, leave me alone," especially from the older guys. The younger guys are more used to reviewing because of the academy culture, so they are a lot more open to it. I don't really care, because I think it's the right thing to do, so I do it. They'll get used to it and it'll be part of their daily work.'

Howe has now moved from his office, with its nerve-centre sense of purpose, to a second-floor corporate box. He is a solicitous host, pouring the tea and exchanging managerial small talk. It's probably not the time to confide that, in similar circumstances, one of his peers referred to him and Tindall as 'the boy band'.

It was a flippant observation – 'They're too bloody good-looking for our game' – which contained a grain of truth. Howe, with his hint of shyness and signs of a creative temperament, would fit the Gary Barlow model. Tindall, slightly taller, dark-haired and a little more rugged, could well appeal to the Robbie Williams demo-graphic. Whatever flight of fancy those comparisons represent, Howe concedes they are a well-rehearsed double act.

'Your number two needs to inspire you in some way.

If there isn't that positivity you're going to get friction in the relationship because you're so close. I spend more time with Jason than I do with my wife, there's no doubt about that. We were teammates but never friends in the time we played. We never gelled socially.

'When I got the job, which I didn't expect to be offered, he had been around the group as number two to Jimmy Quinn. It was strange. I just sort of knew I wanted Jason to stay. I don't know why. I'd chatted with him when he was manager at Weymouth, on his own. I'd gone to see his team play. We'd both given each other a little bit of information. I just thought, yeah, I'd like the chance to work with him.'

Like many managers, Howe, a former England Under 21 defender, is compensating for a playing career ruined by serious injury. His was sustained 51 minutes into his debut for Portsmouth, a 2–0 defeat at Preston North End on March 30, 2002, after he had been signed by Harry Redknapp from Bournemouth for £400,000. The consequences are recalled with understandable clarity.

'I dislocated my kneecap. That chipped a bit of bone underneath so I had a defect which basically meant that any time I squatted, I didn't have any power. I managed to hang in there for a few more years after being out for about eighteen months but I was nowhere near the same player after the injury.

'One surgeon told me I'd never play again. When you are twenty-four and you hear something like that out of the blue it concentrates your mind. I'd always thought about coaching, not management, but hadn't really done anything about it. I was still trying to get back to my best playing-wise, but it was pretty obvious that I was never going to get there. I knew I was on my last legs.

'Kevin Bond, who was manager here at the time, asked me to join the coaching staff. We'd got on really well together when we were both at Portsmouth, but I was reluctant to go straight from teammate to coach. As things turned out, I made that transition very quickly. I'd been friends with some of the players for a long, long time. I wouldn't say I shut them off totally, but that dynamic changed.'

He did not know it at the time, but Howe's direction of travel changed at the Raymond McEnhill Stadium on Sunday, December 3, 2006. He was sent to scout a second-round FA Cup tie in which Salisbury City, of the Conference South, held Nottingham Forest, League One leaders, to a 1–1 draw.

'I think Kevin recognised my work ethic. We had deep, deep talks about football when I was a player and he was a manager. We shared the same views on the game, and I vividly remember that Cup tie. Kevin couldn't get to it, and neither could Rob Newman, his assistant. Our next game was against Forest. We couldn't pay a scout to go, so he asked me to do it. That was the watershed moment.

'I did a report for him, and enjoyed it. We went on to win the Forest game. I played in it, funnily enough. From that moment Kevin looked at me and thought, he might have something to offer me. I was one of the most experienced players in the group. He knew he could trust me. Anything he told me and anything I told him, we knew would be in confidence.

'Now I'm on the other side I understand the thought processes involved. When, as a manager, you have a feeling that someone can help you in any way, you want them close to you. Things change, at a human level, when you are promoted from within the dressing room. People talk about a cut-off point, a line that has to be drawn.

'I agree with that, but you can still have a good, close relationship with players, just on another level. It doesn't mean you don't respect each other, it doesn't mean you aren't close to one another, it's just different. To be honest, I found it easy to come to terms with the different roles and responsibilities.

'You're never going to please everybody. That's something you learn the minute you take the job. You're going to be an unpopular figure, whether that's in your dressing room because you've got to make tough decisions, or whether that's from the crowd because you have to sell a player they love. A leader has to take the route he thinks is right. You have to accept criticism if it doesn't work.

'There was no bedding-in period of two or three months. I felt and thought like a manager the day I was appointed. I don't know why that was. Maybe I'd subconsciously prepared myself for that moment. I think every player dreams and thinks, this is what I would do as the manager. I don't agree with this, but I agree with that. It's natural.

'When I got the job here we were in dire straits. Staying in the league was everything, and behind the scenes things were in turmoil. But I felt normal. Dealing with that sort of stuff is not something you're ever taught; I don't think you can study it on a coaching course, or wherever. It's just intuitive. You know you can do it, so you just get on with it.

'Dealing with players is just the same. I get an instant feel for someone. I don't know how to describe it but I get a sense of them the first time we meet. Sometimes the way I deal with a particular person might evolve over time, but as a general rule you have to nail that as soon as possible. If you manage the relationship poorly, performances will suffer.

'There are several players in the current group I know I can raise my voice to. There are others who, if they have not had a good game, I'll ignore and speak to another day. I know confrontation will solve nothing, because barriers will be raised and there will be unnecessary negativity around the place.

'Being a football manager is a unique job, because

you don't have a teacher, in a formal sense, or someone to shadow. People appoint you and say, "You're supposed to be good at this. Come on, win us some games." I would say I'm self-taught. I watch training back every day; it takes me longer than the session itself, because that's the only way I can determine whether I am improving.

'Every two months I'll sit down and think, right, how has our training been, how are things working? Are our principles right? Do we need to evolve, do we need to change? Nobody is going to come round and say, "Right, I'm going to come and watch you train. I'm going to see how you do your job and I'll give you some tips."

'One, you'd never invite a stranger in. Two, there's nobody who's actually suited to that role anyway. You can't go to a competitor. You've got your courses and occasionally you're lucky enough to get a Premier League manager who will allow you to come in, but even that's getting more difficult now, unless you're out of work.

'Education is not easy. I wish there was an answer. I wish I could have said I'd worked with José Mourinho or Brendan Rodgers for one or two years. I'm sure I'd be a lot more advanced in my way of working than I am now, but the reality is you don't have the time or the luxury of the opportunity to do that.'

Rodgers had, in fact, been receptive to Howe's eagerness to learn. He was developing a reputation as the Sir

Alex Ferguson of his generation, a supportive figure concerned with the collective welfare of those who worked in more humble circumstances. It was a two-way street, since generosity with his time enabled him to measure the potential of those who aspired to his status.

Howe is fresh-faced, softly spoken. He may not fit the mould of a thrusting young executive, but he is expected to possess a professional instinct to go for the jugular. Managers like him, identified as coming men, must plan their career carefully. Loyalty is applauded, but complacency is easily inferred. The right offer to move on must be taken at the right time.

'I really left here because of outside pressures. That may sound funny, but I'd quickly turned down two jobs, at higher-placed clubs than us at the time. It's one of those accepted things in management, isn't it? You don't do that. Everybody told me, "You've got to go. These guys are coming in for you and you've got to leave."

'Peterborough came in first, and Southampton followed. I was like, but I've only been in the job six months. It's my first in management and I'm only thirty-one. It didn't make sense to me. I said no, but then we had a really good start the following season. We were first or second in League One. The speculation began to grow. Suddenly, again, I was in a crazy situation. I had three clubs who were without managers approach me and the club, wanting me.

'I could take my pick from Charlton, Crystal Palace and Burnley. I found myself in a position where I thought I couldn't pass up on the opportunity, because I would be seen to be lacking in ambition, or whatever it is people think you're lacking in if you turn down jobs. I actually had to take one, and that was how it panned out.

'I'd had a bit of a falling-out with the chairman here. That really pushed me over the edge to leave. I made a little bit of a mess of it in the end, because I was torn, and ended up taking the one furthest away, the toughest challenge, because I wanted to test myself and take myself out of the comfort zone of Bournemouth and the south coast. I thought I needed to show I could go away and have a crack at something else.

'I had twenty-one months at Burnley. I look back at my time there very fondly. I really do, even though it was the most challenging period of my managerial career. I never thought I'd made a mistake going there, but it never really got going. In terms of results it was frustrating because we felt we were close but never got there.

'I learned so much. We sold a lot of players and I had to build a totally new team. When you go to a new club, as an unknown, with no playing career of note to fall back on, you have to deal with the question: who is this guy with no name? I had to prove myself to Burnley supporters, and they would probably argue I never truly did.

'I believe I did a lot of work behind the scenes to change everything within the club. We recruited a lot of young players with the intention of starting all over again. We never saw the job through, so I really don't know if we would have been successful or not. Sean has gone on to do a great job and take the team to the Premier League. They were good to me and it is nice to see the club flying.'

The natural follow-up question of why he returned to Bournemouth elicits a revealing response. He leans forward slightly, and looks down at the long, dark table a moment more than strictly necessary. He clasps his fingers, as if he is making a conscious effort to remain composed. The reason becomes clear very quickly.

'I lost my mum. That was a real shock, out of the blue. This is the part of being a manager nobody sees. Mum died on the Saturday morning, and I missed that day's game against Crystal Palace because I was here, with her. On the Monday morning you're expected to get back to work, and you've just lost the key figure in your life. I found that incredibly, incredibly difficult.

'I didn't have any grieving process. All my family were back in Bournemouth. I felt really separated from them. Things just built and built and built, though not to the point where I would say my job was affected, because I was absolutely focused on that one hundred per cent. I was back in Burnley on the Monday because that was the best way to deal with it: to work, and try and forget everything else.

'The reality is, I never saw coming back here as an option until they were without a manager and approached Burnley. The minute I heard that I realised how much I missed this club. Then I thought, I've got people I need to help. I'm not the eldest son, but in a sense, I've always been seen as the responsible one. The opportunity to come back to my family was over-whelming. I had to make it clear to Burnley that was what I wanted. It was nothing to do with football.

'I never really had my dad in my life. My grandad was my father figure as I was growing up. He was brilliant with the football, taking me everywhere. My mum was my rock. She brought up five kids with no money. To lose her was a crushing blow for me.

'You're not superhuman, but as a manager you can't be upset or weak, because players are looking to you for strength. They want you to guide them, lead them and inspire them. I don't think I was truly myself after that period. I'm probably still not. Part of you dies when one of your parents dies. It's a big moment in your life.'

The room is suffused with his sadness. His eyes are moist, and his voice catches, faintly. He admits to standing on the touchline during matches because 'the supporters want their manager to give them emotion' but here, in private, he is as far removed from futile theatricality as it is possible to be. It is no surprise to learn of the influence of Sean O'Driscoll, who has followed Aidy Boothroyd in leaving the club game to become an England age-group coach.

'Sean and I lived in Burwood. He was playing and I was in the Centre of Excellence as a really young lad, of fourteen, fifteen. He used to drive me in. You know Sean, he's a very quiet guy and he'd hardly say a word to me. I was scared of him really, but I used to sit in the passenger seat alongside him. He became my youth-team manager, then my first-team manager, so I've gone on a nice little journey with him.

'I learned an incredible amount, just in terms of his integrity. He was of a new breed, with a different way of thinking. He questioned a lot of the stereotypes in football, in management and coaching – "Why are we doing this? I'm not doing that any more. We're going to do this." You listen to him, and suddenly you're thinking, yeah, he's right.

'Little things stick with you. When I was a first-year pro, at eighteen, Mel Machin, who was a brilliant manager, used to take us for a run along the beach every Monday morning. It was almost a recovery ritual. Get it done, get in your cars, get home. But for someone making their way like me, who hadn't played on the Saturday, it's the last thing you need.

'Sean said immediately, "We're not doing that. We're training. We're going to make you better." I think I've shared a lot of his philosophies. We believe in dominating possession for sure, but not for the sake of statistics. We believe very much in positive football, in combination play, wide. If there's a positive path then take it. Sean is very reserved, a very deep thinker. I've always been the same, an introvert, a deep thinker and an analyser. You can't change your personality, can you?'

That is true, but success in such a high-profile industry demands nuance of character and strength of will. Taking a club of Bournemouth's stature into the Premier League would be a career-defining achievement, a powerful reference. Speculation was becoming the soundtrack to his professional life; he was linked with Newcastle United, West Ham, and even mentioned in despatches as a possible successor to Roy Hodgson as England manager.

'I don't know how my career will evolve, to be honest. I try to play an absolutely straight bat to the questions, because the way I look at it I am simply trying to stay in work. It won't really be relevant until someone taps me on the shoulder and says, "See you later, we don't want you any more," or another club, ten years down the line, says, "We'll take you."

'If you start mapping your career out, saying, "I'm going to do this, this and this," you're going to fall flat on your face, because that is the essence of football management. I can't predict the future, just as I couldn't have predicted everything that has happened to me over the last five or six years. What's the point? Just try and do the job the best you can. Try and educate yourself, become the best person you can be, and see what twists and turns lie ahead, because it will be a bumpy road whichever way you go.

'I am in a very competitive business and this would be a really attractive job for anybody at the moment. The club's in a really good financial state, very ambitious. Why over-think things? That's wasted energy, wasted emotion. Why worry about things you can't influence, like somebody getting in the ear of the owner? What will be, will be. I'm in control, I can influence results.

'I'm still struggling with time management. The work/family balance is probably about ninety to ten to the football club. I really struggle to switch off. My phone is always on just in case. You live it, you breathe it, but you do need an understanding partner and an understanding family. My kids are three and three months, so they don't really know that yet. As they get older I'm sure they will.'

He laughs, and speaks of occasional release, running with Eric, his boxer dog, on the beach as darkness falls on another full day. The laptop is calling, and he intends to update the latest edition of his training diary. One final question: why does he do the job, ask so much of himself and those around him?

'If I wasn't doing this, what else could I do to make

a mark in society? You're only on the planet once as far as we know, and you want to try and do something that affects people's lives. I can think of no better way. Football is such an emotional sport. It affects people positively and negatively depending on results. I've seen the joy given by promotions and the sort of roll we're on at the moment. I want to be able to look back and say, "You achieved something memorable."'

A play-off place was assured, but in a Championship season which contained the elements of baseball's great pennant races, surprise and persistent pressure, four other managers of the highest quality were in there, pitching.

18

Hungry Like a Wolf

Footballers are rarely comfortable speaking openly in group situations outside the emotionally driven confines of the dressing room, so Kenny Jackett took a typically practical approach to preparing his squad for a session with sports psychologist Dave Young. He was politeness personified in requesting them to focus minds on the final seven games of the regular season.

Bournemouth led four clubs pushing for automatic promotion from the Championship. Wolverhampton Wanderers were in a secondary group of four more, which also included Ipswich Town, Brentford and Derby County, who were realistically competing for two play-off places. With margins so tight, the manager sought to assess the dynamics of a group he had assembled over the previous eighteen months.

'You have shown you have the will,' he told them, as they gathered in a first-floor analytics room at the

Compton training ground. 'You have the desire inside of you. We want to give you the tools to complete the job, so your input here will help us all. If you are open-minded for the next thirty minutes I would appreciate it.'

With that, he settled back on the margins, to make notes on an A4 pad. Players, in small groups, were asked to identify the determining factors in their promotion push, which had acquired timely momentum over the previous ten games. They took the task seriously, highlighting the tempo of training, the subtlety of squad rotation, and a tangible sense of unity as keys to their success.

Young then asked them to consider the dangers which lay ahead. Again, the answers were thoughtful, businesslike. They spoke of the need to retain mental equilibrium, to worry about their own performances instead of stressing over things they could not control, like the results of rivals. They promised not to allow a blame culture to take hold.

Benik Afobe, a 30-goal striker signed for £2 million from Arsenal in January, was a galvanising figure, despite his youth. Captain Danny Batth spoke with an authority beyond his 24 years. Richard Stearman, his defensive partner, injected positivity into the discussion, praising the team's growing maturity in seeing out matches by playing in the right areas, at the right time.

It was the sort of unseen ritual which rarely gets remarked upon but reveals much about the art of football management. Jackett was measured and supportive, but he enforced culture change by brutally isolating those players identified most closely with successive relegations from the Premier League to League One.

He had impressed during a three-week, three-tier interview process for the Wolves job in June 2013. His reputation as an exceptional development coach was compatible with a system that featured a Head of Football Development and Recruitment, Kevin Thelwell. The values Jackett had assimilated from his late father, Frank, were tenets of faith. His was a cold-eyed cull, expressed most starkly in physical terms.

The outcasts, christened 'The Bomb Squad' or 'Group Three', were obliged to change on their own, and train as far away from the first-team group as possible. They went through the motions, sullenly. Some, like defender Roger Johnson and midfield player Jamie O'Hara, lingered for more than a year before accepting their fate.

Jackett's clarity of purpose was striking. He understood the sensitivity of underachieving players driving cars worth in excess of £100,000 in an economically depressed area, and banned them from the training ground. He instituted runs through the town centre during the morning rush hour, so his players could see their fans going to do a full day's work. He invited supporters to join him on a tour of the Molineux Museum.

'I have knocked the walls down and built them again. They needed smashing to bits, quickly. There were quite a number of players here who were just waiting for something better to come along. That is not the right way to be. They were being paid very well, and were happy to tick over. You could see it in their eyes, sense it in their body language.

'The club was almost in suspended animation. I had to accelerate the process of change by isolating those who didn't have the hunger to make the most of themselves. I told them straight away they were not in my plans. It is best to get everything out in the open, because if they don't know what I want, they'll just complain, "The manager doesn't talk to me."

'There weren't too many rucks, just a couple of situations where people knocked on my door and said, "I should be in the fucking team." I was polite, said I was going down a different route, and eventually most of the lads drifted away. They needed the move. Naturally, they had their mates, but if anyone else sided with them internally, I got rid of them as well. It had to be that way.

'There had been a complete breakdown in the relationship with the supporters. The crowd needed new faces, a couple of home-grown players, a few fresh ones, and the odd one they'd never heard of. A change in atmosphere has to be player-led. It is a deeper process than just getting results. Fans have to see a sense of togetherness, of pride in playing for their club. It is a great club, a big club, and we have to show what a privilege it is to work here.

'We took five thousand to Preston in my first match as manager, even after all the crap. I've tried to embrace that yearning for what this club could be. I've tried to be humble and respectful, but I've also stepped back and worked out how we can use this to our advantage. It was toxic, horrible, but I had this feeling that this was for me.

'It has been pretty full on. Management can be difficult, especially for families, because moving around can leave you a little rootless. But then I look out of the window, at these fantastic facilities, and I think of my old office at Millwall, a Portakabin which swayed in the wind in winter. It is a great working environment.'

Fate decreed that Wolves' penultimate home game would be against Ipswich. Mick McCarthy, their manager, spent six seasons at Molineux, winning the Championship in 2009 before being sacked in February 2012. Three months later they were relegated from the Premier League after taking four points from their final 13 games, and the rot set in.

Managers see players through the prism of their own experience, and McCarthy was naturally protective of some of Jackett's pariahs, who remained a drain on resources since their wages had to be subsidised during the loan spells which preceded permanent transfers or contract annulments.

'There were a couple in that group I wouldn't have agreed with,' he admitted. 'Although Karl Henry could be a back-room boy, a bit of a barrack-room lawyer, he was fabulous. He came with me the week I got there and was there until I went. But it happens. Managers have to make their own decisions, make their own squad, and Kenny did the right thing in terms of telling people what he was going to do. Once that decision was made he may as well have had them as far away as possible.'

The pair are contrasting characters, but had a similar schooling at Millwall, a singular club that demands resilience and wry, self-protective humour from its leaders. Jackett spent five seasons at the Den, while McCarthy had six seasons there, as player and manager in the 1990s. Admiration is mutual, unforced.

'Longevity in this job is not an accident. I have a lot of respect for what Mick has done. He has passed the test of time and has not always had the best of resources. People respond to him, and he is very highly thought of here. I like to think I know him reasonably well. It is different when you are playing against someone on a Saturday, but when we are on our courses, we talk openly. You pick one another's brains to see if you have missed anything.'

McCarthy, with his silver hair, high forehead and

angular nose, is the more distinctive and demonstrative figure in the technical area. Jackett is a methodical, less expressive man, a wood pigeon to the Yorkshireman's bird of prey, but appearances are deceptive since he feeds voraciously off the human energy of the touchline.

'You've got to be your own judge and jury. You've got to learn to think on your feet. If you can't do that you are in trouble. I know some managers like the overview of being high up, but I couldn't sit down. I stand as close to that pitch as I can. There's a feeling you cannot get when you're in the stands.

'You can see who's blowing out of their arse. You pick up who is uninterested. You can hear who wants it the most. It's all information. You can tell if they're getting a little pissy, sense whether they're going to start losing concentration. There's something in the tone of their voices, or the way they try to disguise the fact they're breathing heavily.

'You sense a crowd at your back and react to their link to the players. One feeds off the other. If they're on them you've got to try to do something about it. You can't just blank them if they are unhappy. Whether you do anything is your choice, isn't it? That's got to be better than being up there in the stands, with all the old ladies shouting. There's too much that can come into your mind and stop you concentrating.

'Management is as mentally draining as you want to make it. It's like any job. Your outlook dictates your experience. You have to make sure that you're the one in control of your life. I mean, it's a game of football in the end. All right, we all want to win, and we might lose our job, but there are a lot worse things in the world.

'Think of the kids in cancer wards, young men being sent to Afghanistan and not coming back. This is a game that strips people of their perspective. You have to be realistic and optimistic, but you can't be blindly positive and not see the shit. A Premier League manager might not be able to go out for a coffee unmolested, but real pressure is getting sacked from League Two, when you're on thirty grand a year with two kids and the chairman says he'll pay you to the end of the month.

'I've got to be honest. There's more money in football than there ever has been at the higher levels and we all get a slice of the cake. For that, they're shining lights up your arse. It's twenty-four seven, but what do you want? If nobody was interested you wouldn't get well paid, because nobody would be buying satellite dishes. It's how it is. There's desperation for every story.'

The hysteria is reflective of the disconcerting speed of the media's evolution. But even if football has become soap opera, its basic truths remain untouched. Jackett was acquiring greater confidence and stature through adapting to a collegiate system which enabled him to concentrate on player development instead of being besieged by agents and the babble of the marketplace.

Long-term stability is achieved incrementally. He sought to establish clear pathways, from the Under 18s, through the development squad, to the first team. Kortney Hause and Dominic lorfa, England Under 20 players under Aidy Boothroyd, were ahead of the curve. Afobe embodied a far-sighted, finely scrutinised recruitment policy.

'The job has greater breadth now. I've got to be aware of a bigger group, not just the twenty-two I worked with this morning, but the fifteen young pros in the under twenty-ones who trained on the next pitch, and the three or four I'm looking to push through from the academy. It is a question of organisation, promotion at the right time.

'The nature of footballers hasn't changed; they're young men with the usual obsessions – cars, television, money and girls – but they are much more receptive to sports science than my generation. They've been brought up with fitness coaches and nutritionists, and are comfortable with technology.

'They bring their smartphones to the gym session, to check their programmes. Their game clips are available in a dropbox. They are more open-minded and the game is better for it. As for the way I do my job, the analysis side of things means I can watch any game from around the world. I try to keep a balance, because you can end up watching a lot but not seeing much.

'Time management is important. I've got to keep

myself fresh, and that comes down to good delegation. I'm still central to the decision-making process, but in terms of transfers Kevin does all the background work. He puts the feelers out, speaking to agents, clubs and parents. I get a steer on where we are financially.

'We want the system to work. There's no point somebody being sat in an office across from me saying, "Yeah, we're going to buy this lad," without my buy in, as manager. It has to be a collective decision. Kevin and I work out how best to present our ideas to Jez Moxey, the CEO, and Steve Morgan, the owner.

'It is something all managers will have to come to terms with. You have to learn new ways, very quickly. If you are going to work for someone you have to assess what he wants, what makes him tick. You need to develop your relationship, because if you don't get on with him, it is not going to work.

'I'm enjoying it. This is a good coaching environment. We felt we needed to change the playing style, by playing out from the back, because at a big club the product has to be right. Now we've got to try and use this momentum. Externally, we have got to be a little cute. No silly quotes, no easy motivation. Internally, we have to attack the opportunity. Our mindset has to be right. The Premier League is a realistic ambition.'

Around 160 miles away, in Mick McCarthy's ground-floor office on the outskirts of Ipswich, the eyes are drawn to a photograph of an old man with a single-word caption: 'Legend'. It is a portrait of his mentor, Norman Rimmington, who, at 90, works in the laundry room at Barnsley, the club he has served as player, coach, physiotherapist, groundsman, kit man, assistant manager and caretaker manager.

Rimmington was tending the pitch when he persuaded a 16-year-old centre half to reject an apprenticeship as an electrician at a local coal mine. McCarthy still calls him for advice, a gesture of humility and fealty which hints at the sensitivity of someone so often judged on straight-talking, wise-cracking superficialities.

'There's a prayer which should be on every football manager's wall: "God grant me the serenity to accept the things I cannot change, the courage to change the things I can, and the wisdom to know the difference." Even if there are certain things you can't change in this game that gives you a starting point.'

He became Millwall's player-manager soon after his 33rd birthday; his first decision was to drop one of his best friends, John Colquhoun, who went on to spend three years as Rector of Edinburgh University before becoming a football agent. Nearing the end of his 23rd season in management, McCarthy was effortlessly transported back to his first half-time team talk, from which he was rescued by his assistant Ian 'Taff' Evans.

'I often get asked the best piece of advice I can offer a young coach or manager. I tell them to get a damn good assistant. He needs to know your character, what sorts of players you like. He needs to be there for you, because this is an in sickness and in health business. Make sure he knows more than you. Taff did, and probably still does. I probably wouldn't be here today without him.

'That first game was against Port Vale. I'd been captain, but was completely wet behind the ears. I was probably seen as a good choice by some, a reasonable choice by others and a complete nonsense by the rest. That's the case of everybody who gets a job. I came in, started babbling and thought I was going to choke. My tongue was swelling up and I couldn't talk. Taff just took over.

'Football is a culture all of its own. You have to understand it to work within it, and Millwall gave me a fantastic introduction to its absurdities. The employment stats are crazy, even though I did my bit to up the averages by lasting four years there, seven with Ireland, three with Sunderland and six at Wolves. Pressure can make you act irrationally, and when you've been around long enough you realise that common sense is not all that common.

'It is strange how people won't differentiate between the footballer and the person. They're the same being in their eyes. When I was playing, people used to ask my missus, Fiona, "What's he like to live with?" I think they thought I knocked her around because of how I played. I am what I am. My wife, daughters and granddaughter have got me around their little fingers.'

He has been married for 35 years, and has learned to compartmentalise family life. A career of such length inevitably contains watershed moments, often private and usually profound. One such came on a Sunday morning, less than two years into his stint at Millwall, when he was driving back from Mass.

'I don't lose the plot very often these days. When you're younger you do, because you want to show everybody how much it hurts you. There's an element of self-pity. Everybody's a wanker. They're all fucking idiots. They're all this and they're all that. Well, they're not. I look back and think, how ridiculous. I'm a winner, and still get fired up, but I can rationalise things.

'I was no more passionate about the game in my first job than I am now, but I felt the pressure more then. I needed a few quid more than I do now. Let's not hide from reality; having no mortgage, a bit of financial security behind you, certainly helps. Anyone who tells me it doesn't is lying, because it does.

'We were coming home from church, and the kids were acting up in the back of the car. I got angry with them and Fiona tore a strip off me. She said, "It's all about you, is it?" and told me in no uncertain terms there was nowt wrong with the kids, it was me. The job was getting to me. It made me think.

'I'd be growling on Saturday night. I'd go out for a

couple of pints with my pals on Sunday, and want to be friends with everybody. Fiona highlighted those facts, and it was a valuable lesson, because I realised that, almost without knowing it, I was letting the job affect my relationships. That changed my thoughts.

'I keep myself right and do my exercise, but the job takes its toll. When I was younger I felt I had to be at my desk, just in case something happened. Now I realise it is nonsense to hang around, just to be seen. To survive in this business you have to take a break when there is a chance to do so. You have to be yourself.

'When I was at Sunderland they used to give me a list of questions I might get asked. I remember saying to Lou, my press lady there, "This is what I have to say? Fuck off. Has this come from above? If it has, you can tell them to poke that right up the hole." God love her. She used to laugh at me. She's a great girl, but I wouldn't have it.

'Sunderland was the first time I got the sack. When I joined the club we were getting shot of Kevin Phillips, Tore André Flo, Thomas Sørensen and a load of other players. We made seventy people redundant. We eventually win the Championship with ninety-odd points, and get into the Premier League. I'm told I've got six million quid to spend, all inclusive.

'I'd never felt as disappointed. Typical me, it lasted about a nanosecond. I thought, right, fuck you. We'll be all right, we'll stay up whatever we do. I didn't realise how naive I was. We couldn't get a result, and I'd signed the players. The sack really is like an Exocet missile; you know it's coming, but you don't know when. I was really upset, but I was part of my own downfall. I can't just turn around and blame everybody else for it.

'That was in March. I started at Wolves in the July with the same script. A million quid, we need ten players. Here you are, get on with that. We won the Championship in the third season and I kept them up for two seasons. Then we lost five–one to West Brom, and that was unforgivable in a lot of people's eyes.

'So I walk away thinking, I've done a fucking remarkable job here, not a good job, but a remarkable job. But, likewise, I was responsible for signing the players. I do own it. I like to think I've been honest and straightforward with everyone throughout my career. That's not easy.

'You see the sorrow, disbelief and resentment in players' eyes when you are giving them bad news. They're not daft. They can see when you are bullshitting. I've been in their position. When I was at Barnsley, Norman Hunter told me I wasn't playing because I'd just served a suspension. He was my manager, one of my heroes, but I almost knocked his office door off its hinges and demanded a transfer.

'Looking back, if a player had done that to me I'd have knocked his head off. Norman empathised with me, because I'd been his player of the year for three years on the bounce, and told me to go away and put it in writing. I went home, came back with the letter, and he was still in the same meeting! Bloody hell! I did everything apart from sing "Please release me, let me go".'

Scars heal, and become conversation pieces. History can be rewritten, even by such luminaries as Sir Alex Ferguson. McCarthy did not flinch from the obvious follow-up question, involving his response to a similarly strident challenge from Roy Keane, which became a global psychodrama when, as Republic of Ireland manager, he sent his captain home from the 2002 World Cup.

'The problem was that situation became personal. There were some really nasty things said. It was as tough a time as I have ever had as a manager, but I would do absolutely the same thing again. I know Sir Alex and I didn't agree totally at the time, but when he went to Harvard, ten years later, he spoke about no one but the manager deciding tactics and training. If someone is ruining the squad, take action even if he's the best player in the world.

'It could have scarred me. It certainly defined me. But it hasn't done me any harm. It polarised opinions and caused a lot of heartache, but you learn a lot from hard times. Big Jack was great with big decisions. Totally uncomplicated, dead straight, dead honest. I mean, he took Liam Brady off before half-time. Wow. Just wow.

'I can't run hard any more, or head it, or cross it, or

tackle, or shoot. My job is to get others to do my bidding. Management is all about creating an environment which encourages people to want to learn, and be better. How do I rationalise all the other stuff, the screaming and bawling? We all do it, don't we?

'We see someone on the telly and we shout, "What are you fucking talking about, you cock?" If someone incenses you, you're shouting, "Are you for real? You insincere prick." He might be a politician, an actor, a celebrity, a journalist, another football manager. It doesn't really matter who. I'm judging someone I don't know, in the way others judge me, without knowing me.'

The Championship makes managers and breaks them. This was shaping into a compelling season. Dramas unfolded day by day, hour by hour, minute by minute. Teams required the flexibility of Olympic fencers, the durability of boxers, and the metronomic efficiency of long-distance runners. Supporters were emotionally engaged to the point of obsession – participants rather than observers.

The pace was ferocious. Ipswich were in sixth position, the final play-off spot, having accumulated 74 points by the time they arrived at Molineux. Wolves were eighth, three points behind. The average required to occupy the last play-off berth, over the five previous seasons, had been 72. The storyline was typically engrossing and nuanced.

There were three people in this broken marriage, Jackett, McCarthy and Terry Connor, who had taken charge for the fateful final thirteen games during Wolves' relegation from the Premier League three years earlier. Connor is a gentle, extremely popular man who, by his own admission, was temperamentally unsuited to management. He was in the Ipswich dugout, alongside McCarthy, who spoke of him tenderly, as if he were a younger brother.

'When I was sacked here, TC's bags were packed and it was understood that when I went, he went. But they were on the phone to him all the time. When he said, "I think they might be going to offer me the job," I told him he had to take it. He'd been at Wolves for twelve years and deserved a shot at being a Premier League manager.

'It was hard watching them getting beat with TC. I wouldn't have wished anything other than for him to do well. Certain people said to me, "He's being disloyal to you. He's your best mate and he's sitting in your chair." I told them to piss off. He had my blessing. He couldn't have done it any other way because had he refused they could have sacked him for gross misconduct. "We want you to take the team. No? Well, we're sacking you." That's it. You're out of a job with no money.'

Ipswich had greater reason to celebrate their point in a tense 1–1 draw on a bright, blustery day with poignant subplots. Stearman, the defender who had been so impressive in the psychologist's session, conceded a first-half own goal, mistiming a defensive header under pressure at a corner. Ironically, his Wolves career had been revived by Jackett, who took him back from a loan spell at Ipswich.

Afobe equalised with his 31st goal of the season, a finely crafted piece of opportunism which involved subtly shifting his body position to convert a ball which had dropped over his shoulder at the far post, but Jackett knew a significant opportunity had been wasted. Wolves' fate was out of their hands.

McCarthy's influence was emphasised by his team's game management. They niggled and nudged, stole yards and wasted time at throw-ins. In the dressing room afterwards the manager observed, 'What a belligerent, stubborn, hard-working, tough, horrible bunch you lot have turned out to be." No praise could be higher. In this particular Wacky Race, Dick Dastardly was in pole positon.

19

The Revolution Will Be Televised

Sometimes there is little option but to accept the absurdity of the situation and surrender to fate. Mark Warburton had a contract to honour and human relationships to protect. He was obliged to deal with the mischief of strangers and the surreal, entirely undeserved, prospect of impending unemployment.

'It's just football being football,' he said, neatly encapsulating the menagerie of anguished bloggers, data evangelists and conspiracy theorists debating his future, following confirmation he would leave Brentford at the end of the season, regardless of whether he had overseen successive promotions from League One to the Premier League.

With two matches of the regular season remaining, Brentford were seventh in the Championship, ahead of Wolves on goal difference and one place outside the play-offs. With eight matches of the Danish Superliga season remaining, FC Midtjylland were 11 points clear at the top of the table. A golden fibre-optic cable stretched figuratively from Griffin Park in west London to the MCH Arena in the market town of Herning on the Jutland peninsula. Two small clubs were signalling a paradigm shift in football management. This was more than a refinement of the principle of achievement through analytics; this was the revolution, and it would be televised.

Managers in Warburton's position, obliged to maintain the pretence of business as usual, very rarely hang around to see the job through. He considered walking away once it became clear Brentford owner Matthew Benham was committed to restructuring the club by employing a head coach to work alongside a new sporting director.

He recognised the shift in philosophy went beyond the hybrid model used increasingly in the British game, in which a head coach retains a modicum of control over recruitment. This was a strategic development which owed more to the austere, predictive modelling of the betting industry than the intuitive traditions of the football business. The power had passed to the mathematicians.

Benham, a former hedge fund manager and professional gambler, took a majority stakeholding in FC Midtjylland in July 2014 and installed author Rasmus Ankersen, a former footballer who specialised in the cultural and psychological aspects of coaching, as chairman. They wasted no time in introducing a radical system in which recruitment decisions were reverse-engineered by statistical experts.

'We redesigned the club based on a question: what would a football club look like if it had no human eye and ear?' Ankersen told Michiel de Hoog of the Dutch online journal *De Correspondent*. 'Of course, it turns out you need a human element. But if you say from the start that it has to be a combination of stats and humans, you won't be radical enough to be able to make a difference.'

Players are judged on rigorously applied key performance indicators, informed by mathematical modelling; coaches are expected to consider real-time data before attempting any interaction with the squad, or the outside world. Training has been extended and radicalised; specialist kicking coaches work with individuals in the manner of swing coaches in golf. Monthly set-piece review meetings between players, coaches and Ankersen feature external consultants from apparently alien sporting environments, like the NFL.

Scouts are being reprogrammed to move away from watching live matches. Ankersen's mantra is 'distrust your eyes'. He argues scouts are better employed studying a bigger sample, a large number of games on video, since 'if you base your opinion of a player on a few games you've attended, it will blur your vision'.

Their mathematical model cross-references results from leagues across Europe. Data confounds conventional logic, suggesting, for instance, that Greuther Fürth, a club from Germany's second tier, would flourish in the English Premier League. Ankersen bought Tim Sparv, their Finnish defensive midfield player, because the model depicted him as 'a no stats all-star'.

This is a concept Benham has borrowed from NBA basketball. It is based upon the ability of a player to influence those around him, stealthily and with little apparent impact until a statistician drills down through the numbers. Football's ultimate heresy, admission that the league table occasionally tells whopping lies, has been repackaged as an article of faith.

The experiment remains in its infancy, and will inevitably be extended to involve Brentford. 'It's important not to make the shock too sharp,' Ankersen says. 'You eat an elephant one bite at a time. I need to keep telling the coaches: trust the model. If this way of thinking about football were stupid, Matthew wouldn't have been able to buy not only us, but also Brentford.'

Warburton excelled during his four years at Brentford. They were three years ahead of their initial development schedule. His peers in the football village, astounded by the naivety which led to the exposure of a clumsy attempt to investigate the availability of Rayo Vallecano coach Paco Jémez, expected him to leave quickly.

Yet he felt a responsibility to his players, who sought clarity and reassurance, often late at night. The fallout threatened to contaminate the close season; club captain Jonathan Douglas challenged the shift in direction at a team meeting with Benham, and the air at the training ground, close to Heathrow airport, was thick with the acrid smell of burning bridges.

Warburton had an affinity with his assistant, David Weir. He also acknowledged a lingering respect for an owner whose wealth, far-sightedness and instinct for unexpected opportunity had helped to transform the club. Benham was, after all, a fan. He had already gone on record with his intention to pass Brentford on to his son.

There was the usual background noise. Message boards hummed with unattributed, unsubstantiated nonsense: Warburton had supposedly been discovered in clandestine contact with Norwich City. He was allegedly plotting to take over at Queens Park Rangers behind the back of his friend Chris Ramsey. He had supposedly turned down £10 million to strengthen his squad, opposing moves for Bernardo, a Colombian centre half at Sporting Gijón, and Marco Djuricin, an Austrian international striker, who instead joined Red Bull Salzburg.

Warburton denied everything with an understandable degree of exasperation, blaming inflated financial demands from agents for the lack of senior recruits in the winter transfer window. Brentford's three January signings, Rangers striker Lewis Macleod, Blackburn defender Jack O'Connell and midfield player Josh Laurent from QPR, conformed to a type: they were young, promising and in need of development.

Warburton's credibility was, if anything, enhanced, since he is known as a man of balance and integrity. He was sufficiently attuned to the ruthlessness of modern business, through his former life as a currency trader, to appreciate the single-mindedness of Benham's approach. He regularly returned to the trading floors, to relate his progress to the world he had left ten years previously.

'Sometimes, in football, we try to convince ourselves that our skill sets are special, unique. In reality we are walking miles behind the City. They've been analysing currencies and trends and commodities for centuries. All of a sudden football starts thinking it is cutting edge because it is analysing the stats.

'You've got dealers there who are very wealthy, and management is governed by the need to create the best environment for them to produce. It's the same in football. You can't rule players on two hundred grand a week with a rod of iron. I go back to refresh myself about dealing with the individual.

'I can draw on the experience of my old boss. He was a big trader, utterly ruthless, but did more than rule by fear. He looked after his team fantastically well.

He treated us as individuals, but when he made a decision that was it. He cut people I'd worked with for five years. They were gone in a heartbeat. Sometimes in football you have to do that.

'He just says, "If they're capable let them work. If they're not, let them go." It might sound harsh, but it teaches you to stand by your decision. I look to treat people the right way, as adults, in a respectful manner, but if there's a kickback against your decision you have to be strong enough to front it out. You have to say, "Here are my reasons. That's all you need to know."

'I've taken David and some of the senior players in there. They need to see what other successful people do. They start at six in the morning and finish at eight at night. They earn seven figures plus bonuses but they are the best at what they do. Footballers get wrapped up in their own world sometimes, and it is good for them to see the teamwork, complexity of communication and the ruthlessness of that environment.'

Among the many ironies of the situation was Benham's initial boldness in appointing Warburton, after Uwe Rosler's ill-judged move to Wigan Athletic, in December 2013. Warburton was initially rejected in 2011 after applying for the Brentford job following a spell assisting caretaker manager Nicky Forster.

'I didn't apply when Uwe left, though I was really pissed off I didn't get it two and a half years earlier. I was with Matthew on the train home from Carlisle, where we had lost in the Cup. I had twenty-seven enquiries about the job on my phone on the way back. There were some big hitters interested and I was thinking bloody hell.

'Matthew said we would discuss it in the morning. At ten o'clock I rang and was given the job, simple as that. It was a brave call on his part, because no one really knew who I was. As one of my trader mates said to me, "I play Football Manager on my laptop. You're now one, in real life." It has its surprises.

'The things people associate with the job, picking the team, choosing the tactics, training the players, dealing with the board, are not the hard part. Dealing with emotions, finding the right balance of when to be firm and when to cajole, is delicate. Handling the hunger and the anger can be a nightmare. I didn't realise how much crap swirls around the game.

'You speak to the Spanish boys and they are top pros. If they're not picked, or they're dropped, their immediate reaction is, what do I have to do to impress the coach? A lot of British players in that situation wonder what they can do to piss the coach off even more. Some don't seem to want to commit.

'We're fortunate with our group. The British boys respect the Spanish lads' attitude and embrace their ideas. They are good people. They're not here to take the money and go. The GPS data tells you they work really hard. It is just getting them used to the intensity, because there is no respite. If they don't do their job defensively for one second, bang, it's in.

'You've got to learn to be patient. The Spanish boys are technically good, very fit and have great desire, but the Championship is a culture shock for them. One of our lads, Marcos Tébar, came to me after we played Bournemouth away. He's a super pro, played twenty-five games in La Liga last season, played at the Bernabéu and the Camp Nou.

'He said, "I've never played a game like that in my life." I wasn't surprised, since I saw him thinking, what on earth have I let myself in for? during the match. But that's the game. It is my job to help him through it, because we have a player on our hands. Ninety per cent of football people and my friends just tell me to survive.

'I've worked in an environment of massive stress in the City. But when I'm working on the sidelines I look around at other managers and think, wow. You can see the stress in their eyes and in their pallor. It drains them. I've got to be honest. I'm wiped out by half past eight after a Saturday game. I find I am so tired. I'm not stressed, just knackered. Everything you do in the week comes to a crescendo.'

There was a paradox in his sudden insecurity, because he was an agent of change. He was a natural ally for someone of Benham's instincts. Innovative, broad-minded and impeccably self-educated, Warburton had travelled extensively on football study visits after leaving the City. He analysed development systems, technical programmes and recruitment principles at Sporting Lisbon, Valencia, Ajax and Willem II. In the longer term, he was attracted by the possibility of working in the Bundesliga.

The deductive powers of Hercule Poirot were not really required to recognise clues to change beyond his control. Brentford's appointment in October 2014 of Ted Knutson, a former professional gambler who had worked for eight years in the development of metrics in football, baseball and basketball, was left field, on both personal and professional levels.

Knutson, a graduate of the University of Oklahoma, emerged as a strange mixture of the coy and cocksure. He was widely acclaimed in the analytics community for his generation of football radars, designed to give player statistics a visual dimension pioneered in computer games, and had a cult following on social media.

He was the co-founder of the StatsBomb website, an exceptional platform for debate about analytical trends, yet bizarrely attempted to make a virtue of anonymity. His Twitter biography read: 'Head of Player Analytics (Secret Club FC) Playing Football Manager with real life'. He left the platform temporarily once Warburton's exit strategy was confirmed, in mid-February, and ostentatiously thanked mainstream media for not exposing him.

Brentford's analysis department is one of the best in

English football, yet Knutson had been imposed on it, above an existing structure. He was so unversed in the ways of football that on a rare visit to the training ground he created a stir by choosing to lean against a goalpost to watch a practice match. To players and coaches, that lapse in protocol is the equivalent of mooning the Queen.

Obvious doubts existed about the transferability of principles from the 12-team Danish Superliga, where Midtjylland challenged the traditional dominance of Copenhagen and Brøndby. The competition lacks quality and intensity, and its value as a test bed for a new philosophy, based upon finely calibrated calculation of the odds, was unproven.

Benham's burgeoning fortune, created by his instant judgement of marginal inefficiency in the bookmaking business, suggests he is not a man to be underestimated. Midtjylland were developing satellite clubs in Nigeria, Ghana and Goa, and working with E4Talent, a consultancy which has expanded from its base in Valby, in the southwestern suburbs of Copenhagen, to Manchester.

They project themselves as 'the future of scouting and performance analysis' through the supply of customised, contextualised data. Their methods chime with Benham's model, which pays particular attention to areas of the pitch from which goalscoring opportunities are seized. Brentford employed Robert Rowan, a 24-year-old Scottish analyst who had spent eight weeks as Stenhousemuir's sporting director, as their new scouting co-ordinator.

In a satellite age, football was being urged to rely on something more substantial than a sextant on its voyage into the void. The conservatism of English management, identified and individualised by Warburton as 'the guy whose only ambition is to make it to June 1 every year without getting sacked', was being challenged.

Millwall's sacking of Ian Holloway on March 14, after 14 months in charge, signalled a move away from an emotionally extreme approach to an increasingly sophisticated business. This time, no one could doubt the veracity of the statistics. Millwall won only 13 of their 58 Championship matches under Holloway. They scored only 28 goals in 29 home games in the league.

There was genuine sadness in his ritual optimism following his dismissal, that 'hopefully somebody will want me'. He retained his ambition of joining the select group of managers who have overseen 1,000 or more matches. He was only 52, and had the experience of 870 games under his belt, yet managers in his mould were slowly going the way of vaudeville drama queens and music hall tenors. Their audience was growing away from them.

He moved house for the 33rd time in mid-April, away from south London and a fanbase who wanted badly to share his vision and be purified by his passion. Millwall supporters reciprocate loyalty, but by the end, a 4–1 home defeat to Norwich City, their hostility was so savage that he sheltered in the dugout to avoid being a distraction. With his pinched face, light grey three-piece suit and big-knotted tie, he resembled a prisoner in the dock.

He spoke of the privilege of blame, and insisted his players were with him despite describing the squad as 'dysfunctional'. He had called in a hypnotherapist, former world super middleweight boxing champion Glenn Catley, to work with his squad, who were in danger of being cut adrift in the Championship's relegation zone. The News at Den website spoke of Catley placing his clients into a 'deeply relaxed state of body and mind' before 're-programming patterns of negative thought and behaviour'.

Players are creatures of habit, who yearn to know where they stand instead of being stretched out on a psychologist's couch. Holloway's selection policy was capricious. He played people out of position, promoted recklessly and rejected prematurely. He was bold to the point of perversity, installing teenaged defender Sid Nelson as captain in only his fourth first-team appearance. The theory that the sight of a boyhood fan leading from the front would serve as a rallying point might have been sound, but it was quickly abandoned. Holloway came close to the sack in January, and recruited poorly when given the freedom to bring in seven new players. He had spoken of developing a fresh young group, but his legacy was a squad with an average age approaching 31.

He was replaced, initially on a caretaker basis until the end of the season, by another traditional figure, the club legend. Neil Harris, who had served an 18-month apprenticeship in charge of Millwall's development squad, sought counsel from Kenny Jackett, his former manager, and Sean Dyche, his former teammate, as he rationalised his approach. Both were impressed by his calmness and focus.

Harris wasn't busking. He knew the unique nature of the role, the alchemy which exists at a much maligned club which stays close to the community, collecting for local food banks and hosting anti-knife crime initiatives. Relegation remained a probability, but he would channel defiance through a reversion to 4–4–2 and faith in street-fighting men.

Such opportunities must be seized when they arise, and Harris could not afford to dwell on those who had fallen short as managers at clubs with which they were most closely identified, like Stuart Pearce at Nottingham Forest and Tony Mowbray at Middlesbrough. Failure in such circumstances feels like a death in the family.

Harris has greater awareness of his mortality than most, having survived testicular cancer. I once spent an afternoon with him, rummaging around the attic of his Essex home. It was a fascinating insight into a substantial career: schoolboy trophies were stacked alongside old programmes, beer-stained flags, a golden boot and deflated hat-trick footballs.

He eventually found what he was looking for. He pored over the contents of a box containing 3,000 letters from fans moved by his successful fight against a disease which is most prevalent among men aged 15 to 49. 'This is my life,' he said. 'I felt alone at that time in the sense you feel you are the only person in the world with an illness.

'These letters mean so much to me because they tell me how people perceive me. They remind me of the dark days, but they are also a highlight of my career. To have them is truly special. You have your family around you, and support from the football club, but it is the fans who make you realise you are not alone.

'Some of the spelling might be horrendous, and a lot of the messages are slang, but I could never have dreamed I would deserve such tributes. Maybe they saw a bit of me in them. I was a trier, and they love someone who gives it everything. They graft, and they want to see you graft. A lot of teams and players play in the way they do because of the fans they have.'

Harris was on the verge of a transfer to the Premier League when he was diagnosed in July 2001. The goal he scored on his comeback against Watford was powerfully symbolic, since it was on New Year's Day, 2002, and led to his being carried aloft by his teammates, in a pose of gladiatorial triumph. The moment, captured by a solitary photographer, has been recreated on a mural at the Den.

Dyche can be seen in the image, gesticulating as he helps to hold Harris up. 'That moment was amazing,' he reflected, with unabashed emotion. 'It still ranks up there as one of my best memories. He was a great lad. He'd gone through a hell of a lot and we were a fantastic group of mostly young players.

'I'm pointing at the screen, going, "Look, look, you really have scored. Let's watch the goal." In another small twist of fate, it was against my mate Alec Chamberlain, who was goalie for Watford. Chopper bent it around Chambo to the top corner, a very Neil Harris-type goal. I just thought, what a glorious moment.

'He's had a great career, record scorer, Millwall legend. But when he had the misfortune to get that cancer, he was really flying. We were thinking, this boy could go again and again. It looked as if he was going to go on to even bigger things, like Timmy Cahill and Steven Reid. That's not to undervalue anything he has done, because he's the sort of person you want to see do well.'

Ironically, Dyche was being widely mentioned as a possible successor to Steve McClaren at Derby County, whose attempt to secure a play-off position, after stuttering form in spring, was complicated by persistent speculation that the former England manager would give Mike Ashley's Newcastle regime a vestige of credibility by moving to St James' Park in the summer.

McClaren's irritation was obvious and understandable. His reputation as a coach had been restored in Holland, where he had won the Eredivisie title with FC Twente in 2010. Though he subsequently made false moves by joining Wolfsburg and Nottingham Forest, briefly, he was an ideal fit for an aspirational club like Derby.

The speculation represented rehabilitation, of sorts, for a high-profile victim of the infantilism of the English game, and the more excitable members of its commentariat. He was the 'Wally with the Brolly', 'Schuper Schteeve'. He was treated as living latex, a Spitting Image puppet.

Jackett, his play-off rival, reflected the concern of his peers: 'The reaction to failure at international level is extreme. I saw it at first hand with Graham Taylor. I mean, it was as if the whole country hated him. The disrespect is so complete you almost have to go abroad, like Steve. You get stick for a while, and then it rolls around to someone else. It is only then you start getting a few backhanded compliments, about your ability to bounce back.'

The search for the survivor led to Moor Farm, a complex set behind beech hedges in Oakwood, one of the largest modern estates in Europe. McClaren was a welcoming host, allowing me to watch him work without losing his instinctive fear of one-dimensional portrayal. He was happy to talk informally, in general terms.

His adaptation of the principles of neuro-linguistic programming was reflected by the ritual of players and coaches maintaining eye contact while exchanging pre-session handshakes. Training was dynamic, varied, competitive. McClaren's reedy voice competed for airtime with the whistle which hung around his neck.

A bustling figure, he broke away from a one-touch drill to meticulously measure distances between cones in the following session on an adjoining pitch. He dragged the goals forward, to truncate space. The losers in a short-sided game did ten wind sprints as a forfeit but he promised the group 'it will be harder tomorrow'.

We spoke at a corner table in the canteen, where he could watch his squad's interaction. Swearing was banned, because, in his estimation, lazy language is symbolic of a lack of self-control. He was encouraging his senior players to guide the younger members of his group.

'It is no longer the leader on top of the pyramid,' he said. 'The manager leads from the centre of the circle.' It was a graphic description of a change in outlook, fostered in exile. He was more inclusive, more inclined to sweat the small details.

Eric Steele, whose title of goalkeeping coach minimises his broader influence, lobbied him to restrict external use of training pitches. 'Are we trying to be the best we can be?' he implored, referring to a spreadsheet which revealed Derby were simultaneously hosting two German teams and Torquay United.

Along the corridor a psychologist was conducting what he referred to as a 'speed dating' session. Young players were obliged to stand in front of their peers, introduce themselves and articulate their ambitions. They changed in a dressing room dominated by a sign which read: 'There is no strength without unity.'

McClaren is a long-term advocate of sports psychology, having worked with Bill Beswick at Manchester United, Middlesbrough and the national team. Steve Peters, guru of choice in football, snooker and several Olympic sports, was helping to create a new culture at Derby, 'a learning environment'.

Even the man in charge needs to be nudged in the right direction. 'Getting inside the heads of players is one of the major components in coaching and managing McClaren reflected. 'The psychologist almost has to coach the coach. Ultimately you are the one at the front. You are the leader. You are the manager. Sometimes only you can deliver the message.'

The Dutch experience had a huge effect on him. It challenged conventional beliefs, and encouraged him to empower his players. He spoke with deep respect about minutely detailed six-week training plans produced by his assistants. Sessions, timed to the second, were adaptable. His input was governed by the principle that less is more.

'When I first got there I really didn't have a clue. I behaved as I had always behaved. I'd be on the touchline, waving my arms about, telling them this and that. But the other coaches just quietly said, "Let them think it through themselves."

'The players conducted their own twenty-minute briefings before matches. "Why not?" they told me. "We've been doing this since we were eleven." I taught them game management, how to win, and they made me realise how much there is to be learned.'

Perspective was readily available. Derby had been desperately unfortunate to lose to QPR in the previous season's play-off final at Wembley, but the fate of Óscar García, who resigned as Brighton manager after being defeated by McClaren's team in the semi-finals, was sobering.

In yet another example of football's hidden networks, García had made informal contact with Warburton to investigate the English job market soon after the start of the season. When asked why he wanted to leave Maccabi Tel Aviv only two months after joining them, the Spaniard sent the Brentford manager a photograph of the ongoing Gaza conflict: a missile flying low across his training ground.

García duly joined Watford in early September, but

stepped down after 27 days, following heart-related chest pains which prompted doctors to warn him off stressful activity. His successor, Billy McKinlay, lasted only eight days in his first managerial job. The volcano was rumbling, ominously.

Warburton was scrupulous in maintaining professional standards, optimistic to the end. Fulham were supposedly interested in his services. His calling card was a team competing against Championship clubs with wage bills which were up to five times higher, and a club, insulated from the harshest consequences of a puzzling philosophical dispute between manager and owner.

'I used to say to Uwe, "If we're sacked tomorrow, let's make sure we leave the club in really good shape." I'm talking about medical care, analytical support, logistical efficiency, the pitches, the players, everything. I like to think what goes around comes around. If we do our job here, whatever happens, hopefully we'll get a chance to move forward.'

He did not know it at the time, but his success was linked, inextricably, to Steve McClaren's failure.

20

View from the Boundary

Another Ashes summer lay ahead. It remained a seductive prospect, despite the growing pains of the England team and the siren calls of a social media phenomenon named Kevin Pietersen. As an MCC member, Paul Tisdale had the first two days of the Lord's Test in mid-July blocked off in his diary. His players, who would be preparing for the new football season, could fend for themselves.

Tisdale's status as the second-longest-serving manager in the top four tiers of English football was substantial without being a substitute for his greatest passion. Cricket, with its rhythms and rituals, was an abiding love; it was a game of multiple layers and infinite variation, a cerebral challenge which required mastery of technique.

Football had chosen him, almost by default. He had a semi detached playing career which took him from the Premier League with Southampton to Exeter City, the club he was appointed to manage in June 2006, via the now-defunct FinnPa in Helsinki and Panionios, in the southern suburbs of Athens.

Exeter, handicapped by a transfer embargo, just missed out on the League Two play-offs. Their defeat at Hartlepool in the penultimate match of the 2014–15 season had the unintended consequence of condemning Cheltenham Town and Tranmere Rovers to the outer darkness of the newly entitled National Conference.

Tisdale worked under considerable restraints, yet maintained his reputation as an inventive, unorthodox and productive development coach: midfield player Matt Grimes had been sold to Swansea for £1.75 million and goalkeeper Christy Pym was also attracting Premier League interest. Two difficult years of managed decline had been negotiated successfully.

The League Two table merely sketched the story. Using it to reach firm conclusions about Tisdale's capability was like judging cricket as a spectacle solely through the binary certainties of the scorebook, without the context of the lyricism of Sir Neville Cardus, the poetry of John Arlott or the socio-political commentary of C. L. R. James.

'People judge you where you finish in the League, but there are so many moving parts at a football club. Last year, for instance, we just stayed up. It is easy to say that's no great achievement. But to keep the club healthy when income was declining needed a brave decision. I knew we had to develop our assets by playing five young players who were not quite ready. That ran the risk of playing well, without winning.

'Ordinarily, you might take a chance with one or two. Those five played between twenty-five and thirty games each. We also developed them in the Under 21 Cup, where we lost in the semi-final after beating big academy teams like Southampton, Blackburn and Crystal Palace. The overall concept was to generate income to give us a chance to move the wheels forward.'

The need became acute when the club required a PFA loan to overcome cash-flow issues in the summer of 2014. The situation was complicated still further by the 'health and safety nightmare' of a pre-season trip to Brazil, for a bizarre friendly to mark the centenary of Exeter's match against the national team.

Tisdale's team were housed in a youth hostel; four players became seriously ill and missed the start of the season. The manager was forced to name himself as a substitute, yet continued with the experiment of playing two veteran central midfield players, Matt Oakley and Danny Butterfield, at the heart of his defence. Their brief was to give Grimes, the principal prospect, the ball as much as possible.

'Matt was a turkey dressed for Christmas for a while. Selling him was our best way of moving forward, so the supply lines to him had to be right. He needed to show what he could do during the autumn months, when the pitches were at their best.'

Wolves passed up on the chance to sign him for £500,000 just before the closure of the summer window. Tisdale negotiated for 11 weeks with Swansea chairman Huw Jenkins before reaching a deal which enabled Exeter to pay off debts, earmark £750,000 for training-ground improvements, and give him a small budget to build a new team.

It was a singular achievement by a singular man who spent the first six and a half years of his life in Malta, where his father worked with the Admiralty. He then boarded at Millfield School in Somerset, where he played rugby and golf at county level, excelled at football, and was drawn towards cricket.

'I was an opening batsman, a captain, a leader. I was considered one of the best cricketers in England at fifteen, but also one of the best footballers. Cricket was sophisticated, but almost amateurish in some respects; you go to university and then they offer you a county place. Football's culture was pushy; you have scouts coming round to your house, trying to nick you.

'Football has a hothouse environment. That's why it doesn't really work in this country. The root is poor. It's just scrap and a bun fight to get who you can. It's all about the here and now. The reason I should have been a cricketer is that I suited the culture better. I could be myself. I could be in a dressing room with senior players, and be full of energy and personality.

'The game suited the way I loved to work, which was very meticulous, very detailed. I would spend hours with a bowling machine. It suited my patience, my discipline. It was a perfect match. Cricket is a team sport with individuals in it. You can tangibly quantify achievement. Football is so subjective. There are so many variables, it's so fluid.

'I was a public-school boy. I was almost too respectful to be a footballer. I was too subtle, my thinking was too detailed. I stayed an extra two years at school to get my A levels, but professional sport was on the table, a three-year contract with a Premier League club. I couldn't take the risk of spending another three or four years at university, so I'm playing a game that's crash-bang-wallop.

'If I'd been born Spanish or Italian it would have been a different story. I'm stuck in the centre of midfield playing the wrong sport at the wrong time, early nineties, with the ball being shelled over my head. I'm listening to information I'm given, considering the way I'm being managed and spoken to. I'm thinking, this is rubbish. The amount of times someone said to me, "How much do you want it?" It's fucking nonsense.

'The miracle is that I managed to stay seven years at Southampton, getting new contracts when others were falling by the wayside. I was dedicated, but never fitted.

I played eighteen periods in the Premier League, but it should have been three or four hundred. That lack of success I had as a player motivates gets me up at six thirty a.m. to drive to work because I know what I could have done.

'I had a nice view of the game, playing in Europe. Greece was terrific because of its technical base. It was like basketball – tactical, patient – and it suited me down to the ground. But as soon as I was out of the top level in England, it became a different sport. I had problems with injury and there was no way I was going to get what I needed to be satisfied.'

Tisdale is speaking in the early afternoon of a sunny day, in his Victorian house overlooking the pond in a Wiltshire village. He has a sketch pad in front of him, on which he is redesigning the walled back garden. He is wearing salmon-pink shorts, a wide-brimmed hat and a familiarly engaged expression. Ashen-faced Ron Knee he is not.

He was 26 when his direction changed through a chance meeting in the gymnasium at Bath Rugby club with Ged Roddy, who was to become a polarising figure as the Premier League's head of youth development. Roddy, establishing a university football programme to complement other sports such as swimming, netball and athletics, needed a head coach.

'I was about to sign a contract at Beveren in Belgium, where there had been some sort of ridiculous takeover.

I was thinking, I'm better than this. I contacted Ged to find out more about the job: "We haven't got a club. We haven't got any players. We haven't got any kit. We haven't got any balls. There's an office. Go and knock yourself out and see what you can do."

'He had the idea of getting players who had been released by clubs, regenerating them and selling them. Within two or three years it was, "Sod that, that ain't going to work." We needed to just win games, gain credibility. We ended up pushing a dozen or more back into professional football, but it was never going to be a big money-spinner.

'I was in an environment I had an affinity with, because I had always wanted to go to university. It was educational, trial and error. I was playing 4–6–0 with students in 2001 and beating Football League sides. I tried every system going. We couldn't sign players during the year so whatever you get, you work with. You become very inventive. I loved it. I had nobody questioning me.' He found a kindred spirit in Brian Ashton, the former England rugby head coach, who shared the disciplines of planning and the intricacies of communication. They participated in Monday debriefs with other coaches from Olympic disciplines, cross-fertilising ideas in an intellectually stimulating setting.

'I was amazed how many ideas are generic. Ten per cent is sport-specific coaching but the rest of it is how you treat people, how you organise, how you timetable, how you deliver, right down to what kit you wear. It made me see myself as a chemist. My job is to get the chemistry absolutely spot-bollock-on. If you get it right, get that colour in the test tube you need, things will flourish.

'I'm in sessions with people who've just come back from the Olympics. We're talking about problems, mistakes and solutions. I'm learning from other team sports. They're asking me questions about the Premier League and I'm thinking, people in football just want to do what they've always done. That's why I've looked at things differently to most.'

His influences are suitably eclectic. His best friend is Ray Kelvin, who founded the Ted Baker business in a Glasgow shirt shop and built it into an £1 billion global empire, run on memorably egalitarian lines. Though publicity-shy, Kelvin greets staff with a bear hug, engages with them as individuals, and insists visitors complete a series of press-ups if they are late to meetings.

Tisdale was appointed lead ambassador for the Ted Baker brand in the summer of 2015. He is in daily contact with Kelvin, and has assimilated his tendency to speak simply, with disarming intensity. He has also transferred more nuanced organisational skills from the company, such as the balance which must be struck between commerciality and creativity.

Steve Perryman is his soulmate, in football terms. He is Exeter's director of football, a catch-all title encompassing everything from organising community recycling programmes to overseeing recruitment and providing a source of support during matches. More assertive by nature, he can be transformed into an attack dog in the technical area.

Julian Tagg is a distinctive chairman, a former Exeter ballboy who played for the reserves, coached in the Centre of Excellence, became a PE lecturer and oversaw the Football in the Community programme. He has been running the club on behalf of the Supporters' Trust since September 2003.

'Ray is my biggest influence. Like-minded people meet like-minded people, so he met Steve. When the job at Exeter came up they said, "do you want to apply?" I've turned down some jobs because I didn't feel an affinity with the cause or to the tone of the place, but I felt I needed to go for it because, again, it was about like-minded people.

'Steve is highly technical in the way he wants the game played. He was a tough tackling player who'd feed the ball to Glenn Hoddle. He was a leader who played nearly nine hundred games for Tottenham. As a coach and a manager, he's a fantastic ambassador for doing the right thing. He adds strength to my thoughts. He has credibility, through enormous achievement.

'Julian is Mr Exeter. Steve is there because Julian is

there. I'm there because Steve is there, so I'm there, indirectly, because of Julian. He's pulled the club back from being four million quid in debt. The club is his sole passion. He has helped us create a culture of drive, opportunity and talent. That takes ten years.'

The secret of overachievement at such a small club lies in recognising the interconnectivity of ambition, belief, commitment and experience. Tisdale holds annual garden parties at his home for volunteer dinner ladies, grounds staff and their families. Perryman embeds the club in its community, and uses his contacts within the wider game. The outpouring of concern, when he was seriously ill with heart problems in 2012, testifies to the respect in which he is held.

Their ethos is based on common decency, instinctive humanity. When striker Adam Stansfield died from bowel cancer at the age of 31, Tisdale and Perryman insisted on paying his two-year contract into his estate in full, far beyond the required statutory minimum. It took 5 per cent of the playing budget but it was simply the right thing to do.

Football is, ultimately, about players. Tisdale takes heed of Ashton's advice – 'Take them out of their comfort zone once a week' – but is subtle and emotionally intelligent in recognising fears and frustrations he once shared.

'My players weren't playing football at the age of twelve because they wanted to chase the ball and stand in shape. I try to get them to remember what it was like when they were the best player at school. They weren't worrying, "Am I fit enough? What are my Prozone stats?" They just played.

'That gets sucked out of them bit by bit, so I try to encapsulate it in their psyche. I've got to get them in the right place at the right time, thinking the right thing. Ninety per cent of what I talk to them about is positive, upbeat. Most businesses operate six-monthly or annual reviews, but in football it's a daily review. People should know where they stand because the business is so transitory.

'One thing that gives me the edge is that I know what it is like to be on the periphery. I know what it's like to be a reserve player, to be on the bench every week. I know what it's like to be looking for new contracts, to be on the outside. It wasn't that my face didn't fit, because I obviously did not play well enough, but I know the deeper reasons why I wasn't selected.

'I was good enough, but didn't present myself well. I was quiet, in my shell. I wasn't comfortable around people. That failure gave me the drive to take an amazing opportunity, which came about through pure chance. I'm about creating credibility over the long term, instead of just grabbing the next job.'

He has had chances to leave Exeter, twice turning down Swansea, in the aftermath of the departures of Roberto Martínez and Paulo Sousa. He rejected the chance to return to Southampton as manager, following Alan Pardew's sacking in 2010. Portsmouth were given permission to speak to him in December 2013, but, by his own admission, he 'left them scared witless by telling them the truth'. He was also shortlisted for the England Under 21 job, won by Gareth Southgate.

'I'm totally in love with Exeter, but I know I'll leave one day. Other coaches and managers say, "Oh, you're not ambitious then." I'm more ambitious than anybody could imagine. I've been in the boardroom and heard people say, "He's never going to leave. He ain't got the guts for it." And I think, you cheeky bastard. You haven't got a clue.

'My determination to succeed is all-consuming, but I've got balance in my life as well. I want to be known for building things, and working alongside the people that employ me. Not working for them, but with them. There's a big difference. I've worked out what type of club we are, where we sit financially, and what I need to do to add value.

'It is a waste of time for Exeter to have scouts everywhere. We can't afford them. We are either the first call a parent or agent makes, or the last. We are the rehab team, the development team. I put a huge amount of time into the players that I have. We're not a win at all costs club, and I'm not necessarily a win at all costs manager, so I fit.

'Being in a bubble in the South West, you don't do

the circuit. You don't do all the nonsense; you go to work, shut the gate at the training ground, and everyone's on the same page. We play good football, the best, I think, in the league. A lot of coaches say they do the same, but let me tell you, they don't. They might for five minutes when they are two–nil up, but when it really matters, when they are one down or at nil–nil, they throw it down the line and hook it on.

'How do I get my teams to play? I don't tell them not to. We do a weekly half an hour meeting with video clips. It's not what I had as a player. Then it was lose four–nil and sit through a five-hour video inquest thinking, fucking hell, I hope it's not me, or win four–nil and have a five-a-side. Now it's a lesson, positive, humorous, full of information. Drip, drip, drip, drip, drip.

'Most players are stifled. I've played a diamond. I've played 3–5–2. I've played 4–6–0 and drawn four–four, so don't tell me you can't score goals in that shape. I say very little, hardly anything, from the touchline. I look at the pitch. I look at space, not players. I'll often know from the first minute that I'll have to make a change in the sixtieth minute.

'When you're a manager, stood there on the touchline, it's all about tone and feel. You need a very tight understanding of the game, what's needed, and what's not. You're dealing with dozens of variables at the same time, and if the structure and coaching are right, it is easier to assess which bit is making the difference.

'Say you're one–nil down with ten minutes to go. You can't describe the pressure you are under. You're picking next week's team as you're watching, thinking what you're going to say to that player, or the press. You're desperately trying to get that goal, blocking the supporters out because they think about it for two hours every week and then they go home. You think about it sixteen hours a day.

'At that point, it's very easy for a manager to think, I want someone on that pitch to reflect what that lot behind me are thinking. They're usually going, fucking get stuck in. So, to take off the player who is putting himself about, running everywhere and putting tackles in but doing all the wrong things, my God, you've got to be brave.

'I know I'm brave. I was criticised for about a year at Exeter for not having any passion, because they expected someone different. I live this, I'm consumed by it. Try thinking about a really important decision and screaming at the same time. It doesn't work, does it? Keep quiet, think clearly. I'm taking everything out of my mind and concentrating on one big decision, the thirty seconds out of ninety minutes where I have to get everything right.'

He looks the part of a dressing-room agnostic. Not for him club shop chic: the tracksuit, baseball cap and Tipp-Ex-white trainers combo. He is straight off the catwalk, a Ted Baker vision in tweed, linen and pastel shades. This is a manager whose trump card is not Sun Tzu and *The Art of War*, but a good, old-fashioned gentleman's fashion statement, the silk cravat.

'I'm an oddity. With what I wear, with how I speak, with the choices I've made. I'm an oddity in how I view players. I really don't mind that perception. It actually gives me an edge. I see it as a positive. There's nothing clever or tactical about it, but the game is so conditioned to distrust individuality it allows me to show how strong-willed I am in what I do.

'How do you make players feel they can beat anybody? That's why I wore a cravat for six months. I said to the players, "When I'm stood there, looking down the touchline twenty yards away, and the other manager's got his tracksuit tucked into his socks, I'm one–nil up. How are you going to be one–nil up before you start?

'"How are you going to be feeling in that crappy tunnel? Well, the other team will be pissed off coming out of their dressing room, because it's damp and tiny. They might be four inches taller than you, but you'll stand alongside them and know the manager's got his cravat on. I'll go out early and be stood in that technical area, with my silk scarf, feeling the bollocks. When you walk out, you'll look at me, and know if I feel it, then you'll feel the nuts too."'

Tisdale is still only 42. He has taken Exeter from the Conference to eighth in League One, after two promotions. He has given them two trips to Wembley and retrenched after relegation to League Two. He has been trained on such analytic tools as Sports Code, and understands the worth of 'true stats, not *Match of the Day* nonsense about how many kilometres they've run or how many passes they've completed'.

He has the instincts and experience to be an outstanding modern manager at a much higher level than the one at which he currently operates. Why, then, is he still at the other St James Park? To his credit, he recognises the validity of the question: 'Football is such a momentary thing. I am probably becoming a bit niche. I'm not getting the calls I used to, because I haven't had a promotion for three or four years. People don't think of me as readily when a job comes up. I know this sounds strange, but because of the way I work, I am more and more attractive to fewer people.'

Old-school methods were having mixed success in League Two. John Still's Luton Town also narrowly missed a play-off place, following a spring slump which detached them from the pacemakers. Micky Adams left Tranmere by mutual consent with two games of the season remaining, following a home defeat to Oxford United in which he was pelted with eggs by protesting supporters.

Rovers lost only two of his first 13 games in charge, picking up 18 points from nine games going into February, when they were 17th. Yet Adams' unease was reflected by his overuse of the loan market, and constant changes in personnel and strategy. His last 13 matches as manager yielded just five points, and Tranmere left the league, following a 94-year tenure, having used 48 players.

Fate, rashly tempted, duly retaliated. Hartlepool, who survived at Tranmere's expense with a 2–1 win over Exeter, were managed by Ronnie Moore. He had been sacked by Rovers in April 2014, when they were 19th in League One, after admitting to breaching rules on gambling. He was also fined £2,000 by the FA and given a one-month ban, suspended for two years.

Moore had placed small-scale accumulator bets using a family online account, the majority of which were under £10. One £1 wager linked Tranmere with Manchester United in a win double and earned him £3.93. He was out of work for eight months, and estimates the case cost him £130,000, since his Tranmere contract was annulled without compensation.

'I'm actually gutted for Tranmere, because it is a fantastic club, a big club, and I feel for the fans,' he told the *Hartlepool Mail*. 'I'm not sounding big-headed, but they would not have gone down last season if I was still there. They would not have gone down this year. What goes around comes around, doesn't it?'

The rise of Wycombe, the previous season's escapologists, was an infinitely more uplifting story, though it risked ending in crushing anticlimax. On the same afternoon relegation issues were decided at the bottom of the Football League, they slipped out of the automatic promotion places in League Two for the first time in the season. Even someone of Gareth Ainsworth's sunny nature would be forgiven for regarding the play-offs as a prison sentence.

'The season might be two matches too long for us,' he confided the day before a fateful 1–0 home defeat by Morecambe, in which he was obliged to play three midfield players in the back four, and could only name three outfield players on the substitutes' bench. His loyalty to the smallest squad in the division had finally been undermined by injuries and suspension.

The year had taken its toll, despite a burgeoning relationship with his chairman, Andrew Howard and the security of a new five and a half year contract signed in January. Ainsworth's long, swept-back hair had turned markedly grey, especially around the temples. He was physically fit and, despite a shock Bracknell Sunday League defeat by Morale Madrid, had helped Finchampstead Athletic to the Berks & Bucks Inter-mediate Cup final.

'I've always been a fit lad, but mentally I can feel the strain when I blink. I know it is a weird thing to say but I feel tired in my eyes. The concentration levels you need in this job are ridiculous. I have never thought so deeply, so much, in my life. My head hurts, sometimes.

'Sleep is another issue. I have closed my eyes thinking of my team and woken up thinking about my team. That was something I promised myself I would never do, but I couldn't help myself. Despite all that, I really enjoy it.'

'The chairman is a fantastic guy. I can't say enough about how he has helped me develop as a person. Next to my dad, and John Beck, my first manager, Andrew has had the biggest influence on me. We've spoken about man management, mental skills, taking the emotion out of decisions. He is totally professional, yet close and supportive. He is a friend.'

'It has been tough for him, too, taking on a Trust-run club with all the suspicion swirling about, all the tongues wagging about what is in it for him. He has not taken a penny out of the club. He is unconditional in the advice he has given me.'

Howard had purchased a five-bedroom house in the town, in order to establish a so-called 'Life Academy'. It was further evidence of a holistic approach, designed to attract a better class of loanee: four young players would live together with a member of staff and be tutored in such basic life skills as cooking, cleaning and financial planning. Aston Villa were the first to be impressed by the initiative.

'You have to be so strong. I have played a game for a living for twenty-five years, and now I have kids of seventeen and eighteen in my team. I try to think back to when I was their age, in my first car trying to pull girls. I am only forty-two, but I can't even remember those days. How young are they to have such weight on their shoulders? I have to be there for these guys.

'I pride myself on not letting people down. Football is a hard world. I am a normal guy and I will give this my absolute best. I have my faith and my family. That keeps me grounded, and hopefully sane. I still get choked up, seeing my parents at games. They drive for four hours, down from Blackburn, when we're at home and they go through the hell I'm going through on the touchline.

'I will do this for my children. They can rely on me and so can everybody else. If I can continue adding tactical nous and some more leadership skills to my good eye for a player, I will have the right components to see this through. I'm hopefully putting my stamp on the club.

'It is flattering to be linked to other clubs because we have done well, but I am not going to be a hypocrite, preach togetherness and then walk out on a whim. There is mayhem going on out there at the moment. Why jump into the whirlpool? I am really happy here.'

There would be no last-day fairy tale, no repeat of the Torquay miracle. Wycombe won 3–2 at Northampton Town in typically resilient manner, Brentford loanee Alfie Mawson scoring with the last kick of the match in the 97th minute, but missed out on automatic promotion due to Bury's 1–0 victory at Tranmere.

Ainsworth spoke of his 'immeasurable pride' in

accumulating 84 points, an improvement of 34 points on the previous season. In any other year, that would have been sufficient to guarantee a place in League One. He refocused quickly, and talked up the prospect of a Wembley appearance in the play-off final, but inner peace was impossible. Fate would prove to be cruel, capricious.

Wycombe were twenty seconds away from promotion at Wembley, when they conceded an equaliser to Southend in added time at the end of extra time. The sight of Ainsworth standing alongside Phil Brown, his opposite number, during the penalty shoot out, which Wycombe lost 7–6 after leading, symbolised the solidarity of their trade. Ainsworth, later named League Two manager of the year by his peers, retained his dignity and perspective without losing sight of a bitter truth.

'It is crazy to think of, but managers are addicted to the lows. It is one hell of an emotion to feel. The highs are never as high, and the lows are simply despair. Maybe we are unconsciously addicted to putting things right . . .'

21

From Darkness into Light

M artin Ling took to the stage in a celebrated sporting setting, beside the Old Course in St Andrews. His audience of more than 40 fellow managers and coaches knew where he had come from, meta-phorically, and were about to share the redemptive force of his journey.

'I'm going to show you how it can creep up on you,' he said, referring to the paralysing depression which provides a punctuation mark in his life, and career. 'You would be surprised how easily it does so. I felt I was the most unlikely person to get it. Everyone I spoke to thought the same way. They said the same sort of things: "You're a joker, Mart . . . you take the piss . . . you're on top of it all." My message is a simple one. If I were you, sitting there listening to me talk, I would have thought, that is never going to happen to me. But it can, and it does.

'Someone recently asked me, "Did you enjoy being a football a manager?" We know a win on Saturday makes life a bit easier, but enjoyment isn't the right word to use, is it? The relief of winning goes so quickly, because there is always another match. This is a hard business to work in.

'It doesn't matter how small and insignificant it seems, if you are feeling down, and you keep feeling down, there may be a problem. There are mechanisms in place for you to get help. Reach out and grab the chance. It makes it easier to deal with.'

He spoke movingly about the commonality of his trade, the emotional and financial support he had received from the League Managers Association, who settled the £60,000 bill for his care. He also highlighted the work of Time for Change, a charity which seeks to minimise the stigma of mental health.

'They are why I am here. There are only so many ways I can say thank you to the people who stuck by me when the need was there. I am in a good place. I have an obligation to speak out. I felt it was time for me to be open and honest, and get my story out there.'

The silence with which he was received, in what was billed as a masterclass in resilience, was as eloquent as his subsequent ovation. Afterwards, he was embraced by Alan Pardew. 'You've still got that inner drive, haven't you?' he said. 'Yeah,' Ling replied. 'I'm desperate if I am honest with you.'

Gus Poyet and Jimmy Floyd Hasselbaink, managers of similar intensity at contrasting stages in their careers, were in the queue to pay their respects. The testimony of one of their own was uniquely powerful, since it confronted a private fear of pushing themselves beyond natural boundaries.

Ling was especially appreciative of the presence of Bolton manager Neil Lennon, who had been candid about his struggles with depression, which struck at his peak as a player at Leicester City and Celtic. Lennon's mood was so dark he remembers being in an exultant dressing room after an Old Firm win over Rangers at Ibrox, unable to recollect a single incident from the game.

'I'm just sitting in the corner relieved it's over, wanting to go home and close the door, turn off the light and not speak to anybody,' he admitted. A high-profile supporter of Mind Games, a Scottish mental health initiative, Lennon operates an open-door policy with his players and is especially sensitive to signs of younger members of his squad becoming withdrawn, or acting in an isolated manner.

He bonded naturally with Ling, since their experiences were so similar. 'The biggest incentive for me is to prove people with depression can manage a football club,' Ling reflected. 'Neil is doing just that. He has shown the light at the end of the tunnel.' Their power as advocates for greater understanding was profound.

Ling's friend Dean Smith, who took Walsall to Wembley for the first time in their 127-year history for the Johnstone's Paint Trophy final, finished the season as the fourth-longest of serving manager in the top four tiers of English football, behind Arsène Wenger, Paul Tisdale and Karl Robinson. He admitted he had re-evaluated his approach.

'When I look at Martin now it is good to see him so sorted,' he said. 'What he went through made me realise how important it is to appreciate there is an outside world, away from football. The support network of your family, friends and staff is integral.

'I have always seen myself as a positive person, and you come to realise you are dealing with the natural sensitivities of human beings. That's why I don't go into the dressing room after games. It is too emotional a time. I would rather wait, and speak to the players rationally on Monday morning.'

Distance offers clarity. Aidy Boothroyd was relishing his role as coach of the England Under 20 team, who finished fourth in the summer Toulon Tournament. He saw management from a different angle, through the eyes of those who attended seminars and coaching sessions at his new workplace, St George's Park.

'Since Northampton I've been to a World Cup. I've watched the best of the best play. Now I can walk down a flight of stairs, go into the analysis room and watch any game from the weekend. There will always be a couple of hours when we get together as coaches and say, "Did you see that? What did you think of this? How does it fit with what we're trying to do?"

'I have to tell you, mate, it's brilliant. I'm enthused and I'm thinking about football. I've got five years here and I'm not even fifty. I'm far better educated and will be ready for it if I get back on the hamster's wheel. You do stop learning, and it takes its toll on you. We're a band of brothers who keep getting our throats slit, but we keep going.

'Someone who has had a bad time and been sacked gravitates towards anyone who has been in that position. You can verbalise the hurt to a certain degree, but it is more about the feelings you share. You have to go through the vitriol, the bitter and twisted rubbish of them singing that you're getting sacked in the morning.

'All those chairmen who tell you, "We're going to make a change, we're going to go in a different direction." Yeah, OK, it'll probably be going backwards but that's fine, you know. There's empathy between football managers that you are not going to get in any other job. I've lived it. I know what the other guy is going through.

'I bumped into a manager at a game recently, and I won't tell you who it is because it's not fair. I competed against him five years ago, when he was fresh and bright. He was at it. Now he's put on weight. His face is fuller, he's lost a bit of his hair, going bald, and he just said, "I'm ready for a change." I can really relate to that.'

Boothroyd had matured. He was no longer too busy doing the job to do it to the best of his ability. The brash young crusader of his Watford days, creator of a culture which nurtured managers of the quality of Brendan Rodgers, Sean Dyche, Chris Powell and Mark Warburton, had grown more reflective without losing his Yorkie strut. Wise heads nodded in approval.

Mick McCarthy, whose Ipswich Town team were beaten by East Anglian rivals Norwich City in the semi-final of the Championship play-offs, was their spokesman: 'Aidy was ubiquitous when he was at Watford. He regrets that now. I used to say to him, "Do me a favour. You were at the opening of a bloody envelope, man. You were everywhere and everyone wanted to know what you were going to say. You were the bright, young thing. And when you're not the bright, young thing, you grow up."

'Ollie [Ian Holloway] was the same at Blackpool. I don't think he's contrived either, because he's bonkers when you meet him. He is what he is. But he was another one. They'd ask him about Man United and he'd comment and you'd be thinking, Ollie, shut up! You can't have an opinion on everything. Even if you think you can, you don't have to give it to everybody.'

McCarthy sent an apposite text to Gary Waddock when he was appointed as Portsmouth's assistant manager: 'Welcome back to the asylum.' Waddock ended the season as caretaker manager, following the sacking of Andy Awford on April 13.

He was on a seven-man shortlist for a permanent position, drawn from more than 80 applicants, including such potential initiates as Teddy Sheringham, who eventually replaced Graham Westley at Stevenage. Portsmouth chose to pursue Paul Cook, who had taken Chesterfield into the League One play-offs. Since he wished to work with his own back-room staff, Waddock left the club on May 18. There had been 58 managerial changes since Waddock was originally evicted from Oxford United, three days into pre-season training: 43 managers were sacked, 15 had resigned. A record 18 changes were made in the Championship alone. The average tenure of first-time managers was just over a year.

Comparisons with the four major North American sports were instructive. According to the *Wall Street Journal*, head coaches in the National Basketball Association and National Hockey League average more three years in the role. National Football League franchises, on average, retain faith in their head coaches for four years and four months. The mean length of employment for Major League Baseball managers is four years and eight months.

The law of supply and demand ensures football managers in England will continue to be treated as Poundland prophets, impulse purchases who have the status of easily disposable assets. Little due diligence is done; shortlists are rarely strategic since they contain managers of different ages, philosophies and personalities.

Too often, recruitment has all the sophistication of a childhood game of pinning the tail on the donkey. Norwich City's success in reaching the Premier League after securing Alex Neil suggests it need not be so; he was discovered through an internal database of Europe's top 250 young managers. Metrics suggested he was in 35th position, abnormally high for someone of his age, 33, and experience, at Hamilton Academical.

Contractual arrangements were similarly haphazard. LMA research found that many were a cut and paste version of former contracts, 'often several generations of manager old and no longer legally current or relevant to modern industrial relations best practice'. They were increasingly concerned by abuse of the 'gardening leave' principle, first applied in the financial services industry.

Aware of 'the practice of some clubs to pursue opportunistic allegations of gross misconduct against their managers when terminating their contracts', the LMA were lobbying to introduce a uniform arrangement, designed to give clarity to an opaque process. In this so-called 'mutual liquidated damages' model, the terminating party, either club or manager, is obliged to pay predetermined compensation. The procedure should result in 'improved and consistent understanding' and 'significant and immediate savings in legal costs'.

The surprising sacking of Shaun Derry by Notts County on March 23 conformed to a pattern. He was ostensibly dismissed after a terrible run of eight defeats in ten games, which culminated in a 4–1 loss at MK Dons, but closer investigation revealed a classic case of a club reverting to type in losing faith with a manager committed to a long term plan. Derry's departure was a precursor of another change in strategy at boardroom level. County began looking for their fifteenth manager in eleven years an hour after owner Ray Trew announced he had made his wife, Aileen, chief executive.

Derry had inherited a club with no scouting structure and inadequate financial planning. His budget was slashed by £1 million before the season started. Expectation soared when they were in play-off contention at the turn of the year, but he lost his three best players when Louis Laing, Stephen McLaughlin and Jake Cassidy returned to their parent clubs.

He lacked the finance to work the loan market effectively, and was unable to recruit players of better or similar quality. Derry became increasingly frustrated, and by his own admission is too honest to hide his feelings. Friction was inevitable. Though chief executive Jim Rodwell was not a natural ally, his departure to Scunthorpe United added to the sense of a rudderless organisation.

'With the greatest respect to the people who run the club, it was difficult,' Derry reflected. 'We just couldn't break the pattern. In retrospect, that good start was probably the worst thing that could have happened. I was thinking to myself, we can't sustain this. This has taught me a lot about the role of a football manager.

'I looked behind the dugout in matches towards the end and saw certain managers sniffing around. My wife said I looked forty-seven, not thirty-seven, when it was all over. It took me two or three weeks just to sleep at night. But despite all that, I will get myself out there again. I won't turn up at clubs where guys are in trouble, but I do want to work again.'

The Trews employed Ricardo Moniz, a Dutch development coach once aligned to Martin Jol at Tottenham, on a three-year contract. County were leading until the 88th minute of their final League One game, at Gillingham, but contrived to lose 3–1 and were relegated. Moniz likened it to 'a funeral'.

More than half his players were out of contract, and he evidently doubted many had the character to cope with the privations of the old Fourth Division. 'When it slips out of your hands it's so hard,' he said. 'It's a massive shock, a disaster, the worst day of my career. It's difficult to say if this squad can bounce back.'

Brentford's decision to discard Mark Warburton seemed even more bizarre when they stole into the Championship play-offs with a 3–0 win over Wigan at Griffin Park on the last day of the regular season. It was an old-school occasion, when it was possible to hear the hum of transistor radios, following events elsewhere.

Warburton's stock was rising. He resisted the temptation to complain, and remained scrupulously respectful towards owner Matthew Benham. It was an impressive, far-sighted exit strategy, measured and mature. Defeat to Middlesbrough in the play-off semi-final did little to discourage prospective employers. He would be named as the new Rangers manager, with David Weir as his assistant, in mid-June.

Benham played his hand within 24 hours of Warburton's last game, a 3–0 defeat at the Riverside Stadium. Rasmus Ankersen, chairman of newly installed Danish Superliga champions, FC Midtjylland, was announced as Brentford's new director of football in partnership with Phil Giles, head of quantitative sports research at Smartodds, the sports modelling company through which Benham offers services to a range of clients, including professional gamblers.

In an immediate challenge to conformity, they were given joint responsibility for overseeing the appointment of a head coach. Akaki Gogia, a Georgia-born attacking midfield player signed on a Bosman transfer from German third-division team Hallescher FC, was the first of a multinational influx of new players, assessed on mathematical principle rather than instinct.

Benham told the club website: "When changes to the

football department were first announced, we were very clear that we wanted Brentford to be a club that could reach the Premier League and stay there. We believe this can only be achieved sustainably with an innovative approach to player recruitment and the overall management of the club. Rasmus and Phil can help us achieve our aim."

Marinus Dijkhuizen was appointed as Brentford's new head coach on June 1. He had a predictably distinctive background, having established Excelsior, a small feeder club for Feyenoord, in the Eredivisie. On the same day Paul Clement, Carlo Ancelotti's former assistant at Real Madrid, was named as Steve McClaren's successor at Derby County.

McClaren was the principal victim of Derby's collapse. Top in February, they finished eighth after winning only two of their last 13 games. Anguished images, which captured him with his head in his hands, summoned memories of dark days with England. He again rejected the desperate overtures of Newcastle United, who wanted him to oversee the final three fixtures of another chaotic Premier League season, and intended to devote at least another year to the Championship club. Yet, following a review conducted by the Derby board, he was sacked on May 25.

McClaren issued a statement to amplify his dissapointment, and made a point of stressing "I do not believe or accept that rumours linking me to the Newcastle

United job were a factor in the team's performance this year, as had been alleged."

Newcastle's problems were largely self-inflicted. John Carver lacked the subtlety and self-control to manage effectively, making an extraordinary attack on the character of his players after an eighth successive defeat, at Leicester City on May 2 by agreeing with protesting fans who called them 'gutless', 'spineless' and 'cowards'.

He challenged a taboo by accusing Mike Williamson of deliberately getting sent off, a charge the defender eloquently and vehemently denied the following day. Carver gave a glimpse into the tortured soul of a manager at bay; he quivered with anger, spoke defiantly, but finally admitted, with a poignant sense of sadness, 'If I'm honest, I have to admit there's a chance they're just not listening to me.' He and first-team coach Steve Stone were dismissed on June 9, a day before McClaren was installed as Newcastle's new head coach, with a brief to revise training methods and enforce cultural change.

The benefits of rational, strategic management were obvious. Kenny Jackett had restored Wolverhampton Wanderers' identity, despite a fractional failure to qualify for the Championship play-offs. They missed out on goal difference after beating his former club Millwall, who had confirmed Neil Harris as manager after their relegation, on the final day.

Swansea City, another of Jackett's former clubs, had

their best-ever Premier League season under Garry Monk, his former captain.

He was praised as a coming man by Alan Pardew and Arsène Wenger. Stoke City, who secured the services of Mark Hughes until 2018, were alongside Swansea as the best of the rest. Burnley's relegation, through a combination of financial prudence and a basic inability to score a sufficient number of goals, did not dull the sheen of Sean Dyche's reputation.

Eddie Howe's status as the poster boy of British management was reinforced by Bournemouth's promotion as Championship winners, following a final day win at Charlton Athletic. The feat earned him the cherished title of LMA Manager of the Year. Thankfully, his sense of perspective survived the traditional lunacy of immediate comparisons with José Mourinho and adolescent conjecture about his suitability to follow Arsène Wenger at Arsenal.

At his moment of triumph Howe summoned, once again, the sacred memory of his late mother, Annie. The maternal influences on his management style might appear to challenge the game's macho culture, but chime with the experience of North America's arguably greatest coach, Mike Krzyzewski, who won his fifth national college basketball title with Duke University in March.

Krzyzewski's unique record – more than 1,000 wins over 35 years – has, combined with his ascetic style, made him a business guru. PricewaterhouseCoopers, the global accounting firm, have sent their 500 most promising employees to study his methods. He preaches interactivity, and acknowledges the feminine influences of his late mother, Emily, his wife, Mickie, and his three daughters, Debbie, Jamie and Lindy:

'Guys don't share insights. If a guy does, we call him a blowhard or a know-it-all, so we don't do it. There's an empathetic part of leadership, and this is where the women in my life have had a huge impact on me. Every night at the dinner table, my wife and girls discussed their day. They remembered details. They remembered the feeling that the detail brought, and the feeling before that, whereas men we remember only the final feeling. We're all about the end of the story, the punchline.'

Karl Robinson, another outstanding, emotionally driven member of an emerging generation, also found fulfilment in dramatic circumstances. In yet another example of football's interconnectivity, MK Dons' elevation to the Championship was indirectly assured by the justification of Colchester's decision to discard Joe Dunne.

Having flatlined in and around the relegation zone throughout the season, Colchester rescued themselves with nine minutes remaining. A George Moncur goal secured a 1–0 win that removed Preston North End from the second automatic promotion place. A system developed by Dunne and regenerated by Tony Humes, his successor, had been validated.

Robinson, 105 miles away at Stadium MK overseeing

the last rites of a 5–1 win over bottom club Yeovil Town, was close to tears. 'I tried to be cool and calm but with ten minutes to go I was crumbling,' he admitted. 'When we knew it was over and Colchester had won, we still had a minute to play. It was the best minute of football I've ever watched. These are things that will live with us for ever.'

Careers hinge on such marginal gains. Had Preston's nerve held, and MK Dons suffered their fourth play-off disappointment in six years, Robinson would probably have moved on. There was a sense of significance about the style and substance of his first promotion as manager: they had scored 101 goals, accumulated 91 points and stuck to strategic principles.

The sight of a beaming Dele Alli parading the prop of an ersatz trophy for finishing as runners-up hinted at a deeper meaning. Robinson's duty as Daddy Day Care was done; the teenager was perfectly prepared for the next phase of his life. It would not be easy, since rumours circulated that a faction at Tottenham resented the implications of Alli's arrival, but he was ready for the challenge.

Robinson lost a soul mate on May 27, when Andy King, his chief scout died suddenly from a heart attack. "This is one of the biggest losses in my life, both person- ally and professionally", he said. "I'm on the floor. I don't think I'll ever meet a person like him again. Outside of my family, he's provided me with more support than anybody else. I'm just so thankful to him for his help and guidance, as well as the love he showed me and my family."

Elsewhere, the trend of subjective judgements being complemented by objective assessment accelerated. According to analysis by Infostrada, a Dutch-based data company which supplies statistics from more than 250 sports, Roberto Martínez was the biggest managerial underachiever in the Premier League, despite Everton's late-season revival.

Brendan Rodgers, under significant pressure at Liverpool following failure to sustain a spring surge, fared marginally better, but was in a 'red zone' in which the availability of attractive alternatives had to be taken into account. The 3–4–3 system, which took shape in his mind as he paced the kitchen of his Formby home during an anxious early morning vigil, had been analysed and neutralised.

His dilemma, in being deemed individually responsible for the shortcomings of a collegiate recruitment system which had frittered away £215 million in three years, struck a chord with his peers since it highlighted the fact he was no longer king of his own destiny. His conviction that he could inspire through the clarity of his communication and the authenticity of his emotions seemed lost on his players.

His public were tiring of his hyperbole. He seemed tired and wan. I last saw him at the Hawthorns, where his relentless positivity in attempting to promote the fiction that Liverpool's performance in a goalless draw was 'outstanding' merely made him appear desperate or, worse, deluded. He needed something more substantive than autocue optimism to restore faith.

Defeat by Aston Villa in the FA Cup semi-final, followed by a 6-1 defeat at Stoke on the last day of the season, raised doubts about his tactical acumen, selection policy and the collective character of his team. Mario Balotelli, who simply refused to buy into the CORE principles on the flip chart in the manager's office, was a source of constant embarrassment. The mists of history swirling around Steven Gerrard in a farewell match at Anfield which bordered on mawkish; could not obscure the delicacy of the club's situation.

Liverpool's failure to qualify for the Champions League had eased them down football's food chain, leaving them, and their manager vulnerable. The limitations of a holistic philosophy, expressed privately by Rodgers in his office at Melwood, were being exposed publicly. The inherent opportunism of Raheem Sterling and his representative, in agitating for a transfer, foretold a difficult summer. Rodgers was further weakened by a board review which resulted in the departure of his assistants, Colin Pascoe and Mike Marsh.

If Rodgers faced a career-defining season in 2015–16, Wenger's status as the dean of football management remained unchallenged. Longevity had given him a state of grace; his legacy was secure, even in an age of lucrative mediocrity and institutionalised cynicism.

Arsenal's retention of the FA Cup allowed him to express quiet satisfaction at the end of another turbulent season. He remained true to his faith: 'We live in a society where everything is now quantified. It is the job of the model manager to select the most important things, and filter out the noise. It is not only about winning, but a deeper purpose, elevating the game above your own ego.'

The number-crunchers considered Ronald Koeman the Premier League's biggest overachiever at Southampton, whose executive director, Les Reed, had set the strategic goal of Champions League football within five years. His watchfulness and certainty of purpose reminded me of one of Sir Alex Ferguson's traits, closely observing his players when they are unaware of the intensity of scrutiny.

'What you can pick up by watching is incredibly valuable,' Ferguson told the *Harvard Business Review* in October 2013. 'Seeing a change in a player's habits or a sudden dip in his enthusiasm allowed me to go further with him: Is it family problems? Is he struggling financially? Is he tired? What kind of mood is he in? Sometimes I could even tell that a player was injured when he thought he was fine.

'I don't think many people fully understand the value of observing. I came to see observation as a critical part of my management skills. The ability to see things is key – or, more specifically, the ability to see things you don't expect to see.'

Attitudes which challenged football's pretentions as a modern, corporately responsible industry complicated an already fraught profession. Alan Pardew reinvented himself at Crystal Palace, a club which suited his character and ambition, and remained diplomatic about his release from the tender mercies of Mike Ashley.

The therapeutic nature of Pardew's relationship with sports psychologist Jeremy Snape was becoming increasingly obvious. He projected an elder statesman's quiet authority, although some chose to misinterpret his remarks about being a standard bearer for home-grown coaches, and a potential England manager, as trademark arrogance.

It was yet another example of the banality of aspects of my trade. Pardew's supposed 'brand' dictated the manner in which he was received. Like most prominent managers, he had grown weary of coconut-shy press conferences, in which he was expected to pronounce on extraneous issues of the day. He used his experience constructively, but frustration bubbled over in the build-up to the overhyped 'Fight of the Century' between Floyd Mayweather and Manny Pacquiao.

'If there is a criticism I have of the Premier League it's the spotlight is so much on the manager,' he told Jonathan Northcroft of the *Sunday Times*. 'It's ridiculous. Sky were asking our opinion on the big fight. What do we know about the boxing world? And what does our opinion matter?

'Eddie Howe is going to be thrust into this world. I'll be one of the senior managers telling him "don't change", but unfortunately it does change us. It's changed me. It's changed Mark Hughes. It's changed Sam Allardyce. We're all a little bit guarded. The spotlight needs to come away, and focus on the players again.'

He benefited from leaving Newcastle on his own terms. That lent distance from subsequent turmoil, which shredded the credibility of Carver, his former coach, and completed Ashley's alienation from a fan base that customarily demonstrates loyalty from cradle to grave. Contempt was mutual, but not uniquely corrosive.

Other clubs were perilously close to becoming unmanageable because of the volatility of owners who seemed to take perverse pleasure in the toxicity of their presence. Leeds United, under the intermittent presidency of Massimo Cellino, operated sub-optimally in an atmosphere of anger and anarchy.

Neil Redfearn, Brian McDermott's former coach, used his academy background to develop young players of the quality of Lewis Cook, Alex Mowatt and Sam Byram after succeeding the ill-fated David Hockaday and Darko Milanič as head coach in October. His reward was to be demeaned and undermined, apparently from within.

Six players associated with Cellino suddenly reported injured for an away game at Charlton after survival had been assured, though the Italian owner distanced himself from what was, seen in the most sympathetic light possible, an extraordinary coincidence.

Redfearn, a thoroughly decent man, was left to spin in the wind. He was unhappy that his assistant, Steve Thompson, had been suspended without warning or explanation. His plaintive cry before his final match in charge, against Rotherham, was both poignant and pertinent: 'All I'm doing is fighting for the club. If that's a crime then I'm guilty.' His cause was just and his fate preordained. He was duly replaced as head coach by Uwe Rösler on May 20.

The place of a football manager in society was evolving. He – and let's not forget it remains an exclusively masculine calling at the highest level – had to deal with excessive, astringent accountability that was reserved, in previous generations, for the political class.

The 2015 General Election reduced candidates to caricatures. Party machines created compensatory myths and legends because contact with the ordinary voter was deemed too dangerous; authenticity was an illusion. Football managers were denied the protection of sham democracy; they couldn't avoid their public, however hard they tried.

Against this backcloth of chaos, expedience and vulnerability, Richard Bevan, the LMA's chief executive, invested £250,000, a sizeable chunk of his £3 million annual budget, in a five-year strategic leadership programme. Managers were studying those in similarly stressful professions, such as air traffic controllers, heart surgeons and prison officers.

The most pertinent example was closest to home. Ling had rebuilt his career in portfolio fashion. He ran his own football academy, coached at the Tottenham Hotspur Foundation and assisted with the first team at AFC Hornchurch in the Ryman League. He earned a nominal match fee of £20 scouting for Dean Smith at Walsall, and was also one of Radio London's most popular football co-commentators.

He reassembled his 2006 Leyton Orient promotion team to play against a celebrity team managed by Harry Redknapp in a match to raise awareness of Prostate Cancer on May 31, and spent the summer surveying the job market. My admiration for his resilience breached professional protocol, since I could not stop myself telling him that, were I his son, I would implore him to count his blessings.

'I have a lovely stress-free life, earning the same sort of money I was on at Torquay. Sitting here now, though, I can't say I will never go back into football management. For my own peace of mind I've already applied for a couple of jobs, though I'd have a real decision to make if it involved living away from home.

'The coffee stain is still there on my CV. If ten

managers are sitting in the room, going for the same job, maybe I won't get it because the chairman can't or won't see beyond the stain. But you can recover from cancer. You can recover from a brain tumour. And you can recover from depression.

'There is always the chance you will be treated badly in football, from the day you go into it as a kid. My son is in it now, at Leyton Orient. Should he know that? I think he should. I often ask myself these days, did you treat your players like lumps of meat? I hope I didn't. You might have to edge a few out, chuck them overboard at the right time, but I always believed I did things honestly and openly.

'I never did anything underhand. Stress and strain have a big part to play in the game but to this day I swear I would have got depression if I was a dustman, rather than a football manager. Sure, football is more cut-throat, more instant. After five straight defeats as a manager you are a lump of shit on the bottom of some people's shoes.

'My record is good, over ten years in management, but I was being judged by five weeks of depression. I never took a club down. I always made my club money, and worked on a low budget. I always brought players through from the youth system.

'I didn't have the best of times at Cambridge, but I didn't make them any worse. I left Leyton Orient a better club than when I started there. The day I left

Torquay is the day they went downhill. I was cut off in my prime, and think they now realise what a good job I did for them. Do I care about football? Of course I care. But I don't worry any more.

'Once you are out of that hole, that black hole and that horrible darkness, the world is a brighter place . . .'

Epilogue

Martin Ling allowed himself 56 days of grace. He returned to manage Swindon Town, one of the clubs closest to his heart, on November 3, 2015 and insisted his depression had 'gone.' Such optimism was redemptive, and received with instinctive warmth, yet it proved to be reckless.

Although he won five of his first six games in charge, and immersed himself in the exhaustive rituals of his trade, he was fighting and failing to keep the demons at bay. The stress of successive defeats over the Christmas period prompted the most difficult decision of his life.

He resigned on December 29 in the knowledge that, to all intents and purposes, his managerial career was over at the age of 49. His son Sam acted as his spokesman, confirming his father had reached the conclusion 'his family and health are more important than anything.'

The respect in which Ling was held by his peers was

undiminished. Recognising, better than anyone, the moral courage required to concede the pressures of the job were too insidious to ignore, they rallied around publicly and privately.

Several managers contacted me, after reading this book, to admit vivid confirmation of Ling's problems prompted profound, deeply personal, questions. One, not featured in these pages, confided he felt powerless to contain his depression, despite seeking professional help.

His mood swings were becoming more pronounced, and his 20-year marriage was over. His reflexive urge to push loved ones away from him had become intolerable. On too many evenings, he would retreat to his study and drink at least two bottles of red wine as he brooded over match videos or analytical sequences on his laptop.

Football's mental health issue was approaching epidemic proportions, and didn't end at the manager's door. A survey of more than 800 players across 11 countries sketched the parameters of the problem: 38 per cent reported symptoms of anxiety and depression. A quarter struggled to sleep and alcohol abuse was rife.

A Premier League manager shared the story of the star he found impossible to select. A multi-millionaire in his early twenties, he hated the game which has enriched him beyond reason, and felt trapped by an extended family which viewed him as a meal ticket.

He had developed into a distant, disinterested character, and often failed to report for training. Traditional forms of punishment, such as a club fine, were irrelevant since he perceived his wealth as part of the problem. The manager had a chief executive, a coaching team, and the player's counsellor to satisfy.

It was not as if he didn't have other preoccupations. In managerial terms, the lack of security was becoming ever more oppressive. At the time of writing, in mid-February 2016, 37 managers had been sacked and another six had resigned during the 2015-16 season.

The Championship remained the crucible, as impatience became ever more institutionalised. Paul Clement, one of the brightest coaches of his generation, was sacked eight months after succeeding Steve McClaren at Derby County. Neil Redfearn lasted only four months at Rotherham United, where he was replaced by the irascible Neil Warnock.

Garry Monk, hailed as a potential England manager in September 2015, was sacked by Swansea in December. Typically he resorted to further self-education; he shadowed Kenny Jackett, a renowned development coach, at Wolves, where Jackett's job was complicated immeasurably by the club being put up for sale by owner Steve Morgan.

David Moyes and Sir Alex Ferguson were reassuring figures, as doubt inevitably filled what Monk described as the 'void' of sudden unemployment. Brendan

Rodgers, sacked by Liverpool an hour after a drawn Merseyside derby in October, was another former Swansea manager to offer support.

Rodgers joined José Mourinho in making a studied announcement that he would wait until the summer to make his next career move. His rehabilitation was complicated by the increasing disconnection between perception, of him as a Brentian caricature, and the reality, that he remains a widely respected coach.

It was hard not to conclude that, somewhere on the mean streets of Melwood, the boy from Northern Ireland had morphed into the brand from corporate central. Rodgers made use of the usual media outlets to maintain his profile without easing the suspicion he was a little too calculating for his own good.

Management is governed also by random chance. Shaun Derry inherited Joe Dunne as his assistant when he resumed his career with Cambridge United in November. They had previously spent a year together on the LMA's diploma course, and dovetailed personally and professionally. Their initial ground work, shedding eight players from a bloated 31-strong squad while remaining in touch with the play off places in League Two, was highly promising.

Brian McDermott's return to Reading in December was a surprise. We had met occasionally on the circuit when he was operating as Arsenal's chief scout; he had lost a little of his intensity without compromising his standards and seemed suited to the rhythm and principles of an auxiliary role.

Yet, when the opportunity arose, instinct took over. He is an appropriate spokesman for his trade, and deserves the final word on management's fatal attraction:

'There is too much drama in football at the moment. I've learned not to read the papers and listen to the radio. I've learned to filter out social media. I've learned to work on myself. I am in a really good place.

'This feels right. It works for me. The bottom line was I really fancied it. To walk away from Arsenal was hard, because they were so good to me, but this was a chance to redevelop a club with a real identity. I feel I am better for all my experiences.

'Owners are not easy these days. There is no point in fighting them. I can't tell you how much I have learned – it is frightening. You have to let things go, make things happen. The madness is worse than ever, if you choose to be involved in it, but what's the point?

'You have the choice to go with the madness, or be controlled and constructive. I've seen things you wouldn't believe, but one day a football club is going to have it off by working together as a group. That simple concept can take you to an altogether different level.'

Index